To the memory of my mother
Margaret (1915–1999)
who supported my dreaming

# INSIDE THE ROYAL SHAKESPEARE COMPANY

## Creativity and the Institution

### COLIN CHAMBERS

Routledge
Taylor & Francis Group

LONDON AND NEW YORK

First published 2004 by Routledge
2 Park Square, Milton Park, Abingdon, Oxon, OX14 4RN

Simultaneously published in the USA and Canada
by Routledge
270 Madison Ave, New York NY 10016

*Routledge is an imprint of the Taylor & Francis Group*

Transferred to Digital Printing 2008

Typeset in Minion by M Rules

*British Library Cataloguing in Publication Data*
A catalogue record for this book is available from the British Library

*Library of Congress Cataloging in Publication Data*
Chambers, Colin.
Inside the Royal Shakespeare Company : creativity
and the institution / Colin Chambers.
p. cm.
Includes bibliographical references and index.
1. Royal Shakespeare Company–History.   I. Title.
PN2596.S82R684 2004
792'.0942–dc22
2003015745

ISBN10: 0–415–21202–2 (hbk)
ISBN10: 0–415–46065–4 (pbk)

ISBN13: 978–0–415–21202–1 (hbk)
ISBN13: 978–0–415–46065–1 (pbk)

# CONTENTS

# ACKNOWLEDGEMENTS

I would like to thank the following for their help:

Norman Ayrton, Clive Barker, John Barton, Cicely Berry, David Brierley, Peter Brook, John Broome, John Bury, David Calder, David Cox, Ann Curtis, Ann Daniels, Lyn Darnley, Susan Engel, Martin Esslin, Abd'elkader Farrah, Kaye Flanagan, Peter Gill, Misha Glenny, John Goodwin, Peter Hall, Ian Hogg, Peter Holland, Pamela Howard, Roger Howells, Sally Jacobs, Alby James, Ben Jancovich, David Jones, Michael Kustow, James Langley, Phyllida Lloyd, Genista McIntosh, Katie Mitchell, Sylvia Morris and other staff at the Shakespeare Centre Library, Stratford-upon-Avon, Richard Nelson, Trevor Nunn, Hugh Quarshie, Leon Rubin, Bronwyn Roberston, Clifford Rose, Anthony Rowe, Maggie Roy, James Sargent, Maggie Steed, Janet Suzman, Di Trevis, Philip Voss, Andrew Wade, Deborah Warner, Clifford Williams, Guy Woolfenden.

Funding for part of the research came from an Arts and Humanities Research Board Small Grant in the Creative and Performing Arts.

# INTRODUCTION

My association with the Royal Shakespeare Company began, as is the case for many, when I was taken to see one of its productions while at school. By good luck, that 1963 production at the Aldwych Theatre happened to be *King Lear* directed by Peter Brook with the mesmeric Paul Scofield appearing in the title role. The RSC caught my imagination and I eagerly followed its fortunes for the rest of the decade. Through the 1970s I saw the company's work in my role as drama critic and in 1979, by one of those curious twists of fate, I came to run its play department, employed on a short-term contract. I graduated in 1981 to the post of literary manager, which I held until I left in 1997. My work there brought me into contact with a vast range of the people who are needed to put RSC productions before the public, from the artistic director and senior management to heads of various artistic, administrative and production departments, actors, stage managers, designers and, naturally, playwrights. Looking back on those years after I had moved on, I realised that much of my time had been spent, as had theirs, in trying to resolve the inevitable tension between creativity and the institution. It is a tension that exists throughout all the processes required to find organisational forms for artistic expression, and it is a tension that persists because the impulse to challenge, to push the boundaries, to refuse the constraints of the institution is endemic in any creative project. It is a problem with which anyone working in a cultural organisation, especially a large one, will be familiar and it lies at the root of this book.

The following chapters trace this dialectic between creativity and the institution as it evolved at the RSC across four decades and four artistic directors. In the opening part of the book, the story unfolds chronologically with an emphasis on the early formative years, which provided a template for much of the remainder of the RSC's life. It is as much a political as an artistic story and begins with Peter Hall's creation of the RSC, Britain's first large-scale, permanent repertoire company, its background in the 1950s and his initial seasons from 1960–62 when the company was finding its identity and fighting for public subsidy. The story continues with the establishment of the company as a socially engaged, vibrant national institution, mainly through the *Wars of the Roses* trilogy in 1963, Hall's final years at the head of the company and Trevor Nunn's succession in 1968. The next chapter looks at Nunn's refinement, renewal and expansion of the organisation to a four-theatre operation, and his making Terry Hands joint artistic director in 1978 as the company enjoyed a remarkable run of productions in both the classical and contemporary repertoire that concluded in *The Life and Adventures of Nicholas Nickleby*. Important changes occur with the move to the Barbican in 1982, the further growth of the company following the opening of the Swan Theatre in 1986, and, with Hands now running the company alone, its loss of direction and the temporary closure of its two Barbican theatres. Finally in this section there is a view of the modernisation of the RSC in the 1990s under Adrian Noble, which leads to the unpicking of Hall's legacy through withdrawal from the company's London base and the abandonment of the RSC's hitherto accepted idea of company.

Part Two of the book offers a more general survey of themes: the RSC's repertoire, both Shakespearean and non-Shakespearean, the company's training, research and development work – an area that Britain is singularly poor at supporting – and its strategies for gaining public legitimacy through exploitation of its image and transactions with the audience.[1] The concluding chapter looks at the issue of company and the future of the RSC under Michael Boyd, who became artistic director in 2003.

The book is neither a memoir nor a catalogue of individual productions, many of which are well documented elsewhere and are among the most analysed in modern theatre studies. Rather, the book offers an account of cultural production at the RSC. It is a many-layered chronicle, which moves back and forth at different tempos across a complex field of inter-related artistic, organisational and economic matters.[2] This reflects the reality of the company as a boundless series of shifting relationships, formal and informal. It is a composite of daily negotiations that depend on interactions between individual character and the particular company context, influenced by a vast assortment of intangible factors such as gender, status, timing and location, the effects of which it is difficult to tidy into a neat mould. Necessarily, however, a book attempts to outline a pattern, even while acknowledging the limitations of the venture. Each participant in the story, myself included, will have a unique and personal experience of the events and a different memory of them. Just as no production can exhaust the potential of a text, no one can offer a complete or definitive account. Hopefully this version will at least be recognisable to those who were there and illuminating to those who were not.

The curve of the RSC's fortunes followed those of theatre in general and was embedded in the enormous social shifts of the latter part of the twentieth century. A child of that fabled decade the 1960s, the RSC was born in a moment of rare British expansion within a period of general imperial decline following the Second World War. It was also the time of a reawakening of politics and of a BBC that could host the most celebrated of television series *The Wednesday Play* and the groundbreaking satirical programme *That Was The Week That Was*. The RSC lasted into the new millennium through the 1960s and 1970s when state patronage of the arts was in the ascendant as well as through the next two decades of monetarism and the rolling back of that patronage. They were years of exceptional technological change and social disintegration. Post-war social democracy had failed and the contradiction between the feel-good ideologies attached to advancing globalisation and the lived experiences of individuals became increasingly fraught. Grand national narratives, which had held sway despite their narrow reading of history, fell apart and were not replaced by convincing alternatives. Culture consolidated its role as the central site for the making of meaning in the secularised society both at the individual and the national level but was subject to even greater commercial penetration and fragmentation. Manufacture was overtaken as the nation's motor by service industries, and culture became a vital business sector. This was not surprising, as capitalism had extended its reach to previously unthinkable domains like genetic identity; even space had become a commodity.

Nor was it a surprise that the public service ethos of the subsidised theatre was worn away under the advancing embrace of marketplace entertainment. Having missed an opportunity for transformation at the end of the war, British theatre had gathered momentum for renovation ten years later in the mid-1950s. Set against a background of wider cultural change, this had occurred through a confluence of influences: Brecht, Beckett and the Theatre of the Absurd, American realism, Theatre Workshop and new indigenous playwriting at the Royal Court. The RSC gave added impetus to this process, which reshaped Britain's theatrical landscape. The company offered a new prototype of what a Shakespearean company could be – a large-scale ensemble presenting in repertoire a classical and contemporary programme relevant to its society. Art theatre was reconnecting with social issues, creating a theatre of national debate that was to become more vivid and diverse than any since Shakespeare's day. This was the theatre John Osborne described as a minority art with a majority influence, yet it was unable to hold on to bright talents such as Joan Littlewood and Peter Brook, who were ushered overseas.

In the 1980s, as part of its broader attack on society, government stirred the national undertow of philistinism and fuelled populist resentment against funding the so-called high arts as represented by the RSC. The demand for public grants for this kind of art was interpreted as an index of financial mismanagement and lack of public support. If the art were any good, ran the argument, it would be popular enough to pay for itself. State funding was thereby characterised as a means by which the less well-off paid for the arcane pleasures of a privileged section of the much better-off. Their very enjoyment of these pleasures, such as Shakespeare, reinforced the feeling of superiority they already possessed. The type of theatre associated with this privilege was further undermined by the multiplicity of performance practices that burst through conventional classifications and forced a redefinition of theatre. The RSC had once been in the forefront of this questioning but it had subsequently abandoned the experiment. Its irreverent image was confounded when it moved into the Barbican centre, a modern temple to culture, and found itself cast as an ambassador of officially sanctioned art.

When New Labour came to power in the late 1990s, seemingly in tune with what the RSC stood for, the visual arts, pop music and fashion were courted instead of what were seen as minority arts like theatre. A muddled debate about 'dumbing down' pushed serious discussion on the role and future of the art to the margins. A target-driven mentality deepened the confusion between value and value for money and completed the replacement of artistic excellence as the yardstick for support with social validation in the form of buzzwords like 'access' and 'outreach'. Theatre had fallen from its high national perch. With Shakespeare coming under attack from a vocal faction of the cultural and academic industries as an antiquated relic of an outmoded cottage industry, the charge of obsolescence was added to that of elitism. No wonder, then, that by the end of the century the RSC was in trouble. In this it was not alone. Public life had been devalued during the monetarist years and, despite being part of a culture that prefers institutions to individuals, all national organisations were in the firing line. None was safe, from the BBC and *The Times* to the monarchy and parliament.

The RSC's natural constituency, the middle class, had turned in upon itself. The arts policy-makers remained fickle, the finances remained uncertain. Long-term growth, therefore, was still impossible to plan. Yet the RSC could not escape responsibility for its own destiny. Whilst still adhering to the notion of company, the reality was becoming that of a corporation. The RSC had lost its leading role in the theatre profession and, in trying to adjust to new times, had become too inward looking. The contradictions at its heart – invention versus tradition, spontaneity versus planning, art versus tourism, and the rebellious versus the establishment – had slipped seriously out of kilter and its future was in question.

This decline of the RSC as a creative force may mark the end of the era of the charismatically led, large-scale company and of the notion of culture that lay behind its institutionalisation in flagship centres of excellence. The RSC was seen atop the pyramid, spreading its beneficence outwards and downwards. The gradual shift towards a more diversified view of culture and cultural provision by the end of the twentieth century offered new possibilities in the twenty-first for what might constitute a national theatrical institution. As it entered a rebuilding phase under Michael Boyd, the company faced the task of reinventing itself once again in order to avoid returning to the star-centred museum theatre the RSC had been established to replace.

Theatre is intrinsically social; the story of a major theatre company is, therefore, also a story as well as a metaphor of its society. As a national institution the RSC reflected the wider historical confusions clustered around the loss of a secure national identity and the evident insecurity in finding new consensual definitions. Having achieved nationhood early, the unravelling was all the more complex and involved many interconnecting layers: end of empire, the Irish war, devolution, the tug between the US and Europe, the rise of identity politics, multiculturalism, the atrophy of democracy, and globalisation. The problematic role of Englishness was a central theme, and the RSC echoed this. Indeed, Peter Brook once described the aim of the RSC as the aim of liberal England – to do things well.[3] The RSC was a very English project, yet, at least at the outset, was simultaneously not very English at all. It was animated by ideas, but was always pragmatic. Stratford-upon-Avon and Shakespeare were archetypally English, linking the present to a defining moment from the national past, the first Elizabethan age. Yet the core inspiration – to create an ensemble – was decidedly un-English, as was the means to secure it – state patronage. Peter Hall, who was neither part of the fusty 'old boy network' that ran the arts nor the commercial theatre's ruling elite, was very un-English in his celebrity and upstart habit of public noise making. But this outsider and his own network came to dominate the English theatre with the RSC in the van. He, however, remained at odds with the political and arts establishment, which dismissed his din, very Englishly, as whingeing.

Culture and economics in their own ways conspired to make the RSC's extraordinary achievements a distinctly English success story: the miserly state gave the company just enough subsidy to keep it alive but not enough to allow it to flourish as it wished, and, when its commitment and collective accomplishment thrived in adversity, the best traditions of heroic English amateurism were seemingly endorsed. The public triumph of *The Life and Adventures of Nicholas Nickleby* epitomised this national paradigm. Created as an imaginative response to the serious financial straits in which the company found itself, its sheer theatrical verve stood in marked contrast to the sombre national mood. While the recently elected Prime Minister Margaret Thatcher, in the name of a return to Victorian values, was to use unemployment and poverty as tools of social engineering in her destruction of the nation's social culture, the RSC production set a different Victorian portrait against hers and offered a pertinent reminder of the cruelty of that age. It was a reminder also of the value of the nation's culture and, in what had become a familiar RSC style, its social criticism was expressed as a celebratory event. It lauded the humane capitalism of moneyed philanthropy, which appealed to English liberal sensibilities – an echo of the story of the Stratford theatre itself, established as a self-financing gift to the nation in the late 1800s. And it affirmed a view of the nation and national characteristics as decent and even noble, operating independent of particular social conditions, inherently linked to a disappearing society and yet enduring as an aspirational ideal.

# PART ONE

# A Short History of Four Decades

# ONE

# ALL IN A STATE OF FINDING

When the Royal Shakespeare Company was founded in 1961, it was not conjured out of the sky. The Shakespeare Memorial Theatre at Stratford-upon-Avon already enjoyed a national and international presence, with its own eighty years of history, culture, values and internal arrangements. The RSC was both bolstered and burdened by this history, which it made anew under the impetus of innovations borrowed from elsewhere in Britain and abroad. In examining the background to the formation and first years of the new company, it is clear the old Stratford model no longer served. A fresh model was required to release resourcefulness and the imagination. But how to achieve this dream? The context in which the seemingly impossible occurred, a context that was social, economic, theatrical and personal, shaped not only the immediate dispensation but also the nature of the institution for the decades to come.

## Stratford-upon-Avon

At the time of the RSC's birth, Stratford was a craft market town of some 17,000 people, geographically and politically the heart of conservative middle England.[1] Nonetheless, it was the repository of much theatrical knowledge of, and expertise in, Shakespearean production yet its theatre was also drenched in the 'bardolatry' of the town, a brand of reverential remembrance given rein by the absence of a national theatre. The location of its theatre on the banks of a swan-rich river and the town's Tudor beam image supported the illusion there of an eternal shrine to Stratford's most famous son. However, this tradition of a particularly English rural idyll, which bears scant connection to the world of Shakespeare's plays, was, like many seemingly perpetual English traditions, an invention of the nineteenth century. In fact it took until 1769 – 150 years after Shakespeare's death – for Stratford to host a celebration to him, but even then no play of his was presented, and it was not until Shakespeare's house was bought for the nation nearly 100 years later, in 1847, that calls were made for the creation of a permanent monument to him in the shape of a theatre. During the tercentenary of Shakespeare's birth in 1864, a festival sponsored and organised by Edward Fordham Flower, the town's mayor and founder of the brewery that bears the family name, did include performances of Shakespeare's plays. This festival began the long association between that family and the commemoration of Shakespeare, a tradition of Victorian philanthropy that laid the seeds for the commercial festival theatre operation that was both inherited and supplanted by the RSC.

Flower's son Charles offered a site and some money towards building a theatre dedicated to Shakespeare and launched a national public subscription to raise the remainder. The response was so derisory that he was forced virtually to fund the project himself. The neo-Gothic theatre that opened in 1879 was unpopular, and commentators were concerned to promote the nation's capital as the only location fit for such a place of pilgrimage. Critics made unfavourable comparisons between the prospects of a self-financed theatre in Stratford and those of Bayreuth, likewise small and removed from its capital but which enjoyed royal patronage for its temple to Wagner. This bias was the product of typical London-centred snobbery rather than a justifiable wariness of the curious quasi-religious approach that links a birthplace with the spirit of its celebrated offspring. The Stratford theatre survived the sneers, and in the shape of Frank Benson's touring company, noted almost as much for its cricketing prowess as its acting abilities, it earned itself a national profile. By way of recognition, in 1925 the theatre was granted a royal charter. However, following a fire, another public subscription to build a new theatre for the nation barely managed to raise half the sum required; the rest came from America. After the Second World War, Stratford took the crown for Shakespearean production from the Old Vic, thanks largely to a string of performances there by Old Vic alumni, and Stratford thus consolidated an international as well as a national reputation. Yet, despite a handful of iconoclastic productions, the Stratford festival seasons soon revealed their own artistic limitations. As the new decade of the 1960s approached, it became clear to the chair of the theatre's governors that radical change was required.

Fordham Flower had become chair in 1944, the fourth member of the family to hold the position in an unbroken line. Head of the brewery and a Sandhurst-trained ex-officer who once considered standing as a Tory parliamentary candidate, he proved to be an adept theatre supervisor and a good listener with a sound understanding of how theatre people worked. His first artistic director, Robert Atkins (1944–45), tried to introduce staggered and longer rehearsals but found this difficult as he was not in overall control of the theatre, which was run by a general manager. His radical if aloof successor, Barry Jackson, confronted this problem head-on, sacking heads of departments, re-organising the workshops and backstage facilities, and refusing to employ anyone who had acted at Stratford before. Jackson wanted to create a permanent company, but he and Flower had a difficult relationship and Jackson left after only two seasons, a missed opportunity for change. His successor in 1948, Anthony Quayle, a plain-speaking military man, did have a rapport with Flower and was able to build on Jackson's progress. He made significant changes to the theatre building, notably reducing the stage/audience distance by bringing the circle nearer. He brought in Glen Byam Shaw and – briefly – George Devine, who together were able to attract artists of the highest calibre. Quayle consolidated Stratford's prestige by persuading Hugh 'Binkie' Beaumont, the most powerful London manager, to join the governing body and help him transform Stratford by means of a West End type of star system. Quayle reduced the number of new productions, brought successful ones back with cast changes, and introduced a two-company strategy, one at Stratford (under Byam Shaw) and one on tour (under him). Quayle was dissatisfied with the constraints of the festival system, and agreed with a critic who wrote in 1956 that the Shakespeare Memorial Theatre needed a common acting style and a studio school open all the year round, where novices and veterans would have time and opportunity to apply and develop the lessons of the repertoire. Without a permanent company this would be impossible, yet Quayle was anxious lest a permanent company narrowed the actors' range by concentrating on one playwright's work. It was also too expensive because 'great stars, essential to a first class performance', as he put it, would not absent themselves from the West End.[2]

Quayle and Flower discussed the obvious solution to Stratford's dilemma: public money supporting a base in London. This would allow for a broader repertoire and would satisfy the needs of the stars. Neither man, however, had much time for state aid, which, they believed, would undermine Stratford's independence. There was also little evidence that it would be forthcoming even if sought. The London idea had surfaced before, not surprisingly, given the excessive grip the capital exerted in a small country like Britain. An earlier Stratford director, William Bridges-Adams, had sought a London outlet in the 1930s but the then chair Archibald Flower had blocked the plan, which involved an association with the Old Vic. Quayle tried again. He looked at the Royal Court and the Embassy theatres as venues for a possible London outpost, and asked Devine if he would run it. Instead, Devine went his own way at the former location with the English Stage Company and thereby entered the history books as the pioneer of the playwrights' theatre that revitalised British drama. Quayle dropped the London idea, and, keen to expand his acting career and tired of politicking, he resigned in 1956, leaving Byam Shaw in charge as a holding operation. In 1958 Byam Shaw duly proposed Peter Hall as his successor. Hall, then aged twenty-seven, had directed twice at Stratford and, as far as can be determined, was the only candidate.

## Peter Hall

A teenager in the war (he was born in 1930), Hall was representative of a new upwardly mobile breed of ebullient 'scholarship boy' determined to make the most of whatever opportunities the post-war settlement offered. He reached his majority at the time of nationalisation and the introduction of the welfare state, and by background and inclination voted Labour but was not of the radical left.[3] Apart from a moment when he was briefly engaged to a woman he had met in the RAF, he had only one resolve: to be a theatre director. The power position in the theatre lay with this relatively new role of director, which had unseated that of the actor-manager. Hall was influenced by the example of Edward Gordon Craig, who believed in the director as superman and who had become an icon for Hall through his book *On the Art of the Theatre*. The survival of the major pre-war reps such as Birmingham, Liverpool and the Old Vic, and the establishment after the war of the Bristol Old Vic, meant that it was not entirely fanciful to crave the notion of a career as a director, let alone for someone who had not also first been an actor (as had major pioneers of the modern theatre like Stanislavsky or Reinhardt, and in the UK, Granville-Barker). The directorial success of non-acting university graduates, such as Hugh Hunt and Peter Brook, made the dream plausible if not obvious for students like Hall.

Although the theatre was still widely regarded as a risqué profession, the curious admixture at his university, Cambridge, of the 'puritan'

F.R. Leavis and the 'cavalier' George Rylands conferred upon him not only an intellectual and ethical justification of such a choice but also a sense of missionary intent. Leavis despised as effete both the theatre and the Rylands Bloomsbury set, yet his notions of textual scrutiny and the moral gravitas of art provided powerful analytical tools and the urgency of an evangelical spirit: good art was not only good for society but essential to its well-being. Rylands, a link to the influential Renaissance revivalist William Poel as well as to Granville-Barker, offered the sensual satisfaction of practising the art with a rigour equal to that of Leavis but with glamour as well. There was the additional allure of Rylands' connections at the highest level of the theatrical profession. The hot-house Cambridge environment in which Hall found himself was famously the seedbed of many who became leading theatrical figures, such as Derek Jacobi, Ian McKellen and Trevor Nunn. As founder of the RSC and later artistic director of the National Theatre, Hall himself was to become the exemplar of the modern artistic director, a defining figure in the shaping of modern British theatre.

Negotiating the student drama jungle was superb training for weathering the vicissitudes of the commercial theatre, and during his twenty student productions, Hall displayed qualities and formed a persona that were to become familiar to those who worked with him at the RSC. He was ambitious (he decided as a fifteen-year-old to run Stratford), could pretend convincingly, easily went over budget, took well-calculated risks and had a huge appetite for work. He enjoyed self-promotion, being in charge and the politics of the theatre. He showed a flair for organisation, was single-minded and usually obtained what he desired with disarming charm. After Cambridge, he moved quickly off the treadmill of the regional reps through the short-lived Elizabethan Theatre Company to running things: the Oxford Playhouse, the Arts Theatre, London, where he made a considerable name for himself directing the English-language première of Samuel Beckett's *Waiting for Godot*, and his own company, International Playwrights Theatre. His reputation was bolstered by having three productions in the West End at the age of twenty-five, including British premières of two plays by Tennessee Williams, *Camino Real* and *Cat on a Hot Tin Roof*. Hall was energetic, articulate, pragmatic, successful and becoming increasingly well connected at the apex of the profession. He was the coming man.

It was the Beckett production that triggered the invitation to direct at Stratford, which Hall had longed for. His debut was not auspicious but he was invited back the following year. He was already a celebrity without being an *enfant terrible* in the Peter Brook mould. The press reported his love of fast cars and his marriage in 1956 to French film star Leslie Caron, which impressed the Stratford governors. Hall says she begged him not to take the RSC job but he was never going to let personal relationships stand in the way, and the marriage did not survive very long after he took up the post. He officially became director of the Shakespeare Memorial Theatre on 1 January 1960, aged twenty-nine, a potent symbol of the new decade, which his youth, liberal views and vigour epitomised.

Hall was seen in the 1950s as uncharacteristically young for such a responsibility, though Hugh Hunt before the war had run the Abbey, Ireland's national theatre, aged only twenty-three. The Stratford governors' anxieties concerning Hall's age were mollified by the appointment at the same time of a new general manager, Patrick Donnell, whom Byam Shaw thought an admirable link between the old and new regimes. Although the governors endorsed Hall's selection, the post was in the gift of Fordham Flower; there were no advertisements or formal interviews. Hall and Flower, the Labour meritocrat and the philanthropic Tory businessman, went on to form what became an unlikely yet remarkable partnership, one of the most important in post-war British theatre. The relationship between chair of governors and chief executive, who at the RSC was the artistic director, is always crucial to the health of a theatre. Too much interference by the chair inhibits the creativity of the institution; too little threatens its capacity to endure. Hall and Flower agreed on the separation of the governors from the artistic management of the company, a division that was followed within the company between the administrative and artistic wings. Future alliances between chair and chief executive officer were similarly vital to the stability of the ever-threatened RSC – there were only three more chairs to the end of the century and three more artistic directors – although it was not until the pairing of Geoffrey Cass and Adrian Noble in the 1990s that a similarly close relationship became central to the direction of the institution itself.

## The plan

Hall impressed Flower with his practical arguments. Hall had lectured on business finance and management in the RAF (by the necessity of accident, as it was not his chief subject), and early in his career had appreciated the importance of the economics and administration of theatre. His time in national service in Germany had introduced him to the concept of public subsidy and his reading, particularly books such as Norman Marshall's *The Other Theatre*, supported the concept persuasively. His hero Craig in 1910 had asked for a five-year subsidy for a standing company of 100, two theatres, and a school for theatre workers. It was an early blueprint for the RSC. Hall argued to Flower that for Stratford to prosper as anything other than a provincial heritage theatre, it had to be transformed into a publicly funded, permanent or semi-permanent company performing classical and contemporary work, built around a core of artists, with a base in London as well as in Stratford. There were signs that British theatre was beginning to reconnect to its society, having previously failed, in Hall's words, 'to take into account the fact that we have had a World War . . . and that everything in the world has changed – values, ways of living, ideals, hopes and fears'.[4] Theatre was staking its claim as a cultural force of significance and a new Stratford–London company could add its considerable voice to this clamour.

Specifically, his aim was to emulate the great art theatre ensembles but without their institutional drawbacks. Hall understood and sympathised with the British caution concerning bureaucratic intervention in the arts and was not seeking the introduction of cultural commissars or artistic jobs for life. On a trip to the Soviet Union in 1958 with the Stratford company, during which time he had the decisive conversation with Flower regarding the future Stratford operation, he saw much that was wrong with the Soviet theatre system. Soon afterwards he met Helene Weigel, Brecht's widow and head of the Berliner Ensemble, who stunned him with her criticism of its spoilt, lazy actors. Hall did not want to replicate a civil service theatre, which he believed quickly became artistically sclerotic, and gave rise to what he characterised as an 'official' Puck syndrome whereby an actor takes a role by right of seniority, not aptness. He recognised that subsidy could make theatre complacent, yet, without it, the experiment could not happen or be sustained. He sought to balance the best of both systems: the collective discovery over time of the subsidised ensemble without its rigidities and the fleetness of the commercial system without its waste.

Flower was familiar with all the elements of Hall's plans to revitalise Stratford except one, and it was critical. The new company had to win public subsidy, and to achieve this it had to gamble everything. The Treasury could not be persuaded to grant Stratford a substantial subvention unless it merited an award on both artistic and economic grounds. The measure of the former would require the company to operate at a level and breadth of activity expected of a major ensemble. The measure of the latter would require Stratford's reserves to have disappeared. Hall's idea was to achieve the former through the latter and vice versa. In other words, Stratford would have to become bankrupt in order to receive state aid, but it would go bankrupt by supporting the vastly expanded work of the new company.

There was a further imperative. Hall and Flower were aware that the putative National Theatre, a shadow that had hung over Stratford since the 1949 National Theatre Act had promised its creation, now really looked like coming into existence. If the challenge presented by a national theatre were not met, Stratford faced a substantial reduction in its appeal, both to audiences and to artists. The climate concerning state aid would change once the NT was launched, and a Stratford–London company could mount a strong argument for similar treatment if it were so ambitious that it could not be ignored. Hall's was a high-risk, 'all or nothing' strategy, but he convinced Flower that it was necessary and practicable.[5] Hall's own personality – a curious mix of the public servant and the pirate – and his appetite for the committee meetings and political manoeuvrings his scheme would entail were important factors in winning Flower's support.

Flower recognised that Stratford faced a clear choice; to continue as before, finding it increasingly difficult to maintain standards, or to expend every effort to become one of the top art theatres of the world, which required a complete alteration in attitude. Accepted commercial notions would have to be abandoned and a new world embraced, in which 'a large annual deficit was part of life'.[6] He expected and received tough resistance from the governors, who were very Tory with a distinctly Midlands flavour. They objected to the shift to London, interpreted as an urban snub to rural Stratford's festival role as guardian of Shakespeare's spirit. Stratford, they feared, would lose its unique character. Opposition to the London move also came from a different angle. Beaumont, the figurehead of the old commercial system Hall wanted to overthrow, saw Hall's London plan as a Trojan horse. By coming to London, Beaumont feared Hall would be attacking the commercial system from within in order to establish the national profile of a publicly backed company. This opposition was ironic, as Beaumont had successfully won government subsidy in wartime to support his commercial operation by presenting classics as educational productions via a separate, non-profit company. Beaumont shared Hall's belief that without subsidy the venture would fail and ruin Stratford, but thought that, with subsidy, the company would offer unfair competition, and would corner the best actors and the best new plays. Beaumont told Hall he would have to resign as a governor, not from personal animus – he had hired Hall himself in the commercial theatre and they admired each other – but to avoid possible conflict of interests. He subsequently stayed true to his word.

The proposed financial strategy, to which the London base was integral, caused the greatest and widespread consternation among the governors. Given the parsimonious level of grant to drama as a whole, this was an audacious, possibly foolhardy plan based on a reversal of the good management upon which Stratford had always prided itself. Flower and Hall won the day but criticism from within the governing body continued throughout the early years of the company.

## The new company

In order to implement his plan, Hall had to fight on several fronts at once in an extraordinary pinball game of frenetic activity – a chaotic creativity as an impresario reflected in the sprawling creativity of the institution he founded. He was not expecting absolute solutions because nothing would ever be settled; the institution would be constantly readjusted. It was being created 'all in a state of finding'.[7]

Upon taking charge at Stratford, Hall was immediately involved in choosing plays, directors, casts and other artists for his first season, commissioning playwrights, implementing institutional changes at Stratford, making various practical changes, such as altering the Stratford stage, searching for his London theatre, lobbying Buckingham Palace to agree to a change of name for the company – which was agreed in March 1961 – and battling for subsidy.

The most pressing issue was to form the new company. The differences in nuance and usage between 'company' and 'ensemble' bothered Hall less than the practicalities. The concept of the ensemble was drawn from music and the ideal of seamless playing. It existed within the theatre as a description of excellent collective work on stage but, despite the efforts of early repertory theatres and smaller utopian projects such as the Group Theatre in London, or the Maddermarket Theatre in Norwich, which he had visited in 1951, there was little tradition of ensembles as such in Britain, which lacked the necessary patronage to support them. Notwithstanding the commonwealth of actors known in Shakespeare's day, the modern version of 'company' was seen as foreign. Foreigners at Glyndebourne had transformed opera in Britain, but opera was seen as foreign in any case. Theatre, especially where Shakespeare was concerned, was different. British theatre and the society of which it was a part had not embraced the idea of 'company' in the sense of a continuing association of people, though the notion featured in many a theatrical debate. Indeed, since the late 1800s when both the Comédie Française and the Saxe-Meiningen troupe visited London, the example of the European ensemble illuminated the arguments of those in favour of a serious theatre. Most notably this was found in the idea of a national theatre to be funded by the state in order to ensure the necessary coherence and stability that would allow it to act as a yardstick of excellence. Charles Flower, the founder of the Shakespeare Memorial Theatre, was inspired by this European model to dream of creating in Stratford an ensemble free from the demands of the box office and supported by an endowment instead. Hall was attempting to make Flower's dream come true.

Hall had been thinking about the merits of the company ideal for some time. As a schoolboy he had been impressed by the fine ensemble playing of the Old Vic company at the New Theatre led by Olivier and Richardson and by the Gielgud repertory of classics at the Haymarket Theatre. Hall had read, if not fully absorbed, books by and about Stanislavsky and the celebrated Moscow Art Theatre, and he had seen the work of ensembles during his national service in Germany. He paid tribute to the impact of the 1956 London visit of the most famous of these, the Berliner Ensemble, as 'the greatest single influence on the English theatre since the war', and the effect of Brecht on all aspects of the RSC's work, from the acting to the scenography, was profound.[8] Hall also said he had an obsession with the Théâtre National Populaire and Barrault/Renaud Company in France, and it was always part of his vision to have such companies performing in the RSC's theatres. He achieved this through the World Theatre Seasons at the Aldwych Theatre, frequently the highpoint of the London theatre and inestimably important in opening up the cloistered world of homegrown drama. His time spent with the Elizabethan Theatre Company (ETC) gained him practical experience, albeit on a different scale to what he would have to confront at Stratford. ETC aimed to maintain a permanent core of actors who would develop a distinctive style of performing. In 1955 he had bemoaned the fact that the Old Vic company changed every season and concluded: 'There is still no company in this country where definite styles of acting can be seen, and where our classics can be played as they ought to be.'[9] One such company that offered a 'definite style' was Theatre Workshop, an acknowledged influence on Hall. He even invited – unsuccessfully – its artistic director Joan Littlewood to direct at the RSC. Theatre Workshop was briefly an ensemble, bound together through dedication, but it fragmented by having to play in the West End due to inadequate state support. Although better publicly funded than Littlewood, George Devine was defeated in his attempts to create an ensemble at the Royal Court for similar lack of public financial patronage.

Hall believed that building a company was the prerequisite for creating a vibrant theatre of reanimated Shakespeare and vital new and modern plays presented in an invigorating symbiosis. Most urgently, a company would provide the conditions for an unprecedented examination of the plays of Shakespeare. Despite his pronounced views on the correct way to speak verse and his immediate introduction of verse classes at Stratford, for Hall a company style – either in a particular production or even more intangibly for the company as a whole – was not a matter of doctrine. It had to be rooted in the choices made by actors, hence the necessity for new ways of working. Freedom in rehearsal to achieve this would be almost impossible outside of a company structure. Related questions such as how a company style that was developed to perform Shakespeare could also serve the different styles of modern work were also to be addressed pragmatically. The motto would be: 'Keep open, keep critical'.[10] The company would be a world of experiment, which Hall recognised would be more consuming of time, energy and patience than following conventional theatre practice. Whatever became identified as the company style – at its strongest, a passionate Puritanism that eschewed individual dazzle for the brilliance of individuals acting impeccably as a group – would be achieved by determined and inventive trial and error. The RSC was not searching for one particular style but, in the process of refining its work within certain common aesthetic guidelines determined by Hall, it produced a recognisable style as a consequence.

Hall had to construct a practical framework that would suit the situation in which he found himself. Ensemble playing would take time to develop, and while there would always be a turnover of actors within the company, he needed to secure a reasonable degree of continuity through the presence of important personnel and adherence to shared beliefs and aims. Peggy Ashcroft was the key to forming Hall's first company of actors. Aside from her own standing as an actress, excelling in both classic and modern plays, she had radical sympathies and had believed in the company ideal since falling in love with the Moscow Art Theatre in the 1920s. She was a link to John Gielgud's attempts in the 1930s to create a company within the commercial system in seasons at the New Theatre and Queen's Theatre, attempts that laid many of the foundations of the post-war Stratford developments. She was also a link to one of the most important of the contemporary theatres, the Royal Court – she served on the artistic committee and had appeared there in Brecht's *The Good Woman of Setzuan*. To Hall she had been a heroine since boyhood, thanks to her 1945 performance in *The Duchess of Malfi*. They first met in 1957 when he cast her as Imogen in *Cymbeline*, his second Stratford production. The following year he directed her in the West End in *Shadow of Heroes*, and, during its run, he asked her to lead the new company. She agreed, and came to be emblematic of the RSC, serving as a member of its Direction. The company subsequently named a rehearsal room above the Swan Theatre in her honour.

The institutional key to Hall's plan was the introduction of what became known as the three-year contract, which was unique in the British theatre. In fact, it was a three-year commitment that in formal terms was made up of three successive one-year contracts, each of which allowed re-negotiation of pay and casting. This reflected the position of Equity, the actors' union, which sought to protect its members' remuneration against inflation as well as their artistic interests by not agreeing to a contract that ran for more than fifty-two weeks. Offering a combination of security and flexibility, the three-year system was designed to gather together a loose nucleus of actors who would regard the company as their permanent home. It gave the company first call on an actor's services for three years but, if the company did not wish to cast an actor, then that actor was free to seek work elsewhere. Provision was made for actors to leave the company on occasion in order to benefit financially and professionally from working in films and television. Hall subsequently sought to provide such opportunities with the RSC itself through TV and film deals. The contract also provided for holidays with pay. In the absence of any public money, the Calouste Gulbenkian Foundation gave £5,000 a year for three years to underwrite the costs of the contracts. Hugh Jenkins, at the time assistant general secretary of Equity (later the Arts Minister), hailed their intro-duction as a 'revolutionary scheme'.[11]

In the age of the commercial theatre, and to a lesser though still con-siderable extent afterwards, classical theatre in Britain had survived courtesy of the hidden subsidy derived from poor remuneration of the actors who performed it. Hall was able to offer pay roughly comparable to that of Old Vic, with a few receiving higher rates, but he was not able to match West End levels. The 'trade-off' was the attraction of more and varied work, better conditions and earnings guaranteed for a definite period. The problem of persuading actors to live in Stratford for many months was addressed by the promise of a London transfer for a few Stratford productions along with the presentation of new work there, and by the artistic dividends of the enterprise itself, resulting from longer rehearsals – on average six weeks for each production – and new ways of working.

These represented a major transformation of conventional theatre practice. In the late 1870s, four plays were seen at Stratford in ten days; in the following decade, and for the next thirty years, the season lasted two weeks. In the 1930s eight plays were rehearsed in eight weeks, all of which opened within a fortnight. This was possible because actors already knew the plays, just as opera singers know the opera canon. If a Mercutio fell ill, at least twenty actors were ready to replace him at a moment's notice. In 1946 Barry Jackson changed the Stratford system by allowing four weeks' rehearsal for each play, and a separate director directed each. This allowed Jackson to open the season in April with three plays and add another five at monthly intervals. At the same time, the boundary between the classical and the modern actor was becoming blurred, a process aided by film. Laurence Olivier, for instance, was known as Heathcliff as well as Henry V, and in the 1950s he completed the journey by playing the seedy music hall artiste Archie Rice in *The Entertainer*.

Hall hoped to stimulate the development of a different type of actor who could make that journey at will, but he recognised the reality of the British theatre lacking a formal ensemble tradition. To many actors, the proposed six-week rehearsal period – a luxury elsewhere – simply meant not having to learn your lines as quickly as before. 'Team spirit' was evident and constituted a willingness to work collectively but defensiveness about craft limited the benefits. A healthy mistrust of doctrine was often mixed with an unhealthy anti-intellectualism, and the emphasis on verse work smacked to some of dogma and the university while to others it was a refreshing chance to develop their skills. Verse speaking came under the tutelage of John Barton, Lay Dean of King's College, Cambridge and Hall's long-time artistic colleague from university days. An eccentric, irreverent, razor blade chewing magus with a fertile mind, he joined the company as Hall's lieutenant and was sufficiently important to Hall for Hall to insist he attend all governors' meetings alongside him.

## First seasons

Setting up the initial seasons without knowing if the company would survive released a surge of adrenalin that saw Hall and his colleagues through difficult and uncharted territory as well as through the problems that can face any theatrical management. The enterprise was carried along by the excitement of creating a new theatre company unlike any that had been seen in Britain before.

As artistic directors had done before and were to continue to do afterwards, Hall unsuccessfully tackled the recalcitrant layout of the Stratford auditorium, which was of proscenium design rather than the open stage of Shakespeare's day. He wanted the audience to feel more as if they were sharing the same space as the actors rather than inhabiting a separate arena. The focal point for the stage was remote for a theatre of its capacity and, from the back of the balcony, further than the normal distance for discerning details of the face. Hall extended the stage to bring it closer to the audience and cut it away at both sides to allow two rows of angled seats to be added to the front stalls. He also added a rake or slope, a platform-like feature that was to become symbolic of the RSC as a theatre of public debate. He set the tone for the future practice of the RSC by leading from the rehearsal floor. He decided to direct three of the six productions in a themed season of comedies, chosen because he did not believe the young company would be able to give a good account of the more mature plays. The first set-back was that Britain's two outstanding directors, Tyrone Guthrie and Peter Brook, were unavailable. Hall turned to university friends, Barton and Peter Wood, leaving only one director from outside the Cambridge circle, Michael Langham.

In choosing the actors who would create his company, Hall immediately paid the price for his pragmatism. He had no interest in being trapped in an esoteric sideshow. He loved celebrity and believed in star quality, if not the star system. Hall wanted star actors who could play within an ensemble alongside the core company actors.[12] No sooner had he secured the services of the stars Rex Harrison and Kay Kendall than he learnt they were withdrawing. He suffered a further blow when, having moved on from Harrison and cast his lead actor Paul Scofield as Shylock, Petruchio and Thersites, he received a shattering letter from the actor a few weeks before rehearsals began, saying he could not face coming to Stratford. Hall held his nerve and gambled. He approached a young actor, Peter O'Toole, whom he had seen playing Hamlet at the Bristol Old Vic the year before. He turned out to be the 'find' of the first season, but in November that year he announced he was to play the lead in David Lean's film *Lawrence of Arabia* and would not be available for London where he had agreed to play Henry II in *Becket*. The company issued an injunction but lost on the grounds that O'Toole had not been contracted to play that specific role. O'Toole's withdrawal threatened the success Hall needed in London in order to persuade the Arts Council to subsidise the company. Not only did Hall want to play O'Toole's Stratford productions in London, he had also won the rights for *Becket* against competition from Beaumont and needed a star to carry it off.

The company he formed was forty-eight strong, with an emphasis on youth, and drew on actors new to Shakespeare who had worked in the committed theatre of the Arts, the Royal Court and Theatre Workshop in addition to those with previous experience of Stratford. The opening production by Hall of *The Two Gentlemen of Verona* was greeted as a disaster. Unrest among senior actors in the next production, *The Taming of the Shrew*, forced Hall to remove its director, his closest ally John Barton, and see it through himself. It was traumatic for Hall and tested his mettle as a company leader. Nevertheless, the critics liked the production and hailed a new star in O'Toole. The season gathered support with each subsequent production. Hall appeared on stage at the final performance to tell the audience his new company had broken Stratford box office records (97.2 per cent), capping even the anniversary season the year before. He considered the season a vindication of his plan. Yet, as he said, as soon as you create a company 'it begins to disintegrate'.[13]

During this opening season, Hall had also planned the second Stratford season, which ran from April to November 1961, along with securing the lease on the Aldwych Theatre, overseeing its refurbishment for the company's needs, and planning its inaugural programme. The struggle to obtain the lease showed the determined and impudent side of Hall that gave the company its reputation for audacity. Hall wanted the Aldwych, where he had directed Peter Sellars in *Brouhaha* two years before, but was rebuffed by its owner Prince Littler, chairman and managing director of Associated Theatre Properties (London) Ltd, and head of the Stoll Moss theatre empire. Hall believed Littler was anxious at Beaumont's opposition and did not think a repertory in the West End would be successful. Hall asked Toby Rowland, who had produced *Brouhaha*, to intercede quietly whilst Hall turned to Prince's younger brother Emile. The brothers, who had been educated in Stratford, had fallen out. Emile was head of a different group of theatre and leisure interests and was a member of the Stratford theatre's executive council. Emile had written, presented and directed fifteen pantomimes, and, according to Hall, yearned for respectability. He responded enthusiastically to Hall's approach and offered him the Cambridge Theatre, seeing the possibility of co-management and making money from guest visits by foreign companies.

Neither this theatre nor this kind of arrangement was what Hall desired but he used the offer as a bargaining ploy to return to Prince, who now changed his mind. Hall's urgency led to a premature announcement in March 1960 of a five-year lease, which had to be revised in July to three. The agreement he struck was necessarily a compromise. Littler charged a low rent but took 25 per cent of the gross box office income. This effectively meant there could be no profit for the company, which also had to recoup its costs in refurbishing the theatre. In November 1960 the company struck a deal with Peter Cadbury, the managing director of Keith Prowse Ltd, the country's biggest ticketing agency, that guaranteed £250,000 worth of ticket income for the first Aldwych season (approximately 25 per cent). It was the largest deal of its kind in Britain and

showed the Treasury and the Arts Council as well as the Stratford governors that Hall was arguing from a position if not of prudence then
certainly of serious practicality and entrepreneurial creativity.

Following speedy work to redesign and modernise the Aldwych to
bring it as much into line with the Stratford theatre as possible, Hall was
able to open in December 1960. The inaugural production of what was
then known as 'The Stratford Company at the Aldwych' was Webster's *The
Duchess of Malfi*, and Ashcroft reprised the role in which Hall had first
seen her sixteen years before. In its first week it broke the theatre's box
office records for that period. Donald McWhinnie directed, a sign of
Hall's commitment to a contemporary sensibility. McWhinnie, who had
directed the play on radio, was known for his recent première production
of *The Caretaker* as well as for his ground-breaking work in radio, commissioning and producing the likes of Pinter, Adamov and Beckett, and
establishing the 'radiophonic workshop', which pioneered *musique concrete* in English broadcasting. *The Duchess of Malfi* was followed by a
Shakespeare transfer from Stratford, Hall's production of *Twelfth Night*,
which sold out for its twenty-five performances. Hall directed Leslie
Caron in the British première of Giraudoux's *Ondine*, which was followed by the world première of the commissioned play *The Devils* by
John Whiting directed by Peter Wood. This caught the mood of the
moment and was revived the following year. In the face of criticism from
many critics when the expansion to London was announced, Hall had
proved his point at the Aldwych. Once he had opened at the theatre,
however, which ran almost the whole year round, the rhythm of life for
the company took on its own new momentum, and fresh demands and
problems became apparent. Acquiring a London base was the most
important systemic change Hall initiated. It was an indispensable element in securing the legitimacy and survival of the company and the
later public subsidy required to support it but also the main cause of the
historic inadequacy of that subsidy.

The 1961 Stratford season, in the meantime, represented a backward
step in terms of consolidating a company. There was a continued stress on
'youth' and 'new faces', with a few exceptions, such as Edith Evans as
Queen Margaret in *Richard III* and the huge error of John Gielgud playing Othello in Franco Zeffirelli's statuesque production that belonged to
a previous era. The high point was Michael Elliott's production of *As You
Like It* with Vanessa Redgrave. The other successful production, *Richard
III*, was also created by a director new to Shakespeare, William Gaskill,
who, like Elliott, would not fit into a company run by Hall. Elliott was a
TV director who had only moved to the theatre two years before and was

subsequently appointed as artistic director of the Old Vic before going on to co-found the Royal Exchange, Manchester, which rivalled and often surpassed the productions of the national companies. Gaskill, who had been directing at the Royal Court for four years, directed three more productions for Hall in 1962 but was humiliated when Hall took over his production of Brecht's *The Caucasian Chalk Circle*. Gaskill claimed Hall had thwarted a collective search for a new kind of theatre practice and the following year joined the newly created National Theatre. He was later artistic director of the Royal Court and established himself as one of the leading directors of the British theatre.

The end of the 1961 London season did see the British première of Anouilh's *Becket*, with Christopher Plummer in place of O'Toole, and Michel Saint-Denis's production of *The Cherry Orchard*, which had played seven performances in Stratford. It broke Aldwych box office records and was shown on BBC TV, directed by Michael Elliott. Ironically, *Becket* transferred to the Globe Theatre, the headquarters of Beaumont's empire, fulfilling the prophecy he had made about the RSC in London. Indeed, while Stratford lacked coherence, the London season had turned out better than anticipated.

## Inventing the institution

Hall's whirlwind approach was creating an organisation by improvisation. He grappled tirelessly with different ways of running the new operation artistically and administratively. After the first season he instituted a collegiate artistic system of associate directors (Brook, who was yet to direct for the company, Michael Elliott, Donald McWhinnie and Peter Wood) and of associate designers (Desmond Heeley, Sean Kenny and Leslie Hurry), who between them had designed eight productions. The extemporised nature of the arrangement can be seen in the RSC careers of those involved. Heeley and Hurry did no more work for the RSC and Kenny designed only one more production. Design, which was central to the RSC, was about to undergo a transformation but at the hands of others. The directors were supposed to direct a minimum of three plays each over three years and be involved in planning yet only Brook stayed, though entirely on his own terms. Elliott transferred *As You Like It* to London and left. After directing two RSC productions in 1962, McWhinnie only returned once, in 1964. He pursued a freelance stage and television career. Peter Wood directed *The Beggar's Opera* at the Aldwych in 1963 and did not return until 1974, and never to Stratford. He found success in the commercial sector and at the NT.

Undaunted, Hall pressed on, inventing the institution in a form of permanent revolution. Following *The Cherry Orchard*, he asked Saint-Denis if he would join the company in a leadership role. Hall had discussed the formation of the RSC with him in the early days of his thinking and in February 1962 he announced that Saint-Denis was to become the RSC's general artistic adviser with a special responsibility for training in charge of a Studio in Stratford. Saint-Denis had great standing. He was a living link with the major influences of twentieth-century continental European theatre through his personal acquaintance with Copeau, Artaud, Stanislavsky and Brecht. Leaders of the British theatre such as Gielgud, Olivier, Ashcroft and Devine revered him for his work over three decades, which included directing the influential Compagnie des Quinze, the London Theatre Studio and the Old Vic School. In April, Hall trumped this appointment by announcing the company was to be run by a triumvirate, with himself as managing director (borrowing a title from industry) alongside Saint-Denis and Brook as directors.

That year, 1962, Hall turned the RSC into what one commentator described as 'the biggest single theatre venture in the world'.[14] By hiring the Arts Theatre in London, he expanded the RSC empire to embrace three theatres, in addition to the Studio in Stratford, two West End transfers, a small-scale tour to mainland Europe and an ambitious large-scale tour of the UK presenting challenging Shakespeare and two world premières. Its company of actors and staff (numbering almost 500) presented twenty-four productions in an unprecedented range of classical and contemporary work to some 700,000 people. As if this size of operation were not enough, Hall harboured other ideas for expansion. In order to make the RSC's stages better able to accommodate the free-flowing production of Shakespeare that he intended, he embarked on two major building schemes. One, in partnership with Ballet Rambert, was to build in London their own 1,600-seat flexible theatre with a smaller space alongside. The other was to turn the Stratford theatre into a 2,000-seat thrust stage amphitheatre – in Hall's words, 'the most exciting theatre building in Europe'.[15]

In fact, occupying a smaller space had become a necessity as soon as Hall had secured the 1,000-seat Aldwych Theatre. In the expectation of a public subsidy that did not arrive, he drove through an interim solution: to open a play a month at the 330-seat Arts Theatre, which he had run in the mid-1950s. To those who thought taking a London base was foolhardy, this further extension of the RSC seemed the sign of insanity, yet much came out of the ambitious but short-lived season that opened in March 1962. *Everything in the Garden* by Giles Cooper transferred to the

West End. A production of *Nil Carborundum* by Henry Livings led to a successful Aldwych production by Hall in 1964 of his comedy *Eh?* A production of *The Lower Depths* began the RSC's association with Gorky, a hallmark of the company's modern work in the 1970s. A production of Middleton's *Women Beware Women*, said by the RSC to be possibly the first for 300 years, followed up the success of *The Duchess of Malfi* and presaged the company's explorations of Jacobean plays at The Other Place and the Swan. The director David Jones, who became the mainstay of the RSC's modern work at the Aldwych, made his debut, the future leading actors Nicol Williamson and David Warner came into the company, and Sally Jacobs, who designed two productions in the Arts season, became Brook's RSC designer.

The main discovery, however, was the playwright David Rudkin, a twenty-five-year-old Oxford University graduate and Birmingham schoolteacher whose play *Afore Night Come* proved ideal for the RSC. Set in Stratford country, it has an urgent, sharp sense of language as well as a tramp called Shakespeare, and taps into the darker dimensions of existence, which the RSC was to explore in several contemporaneous productions. It was revived at the Aldwych and became dubbed a modern 'classic'. Rudkin later became 'unofficial' house dramatist for The Other Place. Hall acknowledged that *Afore Night Come* and other productions in the season helped him understand the ritual violence of the *Henry VI* plays in *The Wars of the Roses* trilogy and fed into the strand of company work represented two years later by the *Theatre of Cruelty* programme and Peter Weiss's *Marat/Sade*.[16]

Before the fringe existed, the Arts season raised the profile of the company as daring and open-minded, and it turned out to be the first of regular and necessary injections of challenging work outside of the RSC's regular spaces. But Hall was forced to end the Arts experiment after just over six months for financial reasons, which meant new plays by John Arden, David Mercer and others had to be returned. Hall still hoped to present three plays a year at the Arts but that ambition, too, was beyond the company's budget.

Just as the company was reaching new heights in 1962, it was also at its most vulnerable. It was now enjoying mixed fortunes at both the Aldwych and in Stratford. Although the press did not butcher it, the production of John Whiting's *A Penny for a Song* was a box office catastrophe at the Aldwych. In Stratford, another box office disaster threatened but of a different kind. Paul Scofield had again agreed to come to Stratford, returning after a fourteen-year absence as Lear in Peter Brook's production. It had already sold 30,000 tickets when Hall had to announce that due to exhaustion caused by acting continuously for two years in England, America and Canada, Scofield could not meet the schedule. Hall could either extend existing shows or hastily insert another. The anticipated 'banker' *Macbeth* was not performing as expected and Hall's buccaneering instincts preferred attack rather defence. *King Lear* was postponed and in its place Clifford Williams was asked to direct *The Comedy of Errors* with only three weeks' rehearsal. The story of its success has passed into RSC folklore as the first untrammelled public validation of the company ideal and an exemplar of the company's recurring triumphs over adversity in the best Dunkirk spirit.

Despite its popularity in the previous century, it was then a little-known play and had not been seen in Stratford since 1938. It represented a huge risk, and Williams, who was not part of the Cambridge circle, was himself another gamble in Hall's eyes.[17] Hall had hired him as a staff director – there were no assistants then – on the explicit understanding that he would not direct but oversee productions after they had opened and supervise transfers. The very size of the RSC had given Williams his first chance when the original director of *Afore Night Come* became unavailable and he was on hand to plug the gap. Now he was to repeat the act. John Wyckham, the RSC's technical director, designed a simple, raked wooden platform as the set and future Oscar-winner Anthony Powell designed the costumes, which were based on rehearsal dress. The cast was drawn from the *King Lear* company with the addition of actors whose own schedule allowed them to take part. Williams was known as a movement not a text man, and he relied on the actors in that latter department. Thanks to the RSC's verse classes, they were able to meet the challenge. It was fun for the actors and became the first seminal RSC production, even though Hall disliked it.

In an attempt to build a collective approach, Hall and other senior directors attended dress run-throughs – hence the nickname actors gave the occasion 'the night of the long knives'. Williams recalls that Hall took everything to do with the RSC personally: 'A failure was a failure for him.' Saint-Denis and Brook accompanied Hall on this occasion, a formidable trio. Williams believes Hall, whom he found to lack a sense of humour, had decided not to like the production before he had seen it, and asked Saint-Denis to comment first. 'You like *commedia*,' he opined. Brook said he had nothing to say and Hall then declared the production a total disaster. He was offended by actors prancing around, says Williams, and thought the production misshapen. He was not going to allow it in his theatre. Time, however, was against Hall. Williams, crushed but brash, proceeded without changing it. The production was hailed as delivering an ensemble RSC style. The critic Kenneth Tynan wrote that it was 'unmistakably' an RSC production. 'The statement is momentous: it means Peter Hall's troupe has developed, uniquely in Britain, a classical style of its own.'[18] Williams did not expect Hall to say he was wrong – and he did not. The production remained in the RSC repertoire on and off for the next ten years.[19]

Its success in the 1962 season lifted the Stratford company's spirits and braced them for the demands of Peter Brook and *King Lear*, which opened nearly two months later to even greater acclaim and eventually legendary status. A year in the planning, its groundbreaking, unsentimental approach, its stark, bare stage with battered leather costumes and corroded metal shapes under harsh white light, confirmed and defined the RSC as a new theatrical organism beyond the brilliance of its individual efforts. *King Lear* and *The Comedy of Errors*, the ideal combination of a tragedy and a comedy, toured abroad to rapturous praise and achieved Hall's ambition of having the RSC regarded as the equal of the towering continental ensembles that were the company's inspiration. It was a remarkable achievement in three seasons, and all without the public subsidy Hall knew the company needed to survive. In fact, just days before *King Lear* had opened, he had learned the outcome of that crucial battle, which was to shape the company's existence for the rest of the century.

## The fight for public subsidy

For the RSC, the move from fiscal independence to reliance on the state, however partial, was a defining moment ideologically as well as financially. While there is no simple correlation between the art and its funding – lavish can be abysmal and shoe-string exhilarating – the economic basis of the company's life was profoundly important in its ambition and achievement. The battle was intricate and protracted and took place mainly in private. Its outcome not only determined the kind of future the RSC could enjoy but also moulded the pattern of the nation's major performing arts funding for the next four decades. It reinforced the pole position in the funding firmament of the Royal Opera House, saw the birth of the two national theatre companies that dominated their own field of activity, and gave rise to the subsequent formation out of the Vic–Wells Opera of the English National Opera at the Coliseum. It was a battle that changed the face of the British arts world.

After Hall's appointment, he recognised that, paradoxically, the best chance of realising his own grand plan was to support the creation of the one institution that might obliterate it, the National Theatre (NT). Its establishment would act as a lever in the campaign for greater drama subsidy in an environment that was by European standards noticeably parsimonious. The Comédie Française on its own received more than one and a half times the amount the Arts Council gave to British drama as a whole. Britain's lack of tradition of state support for the arts was embarrassingly evident in its failure to establish a national theatre despite more than a century of debate. Yet this absence had provided an opening for Hall and the future RSC, however reluctant the arts establishment was to see him fill it. Hall had long supported the creation of a national theatre as consonant with his belief in a better ordered and publicly funded theatre system. Now the births of the two organisations that redrew the map of that system were to be inextricably linked, and they remained umbilically connected thereafter.

Since the first project for a National Theatre was mooted in the mid-1800s, the idea had been linked in one way or another to Stratford and the veneration of Shakespeare. Indeed, the very idea was triggered by the purchase for the nation of Shakespeare's birthplace. The movement for a national theatre, however, meandered until 1959 when, after many false starts and more than a century of debate, there appeared a real likelihood of a National Theatre being established at last. The Chancellor approved a scheme for the NT to be built on the south bank of the Thames. The scheme also involved building an opera house, and the Royal Opera House voiced its opposition in order to preserve its place at the top of the arts establishment's greasy pole. The Chancellor responded by offering a more favourable funding formula for opera, which subsequently distorted the funding available to the NT, which in turn was to mean even less for the RSC.

Laurence Olivier, the unofficial but generally acknowledged director-in-waiting of the NT, knew of Hall's plans to launch an ensemble and, not long before he appeared in Hall's 1959 Stratford production of *Coriolanus*, he made a pre-emptive strike. He asked Hall to be his number two at the NT. Hall preferred to be his own number one and declined. The NT bloc, however, needed Stratford's support to ensure the NT plan progressed. Resistance within the arts establishment centred on the argument that regional theatres should be supported first, and Stratford was a leading regional theatre. Moreover, the NT faction was keen to use Stratford's political weight in view of the less than enthusiastic participation in the campaign by the Old Vic representatives, who had the most to lose from the creation of a national theatre as it would absorb their theatre. The unspoken tension between Stratford and the NT group was the competition each would face from the other, but engagement might fend this off. In 1960, Stratford was formally asked – and it agreed – to join the NT–Old Vic Joint Council. Stratford did not want to be excluded because Lord Cottesloe, an ardent NT supporter who had just been appointed chair of the Arts Council, was preparing a report for the Treasury on the priority to be given the NT within the Council's limited drama budget. Stratford, therefore, needed to be involved, as crucial decisions about public money were about to be taken, which would set the funding pattern for the foreseeable future. Flower and Hall saw their opportunity to secure public funding through Stratford's association with the NT, and if Stratford missed out now, the chance might not come again before Stratford was bankrupt.

The Joint Council submitted a memorandum to the Chancellor, endorsed by Cottesloe, which proposed a 'tripod' arrangement involving three constituent groups: one on the south bank in a new building, one at Stratford and one on tour. In the interim, while the new building was being built, the Old Vic and Stratford would pool their resources, the Old Vic grant would be raised and the Stratford company would receive its first grant – the key to Hall's plans. Cottesloe submitted his own report, which backed the building of a national theatre but also expressed support for regional theatre. To everyone's surprise when a government reply came, in March 1961, the Chancellor pledged monies for the Old Vic and Stratford but rejected the NT plan as too costly. It was the ideal answer from Stratford's viewpoint, and on the strength of it Hall took the short lease on the Arts Theatre. With the Queen having agreed to Stratford's request for a name change, the Royal Shakespeare Company, it seemed, would have no competition for the title of the nation's theatre.[20]

Hall, meanwhile, joined the vociferous protesters on behalf of the slighted NT. Cottesloe followed up the Chancellor's announcement by writing to the RSC, asking it to provide figures and begin negotiations on a possible three-year grant. When the council saw the figures in May, it expressed surprise at the size of the RSC's demands: £124,000 to cover the current deficit, and an appeal for £400,000 to fund the new design for the Stratford theatre. Hall was in expansive mood but had to agree to drop the Stratford scheme because the only way it could be afforded was for the RSC to take out a loan, and this would have to be paid for out of company profits. Hall's strategy was based on the company reducing its profits in order to win public subsidy. A loan, therefore, was not compatible with the greater plan. The nation lost what might have been an extraordinary theatre space in order to gain its first large-scale theatre company.

A further blow to the nascent RSC came that July when the Chancellor was persuaded to change his mind on the NT, not by Tory grandees but by the Labour-controlled London Country Council, or, to be more precise, by the money it promised. The LCC pledged more than half the esti-mated NT building costs and offered the south bank site rent-free. For the Chancellor the appeal was made more attractive by the inclusion of Sadlers Wells in the NT scheme along with the Old Vic and the RSC; three funding streams, to each of the existing organisations, could be united in one. He insisted that the condition of securing any future sub-sidy by any one of those bodies was participation in the new merger plan. The RSC was not told this until after it wrote to Cottesloe to ask when and how much it would receive. His reply was a shock: Cottesloe explained that there would now be no interim money for the RSC until the new NT plan had been agreed upon in all its detail, and that could take a long time. The RSC, which had drawn up its budgets on the expectation of govern-ment money, was stumped. It had commitments to three theatres and no prospect of immediate subsidy even if they were to sign up to what Hall described as the 'British Leyland' solution where big was beautiful.[21]

The Joint Council had to draw up a revised plan and a constitution for the new NT organisation. Stratford became distinctly nervous, believing the Treasury had reneged. Flower and Hall suspected Olivier of empire building, of wanting to be in charge of everything while appropriating Stratford's skills and killing off any competition to the NT in London. With the Arts Council run by an NT man, they saw Stratford's inde-pendence disappearing, a feeling exacerbated when Olivier approached several Stratford actors to appear in his first season running the new Chichester Theatre as the NT in waiting. Olivier, on the other hand, believed with ample evidence that Hall was the empire builder and wanted the RSC to become the NT. Hall later insisted he never wanted the RSC to be the National Theatre, and that he always wanted two national companies. His main concern was that the NT would harm Stratford, particularly because opinion within the Arts Council suggested that Britain, let alone London, could not afford two national theatres. The timing of a visit to Stratford by solicitor Arnold Goodman, a fixer who had been hired to draft the NT constitution, seemed to focus their minds on the reality of the scheme, coming just after they had received Cottesloe's news that there was no immediate subsidy in sight, and none in the long term if they did not agree to a merger. A September 1961 meeting of the Joint Council worsened relations between the Stratford and NT factions. Flower and Hall gambled again and pulled out of the amalgamation, although the decision was not made public for some months. Flower's idea of a loose federation was rejected by an increasingly confident NT group.

When the RSC appealed to the Arts Council again in January 1962, Cottesloe replied that it was too late for the company to receive a grant for 1962/63 but said that an amount of £10,000 had been put aside for the company. This was confusing as the sum was unrelated to any discussions or figures the RSC had submitted, and contradicted his earlier assertion that no money would be forthcoming yet. The following month the mystery deepened when the drama panel discussed money for provincial theatres, and voted them £150,000, but the RSC was not mentioned at all.

Hall decided to instigate a press and political campaign in support of the RSC's appeal, leaking in March 1962 the story that the Aldwych would close if subsidy were not forthcoming. In the media, it was the RSC's 'relevance' – its presentation of new plays such as *The Devils* and the Arts Theatre season as much as its Shakespearean productions – that featured as grounds for the company to be supported from the public purse. In May, a senior Arts Council member told Flower unofficially that the Council had no official knowledge of the RSC applying for a grant. Flower wrote to Cottesloe saying this was nonsense and asked for £50,000. Cottesloe repeated the £10,000 figure as a ceiling, but added there was every hope that £50,000 might be released the following year. This appeared to offer the RSC some immediate respite but Hall continued with the press campaign. This was not the 'done thing' and upset the leading players, especially the Arts Council, which had promised money and resented being exposed to such public pressure. The campaign was important for the RSC's image but appears not to have been decisive in determining the outcome of the struggle for subsidy, which was decided by the Treasury on pragmatic grounds. The campaign climaxed in July just after the revised NT plan was finally settled, and the Chancellor agreed to release money to deliver it. There was no reference to the RSC, which was forced to end its Arts Theatre experiment.

Hall's dream could now have become dust. It was clear that neither Olivier, who was officially appointed artistic director of the NT that August, nor the Arts Council accepted the RSC's London presence or even believed there was money for more than one national theatre. The Treasury saw the proposed annual sum of £400,000 to be given to the South Bank as generous and left no room for other major clients as the commitment would be unsustainable. Hall and Flower believed fiscal power would achieve what persuasion could not. The public purse, it seemed, would not support the RSC adequately, and would thereby weaken it to the point where leading actors and directors would refuse to work for the company. It would be left with no alternative but to accept amalgamation into the NT on terms that were not of its choosing.

Olivier made an unsuccessful last-ditch move in October 1962 to bridge the gap between the factions. Accounts differ of his intention. He invited the RSC's ruling triumvirate of Hall, Brook and Saint-Denis to serve on the NT building committee and (in the Stratford version) said there could be an annual three-month RSC season at the NT – provided the RSC quit London. Olivier, on the other hand, insisted that the offer was a goodwill gesture, made in case the RSC failed to receive any funding at all and was forced to abandon the Aldwych. He believed that it was not the company's presence at the Aldwych that was the problem but the apparent necessity of funding it out of too small a pot of available money. Following Olivier's failure, the situation changed rapidly.

At the end of October Cottesloe told the RSC that it would receive a grant and this should be read as acceptance of the RSC operation in London. A week later – before such announcements would normally be made – the RSC was informed of the sum, £47,000 for 1963/64. It was about half what the RSC judged it needed and meant no pay rise for actors, no reopening of the Arts experiment, and no new building for the Studio in Stratford. More worryingly, there was a warning from the Treasury that has haunted the company ever since. It was not issued directly but by the messenger, in this case Sir William Emrys Williams, secretary-general of the Arts Council. He was told to pass on to the RSC the following advice: while the RSC might assume that 'it will be necessary for them to operate on a National Theatre level', the Treasury would not be able to accept 'any wider implications which might be held to flow from any such assumptions'.[22] In other words, the RSC would not receive a commensurate level of subsidy to the NT's even if it performed commensurately. It would always be the poor relation.

Why the Treasury changed its mind having insisted on merger with the NT as the prerequisite for subsidy is hard to divine. The press campaign seems not to have affected either the principle or the amount, though it must have made rejection of any support for the RSC politically harder as the NT was to be in receipt of subsidy. Perhaps the idea was to keep Hall quiet by giving the organisation some, though not enough, money in the hope, as the RSC believed, that the company would eventually buckle. Clearly the decision was made possible by the little publicised fact that the LCC had offered an additional grant to the NT of £100,000, and the NT had renounced from its Treasury monies exactly the same sum and suggested it go to the RSC instead. The RSC, however, was awarded less than half.

The RSC had won its battle but, as it turned out, had lost the war; it had gained the public subsidy and recognition as a national institution essential to Hall's plan, which meant the London base could be maintained, but it was not sufficient to fulfil Hall's ambitions for the company. Nevertheless, the settlement rankled with regional theatres and remained a divisive issue in the disbursement of the national funding cake. From the perspective of state arts funding in Britain, awarding a grant to the RSC represented an act of faith the like of which was not to be seen again that century. However, the sum awarded was arbitrary and nearly three times less than the NT received. This historic imbalance remained a constraint for the rest of the RSC's life. There was never enough money to support long-term experiment or training, or to reduce ticket prices substantially. It also meant in later years that the RSC had to do more and different things not always for artistic reasons but to attract necessary additional funds.

## The two companies

Neither the RSC nor the NT could ever shake off comparison with the other. The NT even had associates and also aimed to be a permanent company. The two organisations did briefly hold joint meetings on salaries, and when the NT raised its top actors' pay in 1963, the RSC followed suit the following season, with much difficulty. There was occasional sharing of repertoire plans to avoid duplication and discussion on contracts, touring, and the streamlining of the workshop facilities (which came to nothing). The work and the balance sheets of both were regularly contrasted, although the early distinction – defined by the NT's first literary manager Kenneth Tynan as the difference between the roundheads (the RSC) and the cavaliers (the NT) – did not outlive the Hall and Olivier regimes. Their personal tussle, like Hall's confrontation with 'Binkie' Beaumont, represented a clash of the new against the old, the director as king versus the actor-manager of yore, and when Hall succeeded Olivier, the ascendancy of the director was complete. From the mid-1970s, the RSC's appropriation of Shakespeare apart, the two came to share programming tastes and personnel – and even occupied similar concrete bunkers – to the point at which it was not always easy to distinguish between them.[23]

Yet, judged by 'national' criteria, such as the spread of its repertoire, especially the range of contemporary playwrights presented, and its national reach through touring and educational work, the RSC equalled and often surpassed the NT. It also frequently outperformed its only comparator in the statistical stakes beloved of arts administration: number of productions and performances, box office income, and amount of subsidy per paid admission. Nevertheless, the Arts Council refused to rectify the funding injustice. It would not deny the excellence of the RSC's performance but would reiterate the original Treasury position that, regardless of achievement, the RSC was *not* the National Theatre. Furthermore, it would riposte that it was inhibited by the size of its total grant, over which it had no control, and to reward the RSC to the level requested would require other clients to lose out significantly and unjustifiably.[24]

The RSC, which did not have the burden of the NT's huge building maintenance costs, did achieve some kind of even-handed treatment twice – in the mid-1980s, following the government-sponsored Priestley scrutiny, and at the start of the following decade in the wake of the short closure of the RSC's Barbican theatres. On both occasions the disparity was reasserted straightaway. The RSC mostly resisted attacking the NT in its lobbying for a fairer disbursement, but saw the horror predicted by Flower and Quayle of the NT paying higher salaries and offering lower ticket prices become a reality.

Crisis management is to an extent inherent in theatre; creating art involves questioning and challenge, and in Britain, with few exceptions, the institutions supporting that creativity are under-funded. A tension between aspiration and resource is inevitable and important for a creative theatre company, otherwise only dull theatre would be produced, but for the RSC the balance always fell just a little too much on the side of restriction.

# TWO

# IN THE MARKETPLACE OF NOW

Hall had a deep love of Shakespeare; at college he studied not only Elizabethan verse speaking but the punctuation and printing practices of the time and the authenticity of different versions, and he both acted in and directed Shakespeare. Yet Hall came to Stratford not as a classicist but as a director of modern plays. It was this reputation, as well as his continuing direction of new plays, that made his arguments for the company to be 'relevant' convincing. He believed the RSC had to be situated 'in the marketplace of Now . . . expert in the past but alive to the present'.[1] This was its legitimacy with the public, whom he was trying to woo both as potential audience and as taxpayers funding the company from the public purse. Leasing the Aldwych and, albeit briefly, the Arts to add to the Royal Shakespeare Theatre in Stratford allowed, in theory at least, cross-pollination between the RSC's classical and contemporary work. In setting up the Studio, Hall offered institutional artistic support for exploring the connections.

He wanted the RSC to recreate what he imagined must have been the intensity and daring of theatre in Shakespeare's day, an appeal to energise the troublesome present through reference to an iconic past that would characterise much RSC thinking. He felt the two Elizabethan periods shared similarities as times of change, of confusion, of censorship, of scientific and philosophical discovery and of an historic shift in class power, which, in the earlier period, led to a rising bourgeoisie decapitating the King. The present period was characterised by the complacency of Prime

Minister Macmillan's 'You've never had it so good' slogan. This concealed a darker underbelly to society, which became more apparent as the new decade of the 1960s unfolded.

The first Elizabethan period had seen the birth of modern professional theatre, a collaborative as well as a competitive affair with the flowering of acting companies, theatres and an extraordinary number of plays, of which those by Shakespeare represented but a tiny fraction. To the audiences of those days these plays were new plays, and the form was new too. Theatre was an autonomous, radical force, later to be seen as the one and only expression Britain has experienced of a truly popular theatre that crossed the classes. Although scholars are still disputing the nature and extent of this popularity, the myth as well as the plays themselves have been inspirational. Elizabethan theatre became the wellspring of many important innovations in the twentieth century, especially for Brecht and Artaud, the two immense theatrical spirits that hovered over the fledgling RSC. It also featured in the movement of British theatre in the mid-1950s to reconnect with its society as 'vital', 'committed' and 'relevant'.

Although the question of relevance was at the forefront of Hall's thinking for the RSC, in the company's first seasons he was only just beginning to investigate the complexities of what this implied for his own Shakespearean work. 'Relevance' touched on questions of style and the quality of theatrical liveliness on stage as well as more obviously on relating to society and politics. This exploration became the defining journey of the RSC by asking the question 'Why do we need theatre?' and 'What does theatre "mean"?' Questions that in turn ask, 'What does it mean to be human?' Yet for his first season in charge at Stratford, Hall had pragmatically distanced himself from the worthiness of the Royal Court, which, with companies like Theatre Workshop at Stratford East, was laying the basis for the new theatre of national debate to which Hall aspired. Conscious of the delicate balancing act he was undertaking in launching the RSC at Stratford, Hall had said he wanted the opening season to be entertaining and glamorous rather than 'improving'. By 1962, when Peter Brook arrived, Hall had embraced the more radical lexicon of the movement of which he wanted the RSC to be a leading player.

Brook, who was not political in the narrow definition of the word and saw politics as an anthropologist might, was nevertheless a vital influence in pushing Hall to examine 'relevance' more closely. Although Brook did not direct at the RSC until 1962, he had been advising Hall from the company's inception. Brook had introduced him to the writings of Artaud and, through the production of *King Lear*, to the notion of 'Shakespeare our contemporary' in practice. Hall's own next Stratford productions would reveal his growing interest in the mechanics and rituals of power as his pathway to 'relevance' in the theatre and demonstrate that the arrival of an identifiable 'company' and a discernible 'style' – sparse, rigorous and muscular – was neither accidental nor to be short-lived.

As was often the case with the RSC, the acute crises in which it found itself shaped the most astonishing theatrical responses. The first three years of impromptu invention had seen the company establish itself, notwithstanding the unevenness of quality in the work. The company's sheer size and fecundity were breathtaking, but it was in deep financial trouble. Hall was not cowed, however, by the knowledge that only half the necessary public subsidy was on offer and that the RSC finances were haemorrhaging. He was determined to drive on and consolidate the genuine sense of company that had been created. His response was to go for broke. In the autumn of 1962 he cancelled or postponed Stratford productions planned for the latter part of the 1963 season and decided to replace them with *The Wars of the Roses,* an epic trilogy telling the stories of Henry VI, Edward IV and Richard III. The announcement was greeted with amazement as being reckless and daring in equal measure.

## The Wars of the Roses

Hall had been thinking about Shakespeare's history plays for several years, although not for himself. In 1960 he had approached Anthony Quayle, who had directed and acted in a cycle of four history plays at Stratford in 1951, but nothing came of the enquiry. In 1961 Hall had asked Joan Littlewood to direct *Henry IV Parts 1* and *2* as part of a history cycle but she did not like the Stratford set-up – which she nicknamed Stratford West – and departed. Hall had also invited Brook, twice: once in his first year as director and again when Brook joined the company's triumvirate. Brook replied it would take him three years to plan and suggested Hall direct the plays himself. Hall believed he could not risk full productions of all three Henry VI plays, which were hardly known. Instead, he would stage a two-play adaptation of them as well as *Richard III,* a likelier box office success, which, in the context, would be seen in a fresh way. Barton, who had long wanted to work on this project, had prepared a draft by the end of 1962 with substantial sections written by him, following Hall's remit to cut and condense. In early 1963 Hall called him back from the US, where he was on tour with the RSC production of *The Hollow Crown,* to redraft the text to allow all three plays to be performed in one day. Hall rewrote some of the passages Barton had contributed, and changes to the text continued through rehearsal.

Hall's thinking on the plays had been evolving, and went on developing during the production of the trilogy and the subsequent staging of the whole *Richard II–Richard III* cycle. Events played their part. The world had been brought to the edge of nuclear war in the Cuban missile crisis of October 1962 and the newspapers were full of espionage stories, culminating in the defection to the Soviet Union in 1963 of Kim Philby. The Conservatives, the so-called 'natural party of government' that had ruled Britain since 1951, were in disarray. Prime Minister Macmillan sacked his Chancellor and seven other cabinet ministers in July 1962. When the national sex and security scandal involving Stratford's MP, War Minister John Profumo, broke just before the trilogy opened, it led to Macmillan being replaced not by a moderniser but by a reminder of the Tories' aristocratic past, the 14th Earl of Home and a Knight of the Thistle who had served on Neville Chamberlain's staff during the Munich appeasement of Hitler. Politics, however, interested Hall only in so far as they revealed recurring patterns of what he called 'man's basic passions', and in this he was influenced by aspects of Artaud that focused on archetypes.[2]

Crucially for Hall, there was the impact of designers, whose visual and spatial transformation of RSC productions had widespread importance. Leslie Hurry's sandpit design for Hall and Barton's 1960 production of *Troilus and Cressida* was an early indication of a new trend. This was not typical of Hurry yet broke with the decorative designs Lila de Nobili had produced for Hall. A series of anti-illusionist productions allowing fluidity of staging through abstract design heralded a new RSC scenographic style: Jocelyn Herbert's design for *Richard III*, Sean Kenny's *The Devils*, John Bury's *Measure for Measure* and *Julius Caesar*, Brook's *King Lear*, Abd'elkader Farrah's *The Tempest* and Ralph Koltai's designs for *The Caucasian Chalk Circle* and *The Representative*. For the trilogy Hall turned to Bury, who had been Theatre Workshop's main designer through the 1950s. Hall had asked Bury to design for him in 1959, having seen his set for Theatre Workshop's production of *A Taste of Honey* but Bury declined when Hall wanted to see his drawings. Bury did not do drawings. In keeping with his company's improvisatory approach, he extemporised too. Significantly, during preparations for the trilogy, he returned to Joan Littlewood to design *Oh! What a Lovely War*, a seminal production that became a benchmark for anti-heroic reassessments of armed conflict.

Hall and Bury agreed they had to avoid the fey, 'pop-up' look of heraldic Shakespearean history play production recently satirised in *Beyond the Fringe*. The image Hall saw was of a sword – a world of steel stirred up by a visit to Warwick Castle armoury. For Bury, material was fundamental. He designed a complete stage world made from metallic materials – what he called 'unconventional realism'.[3] This approach, and the fact that he offered only ground plans but no finished design drawings, raised eyebrows in the Stratford workshops. Hall gave Bury a free hand to change the practice of the workshops, where the tradition was a fine art one. He met resistance as well as enormous professionalism and enthusiasm. In the paint shop, there had already been problems earlier that season. Farrah's use of Perspex in *The Tempest* – which they had stayed up painting all night because it lost colour when lit – was a sign of things to come. The plastics industry was growing and producing synthetic materials, such as polystyrene and polyurethane, which changed the function of the paint shops. Instead of simply painting a surface, they now had to worry about achieving the right weight, density and reflective index as well as colour. Designers at the RSC were creating environments in which anything painted on canvas would seem unreal.

To find the right texture Bury experimented on iron sheeting and thin steel. At a distance, however, it looked no more metallic than plywood. With Desmond Hall, the production manager, he used various corroding agents such as acids on the iron and steel but this achieved only a patchy rustiness that Bury found romantic and weak. He then adapted a procedure used by Koltai in *The Caucasian Chalk Circle* where he had tarnished copper foil with sulphides. After applying ever-stronger solutions of ammonium sulphide to prevent the copper from going patchy too, Bury achieved the effect he wanted, but only for the moveable walls and arches. The floor, with a one in eight rake, was made of steel treated in an acid bath, mounted on block board and covered with a wire mesh, described by the actor Clifford Rose as 'the cheese grater surface'.[4] So hazardous was this surface that the following year Tony Watts, the RSC armourer, produced special metal knee caps to protect the actors when they had to kneel on it.

Stratford was still using lightweight theatrical swords, but this did not satisfy Bury. Several nearby blacksmiths were commissioned to make steel swords that had the right 'ring', and if they looked too new, they were hammered to achieve a battered look. Like the other props and furniture, such as the council table and throne, many of these heavy swords were also huge: six-foot long and two-handed. The thrilling fights arranged by Barton, enhanced by amplification of the sounds of the boots and swords scraping the floor, became highlights of the production.

For the costumes, Ann Curtis, a ladies cutter in the wardrobe department, collaborated with Bury and helped him overcome opposition in the workshops to his new approach. Bury did not want a peacock production and urged the wardrobe to make what he considered to be clothes rather than costumes. The characters needed to be dressed in line with their role in the story and in harmony with the metallic setting. The solution was to coat the costumes in liquid rubber 'gunk' and embed them with tiny objects. There were only a couple of months in which to design and make hundreds of costumes. The overall look was fifteenth century, though not literally accurate. Modern materials and textures were used within a limited range of fabrics, which helped tighten the focus. As with the set, the costumes changed with the story: the once proud red rose became rusty and colour drained from the stage until among the drying patches of scarlet blood, the black night of England settled on the leather costumes of Richard's thugs.

The costumes were taken next door to the paint shop where Bury organised groups of local people and art school students to 'gunk' them. When colouring agents were subsequently applied to the thick latex coat to add texture, the costumes fell to pieces. Bury experimented with different ways to achieve texture. Glue crystals, marble chippings, chicken grit and stone gravel swept up from tennis courts in Southern Lane were all thrown onto the 'gunked' costumes while still wet. The costumes were then shaken to dispel the excess grit. Hall thought the costumes looked like rags but admired the lustrous effect under light. Boots were also 'gunked'. Metal armour from Barry Jackson's days was brought into service, while an army of volunteer knitters produced chain mail round the clock. They knitted thick butcher's string into 5-foot strips, which were then covered with silver lacquer and beaten flat. The actors had problems with these innovative costumes, which were heavier than promised, and at first rebelled against wearing them because of the rake, the fights, and having to dodge the moving walls of the set. Ashcroft's costume made her bleed and had to be 'toned down'. Also, the costumes could not be altered because they had no visible seams and over time went stiff, which made them even heavier. At first, the costumes wore the actors but the actors did acclimatise and eventually grew into them.

Bury lit *The Wars of the Roses* himself, an unusual practice at the time. He used primarily white lighting because advances in lighting power, which exposed the unreality of paint, revealed the texture of real materials and changed the way actors' faces were seen on stage. He believed the face should be illuminated rather than lit, hence his preference for the 'natural' face, without make-up, which had implications for the make-up and wig departments as well as for casting.

Hall's music adviser Raymond Leppard, who used a wind band in favour of the traditional strings, had been too busy away from Stratford to compose the music. Another Cambridge graduate Guy Woolfenden, who had joined the RSC that year as assistant music director, had taken his place.[5] Hall told him to find a musical interpretation of the dangerous world of the plays; as with the design, it should be neither historically accurate nor totally modern. Woolfenden used slackened drums to achieve a low and ominous tone, short, sharp fanfares and strange noises from the brass ensemble with percussion to match the feeling of the set. On stage he had seven musicians in costume, who concealed small notebooks containing their music as conducting was not possible. He had instruments specially created for the production, such as a curving bronze horn, which was played in duet with a long coach horn. To create a strange, eerie sound, he and Leppard invented an oblong box, approximately seven-foot high and fitted with tautened piano strings, across which the edge of a dagger was drawn. There were problems with the cannon and explosions, the recordings of which sounded terrible. Woolfenden made his own recordings, of about ten people, including Hall, blowing up empty crisp packets and bursting them in quick succession. He played back the recordings at half speed with the gaps edited out.

For Hall and his collaborators, the approach to the project, and therefore to a notion of realism, was organic: '[W]e started with a texture, a style of speaking, a style of presentation, a style of looking, which was all one.'[6] The project showed the creative value of the company in releasing imaginative co-operation across the disciplines through a unified vision.

The pressure was immense when rehearsals began because the season had not started well. A production of *The Tempest* co-directed by Brook and Williams was ill conceived and owed more to expedience than to a desire for collaboration or new forms of collective work. The next production, *Julius Caesar*, was also poorly received, although praised for its clarity. A revival of *The Comedy of Errors* was a relief but, as an eight-month old production, could not provide the necessary impetus for the acting company about to face the rigours of the trilogy. They needed all the time that was available in their rehearsal period. The performance texts of the first two plays, known as *Henry VI* and *Edward IV*, were ready only the day before rehearsals began. These two plays were rehearsed as one and the text was constantly reshaped, with lines and scenes being moved or cut. The original plays' relative lack of exposure allowed Hall and Barton greater interpretive freedom, which was both exhilarating and exhausting. The strain was exacerbated two weeks into rehearsals when Hall collapsed. The cumulative stress of launching the RSC and now the trials of this production had taken their toll. Saint-Denis took over as company director and the cast asked Barton to fill Hall's role. Hall had a young assistant Frank Evans – the scale of the RSC by now necessitating the introduction of such a function – and he took on more responsibility. Hall returned a fortnight later. A more complicated rehearsal schedule based on the two plays being divided into some thirty blocks was introduced. Hall rehearsed one block on stage, concentrating on the narrative drive, which became the backbone of the first two plays which allowed the actors to build their characters; that block would then be rehearsed by Barton in the Conference Hall situated behind the stage, with an emphasis on verse speaking and textual understanding; and then in the dress circle bar Evans would consolidate the work already carried out on the block.

Among the actors, the greatest contrast was between the veteran Ashcroft playing Margaret and as Henry VI the tyro David Warner. He spent the early part of rehearsals apologising for having the part. Hall encouraged him to be instinctive, and this allowed his own unheroic, contemporary persona to come through, sheltered in the knowledge that the role was little known. Ashcroft, who gave an astonishing performance as she progressed through the trilogy from the girlish bride in her twenties by way of the ferocious she-wolf to a defeated queen in her seventies, began by refusing to say anything that was not in her Temple edition of Shakespeare. Barton smuggled in a speech he had written, which he convinced her was 'genuine', and thereafter she had no qualms about the text.

The company rehearsed six and sometimes seven days a week, often into the night. Barton would pursue actors with his notes into the Dirty Duck, the local pub frequented by the actors, and even tried to rehearse when breaks were being taken. Nevertheless, in late May the decision was taken to delay the opening by two weeks. When the first two plays did finally appear – at a Saturday matinee and evening performance in mid-July after the RSC had opened *The Beggar's Opera* at the Aldwych the night before – Hall's gamble was seen to have paid off. It was received as a triumph for Hall and the company ideal. Bernard Levin described it as 'a landmark and beacon in post-war English theatre'.[7] When *Richard III* was added, the superlatives reached hyperbolic proportions. Almost thirty years later, the critic Irving Wardle could still write that *The Wars of the Roses* was 'the greatest Shakespearean event within living memory'.[8]

In the following season, 1964, the quatercentenary of Shakespeare's birth, Hall added the rest of the history cycle, Williams joined the directorial group as a named director and the series was performed in historical order, possibly for the first time. Hall continued to suffer enormous strain. He publicly separated from Leslie Caron in April 1964 and during rehearsals collapsed again, even more spectacularly. He was carried out of the theatre on the royal bier. Peter Wood came in to lend a hand but to his later regret told the company not to credit him. The collective system of directing the RSC had evolved to meet the demands of the work and proved robust enough to see the productions through to general acclaim, topping the extravagance of the earlier reviews. When *The Wars of the Roses* was broadcast at the end of that season on BBC television as three separate programmes lasting approximately three hours each, it was a small-screen event of major significance. It was also broadcast in Australia, the USA and Canada.

Shakespeare's history plays hold a special place in Stratford, and particularly RSC, folklore. The new theatre was launched in 1932 with *Henry IV Parts 1* and *2*, as were the RSC's new London base at the Barbican Centre in 1982 and Adrian Noble's reign as artistic director in 1991. Noble had already directed *Henry V* and his version of the Wars of the Roses sequence, *The Plantagenets*, a history trilogy that sealed his future as artistic director in succession to Terry Hands, who had staked a similar claim with his history productions in the 1970s. Anthony Quayle's finest moment in charge of Stratford is commonly regarded as his 1951 breakthrough history cycle, showing *Richard II*, the two *Henry IV* plays and *Henry V* as part of a continuous story. The RSC's millennium project was the history cycle, and Michael Boyd, who was to be Noble's successor, made his mark in that project with productions of the three parts of *Henry VI*. In the history plays, Shakespeare is clearly writing about his own time, both socially and politically, and is putting the nation on the stage, although his exploration is necessarily heavily coded. Among other questions, the plays ask 'What is history?' and 'How do we make it culturally?'

In *The Wars of the Roses*, Hall used the specificity of history to emphasise its generality: history – and the making of the nation – was a corrupting power struggle in the past and remains one now, and, like the working-through of a curse in ancient drama, there is not much anyone can do about it. Modern democracy, Hall asserted, required ambitious people to run it – like the RSC – but they had to be curbed and checked or their ambition would ruin the very ideals they were trying to serve. The productions caught the mood of Sixties Britain at the fag end of Tory rule and when the full cycle was played, it coincided fortuitously with an upsurge of optimism at the first election victory of Labour for thirteen years. They also spoke more widely of politics across the 'Cold War' world and were seen as an apt commentary on the violence of the era. The view of politics was changing and *The Wars of the Roses* symbolised the new imagery. By the time Hands was directing all three *Henry VI* plays virtually uncut in 1977, Hall's view of 'relevance' had become an outmoded idea and romantic aesthetics had removed politics and history altogether, a trend that continued through to Noble's pictorially vibrant *The Plantagenets*.

Of all the history productions, the cycle under Hall's overall control was the most momentous. It was the single most influential event in the early careers of many of the actors who took part, and it reunited Hall and Barton, who remained with the company as a guiding spirit from then on. It established a pattern that for both the company and the artistic director it was crucial he secured an unalloyed artistic triumph on an emphatic scale. The cycle also began the RSC practice of staging what one critic called 'orgiastic theatrical marathons' such as *The Greeks* and *The Life and Adventures of Nicholas Nickleby*.[9] Institutionally, as the availability of actors for rehearsal became increasingly complex, the cycle produced a refinement of the planning system that served the company well in future years, and it produced a re-organisation of the workshops within a new sense of overall company spirit. It established the number of people required to run the dual theatre policy and, following the demise of the triumvirate, consolidated the idea of associates. It was an iconic marker for the RSC in establishing the idea of shared artistic vision, in the unity of acting, design and music, and in showing that the RSC defends itself best when it attacks. It trumped the National Theatre, which opened a few months after *Richard III* with a weak production of *Hamlet* featuring Peter O'Toole, the lost star of Hall's first season. Shakespeare was RSC territory, and both Shakespeare and the RSC were news. Ashcroft, herself revitalised by the experience, wrote: 'It consolidated in those two years the inspiration of Peter's vision of a company, and was a living representation of what such a company could achieve.'[10]

## Public legitimacy

The RSC was now in full stride. Along with the histories and the international tour of *King Lear* and *The Comedy of Errors*, in 1964 the RSC hosted the World Theatre Season, then planned as a one-off but which became a regular and stimulating fixture for the next decade. Hall also gave space to Brook to run his *Theatre of Cruelty* experimental programmes, without the pressure of a particular public outcome. This work led to the production later that year of Peter Weiss's *Marat/Sade* at the centre of a bold Aldwych repertoire.

Bravery in the repertoire accompanied daring in Hall's thinking about the company's public face. Having secured public funding, he knew he had to secure public legitimacy. He tackled this on several fronts and saw it as an integral part of the RSC's contribution to the building of a modern and more democratic society.

Alongside skilful use of the media, the RSC had overhauled its image in 1963 and given visual coherence to its publicity and published material. New graphics and typefaces and the swan logo featured against bright yellow, evoking the gold of Shakespeare's family colours. Free cast lists were introduced alongside redesigned and more attractive programmes dedicated to each production. They contained notes and commentaries, and set the format still used by the RSC forty years later. This contemporary feel to the company was to be underpinned by the planned move into a new London theatre with Ballet Rambert, but in 1964 the RSC announced it was pulling out of the scheme. In its place, however, the RSC would occupy a grander purpose-built theatre in the proposed Barbican Centre in the City of London. Hall believed this would offer the company greater opportunities to present the full array of its work and attract new audiences.

Also in 1964, emulating the audience-building achievements of the Théâtre National Populaire (TNP), the company launched the RSC Club with its own magazine *Flourish*. It was edited by Michael Kustow, a new member of the press and publicity department who had worked at TNP and whose idea it was to establish the Club. Membership began at 12,637, comprising individuals and groups, which included along with the expected range of drama and educational organisations, a US Air Force hospital, tenants' associations, ramblers' societies, a midwives' group, factories and two convents. The Club offered priority facilities, price reductions and special events, the forerunner of subsequent programmes of talks at the RSC and the more sustained Platform sessions at the National Theatre. The Club, said Hall, was 'the means of preventing the English theatre from becoming bourgeois, institutional and dead'.[11]

This opening up of the RSC to its audience gave rise the following year to the RSC's first mobile unit, which became known as Theatregoround (TGR). As would become a guiding principle of much of the alternative theatre of the next decade, the idea was to overcome the socially divisive protocols of theatre-going and take performances to potential audiences in venues of their own milieu instead of expecting the audience always to enter the company's territory. It was introduced at a time when actors were shedding their image of the respectable player in suit and tie or twin-set in favour of the 'ordinary' person in jeans.

The first stirrings came in March 1965 when the Club sponsored four Stratford-based actors in a thirty-minute programme of excerpts from

Shakespeare and other writing to tour local halls and works' canteens, followed by a talk with the audience afterwards. Actors Commando, as it was known then, continued through to the autumn, by now with six actors and programmes lasting ninety minutes. Attention switched to London where Kustow set up the Human Trailer project with a pilot programme 'How to Stop Worrying and Love the Theatre'. This included jokes and conjuring tricks and was aimed, as he put it, at people lost to the theatre through snobbery or bad teaching. Long titles were the fashion and might not have immediately won the attention of the desired audience but it was an attempt to proselytise without appearing to preach. The project's first full programme was called 'Theatregoround' and played in the East End of London. It included a potted history of theatre from Aeschylus and Aristophanes to Shakespeare, Molière and Pinter. Hall admitted the RSC was not ready to launch a venture like TGR but as with most things, '[I]f we'd waited until we were ready to do things, we wouldn't have done anything at all.'[12]

In April 1966 the RSC received an anonymous donation of £10,000 for TGR and Hall advocated its activities to Stratford's education authorities. Two months later, in the spirit of Ken Kesey, TGR set off on its travels in a double-decker bus which carried a 'fit up' stage, a mobile exhibition and a box office.[13] The bus, sponsored by *The Sunday Telegraph*, was emblazoned with pop art decorations of stripes and circles, courtesy of the Royal College of Art. TGR's staple diet consisted of demonstration sessions by actors, anthologies, 'docudramas' and short plays. Courses for teachers and educational programmes like *The Trial and Execution of Charles I*, linked to a package of documents and materials that could be used in class, prefigured future activities of the RSC Education Department, still almost two decades away. TGR had a recruiting as well as an educational aim. Its programmes would be followed by an invitation to see a regular RSC production at reduced prices. Playing in smaller and usually unconventional performance spaces, TGR sustained the RSC's profile around the nation and established important links with its new audiences, underpinning its claim to 'relevance'.

This 'relevance', however, also caused the RSC problems as a public body. A few, internally and externally, saw its style, repertoire and behaviour as subverting the British way of life. Far from being the guardian of Shakespeare's shrine, the company was believed to be corrupting the texts and spirit of the Bard. Some of the contemporary work was considered offensive and undermining of national institutions, such as the Lord Chamberlain (the stage censor and a member of the Queen's household), as well as the monarchy itself. The company's performance of plays that were not written by Shakespeare was even questioned in the House of Commons, as was its decision in 1963 to drop the playing of the national anthem. Stratford's mayor requested the anthem be reinstated yet the RSC stood firm. One governor in particular, Emile Littler, became the voice of local dissent. Littler was the member of Stratford's governing executive council whom Hall had snubbed in securing the Aldwych Theatre, and had long been a private thorn in Fordham Flower's side. Ideological objections to the London end of the RSC operation (independence versus the state) fuelled by genuine economic worries (and in Littler's case, commercial competition) were overlaid by dislike of the RSC's artistic approach In 1964, Littler made public his disgust at the 'dirty plays' the RSC was performing.[14] A fellow governor, the Midlands manufacturer Sir Alexander Maxwell, expressed astonishment that the RSC executive council did not vet scripts.

The rumpus brought to a head a series of disputes over censorship that had placed the company firmly on the side of the progressive, liberal forces in society. As a director before he joined the RSC, Hall had clashed with the censor several times. In management at the RSC, Hall renewed hostilities and played a significant part in the campaign to end the Lord Chamberlain's centuries-old powers. John Whiting's *The Devils* heads the list of RSC transgressors. It was followed by, among others, Rolf Hochhuth's *The Representative*, David Rudkin's *Afore Night Come* (on its transfer from the Arts Theatre to the Aldwych), Roger Vitrac's *Victor* and *US*, the company's response to the Vietnam War, which the censor and other parliamentarians considered anti-American. The Lord Chamberlain, who prevented the company from presenting *In the Matter of J. Robert Oppenheimer* by Heinar Kipphardt because it represented a living person, had also disapproved of Jean Genet's *The Screens*, thereby inadvertently prompting Peter Brook to organise the *Theatre of Cruelty* programme. During this season scenes from the play were performed under club conditions and the list of the censor's objections were mockingly read out. Such irreverence signalled a public battle between the two national institutions, which carried on throughout 1964. The Lord Chamberlain banned lines from a poem by ee cummings that was included in an anthology production at the Aldwych called *The Rebel*.[15] The prohibited words were printed in the programme, and at the appropriate moment the house lights were turned on and the audience invited to read the corrupting passage. The programme for *Afore Night Come* carried a biting attack on the censor by Hall, who gave lengthy evidence to the royal commission on the subject, which led in 1968 to Parliament granting abolition.

The early bursts of rebellion helped the RSC build its image as unstuffy and even radical, which appealed to an emerging, open-minded definition of the nation but not to governors like Littler. A delegation of actors lobbied Flower in support of Hall, and Flower threatened to resign if Hall did not receive continued backing. Governor criticism thereafter remained private, although no less intense and no less prone to lobbying within the arts establishment. When the RSC's London manager John Roberts retired in 1964, he wrote to Flower:

> Our policies have been pursued with the grudging permission of the executive council and the finance committee, who, I feel, would have blocked them altogether if they could . . . The fact that Peter [Hall], Paddy [Donnell, the RSC general manager] and I, with the background of . . . a public of 750,000, have had to play the role of naughty and irresponsible children at finance committee meetings has been extraordinary.[16]

Hall could not deny that the Aldwych posed a problem. There was no settled policy there, it was difficult to find suitable plays with large enough casts to meet the needs of the contracted actors, and new plays that might have filled the smaller Royal Court were playing to 60 per cent box office or less. Under pressure of late planning or insurmountable company casting problems, actors were being hired for only one play, which undermined the basis of the company notion. At Stratford some productions still only ran for twenty to thirty performances and few transferred, which sustained the special quality of Stratford but meant the waste of the old system had not been overcome. The three-year contracts were not artistically as flexible as had been intended and were very expensive; 75 per cent of actors' salaries had to be paid when they not working for the RSC unless they found other employment. Some of those who had become celebrities through the RSC system did not want to be tied to the company, even by the generous provisions of the three-year contract. Hall had, therefore, introduced an associate artists' scheme – later refined by adding an honorary tier – through which well-known actors could better exploit their status commercially while still retaining the RSC connection. At the same time, the three-year contract was modified to include named parts as a way of overcoming the drain on RSC money if an actor rejected a role and remained unemployed elsewhere.

Planning was difficult enough in an organisation as complicated as the RSC, but it was made harder by the vagaries of the funding system, such as the irregular flow of funds and conditions attached: grant decisions made for only one year at a time and made relatively late for forward planning, and the encouragement of 'deficit' funding whereby 'profits' were not allowed to be carried forward or reserves to be accumulated to offset poor years. A rise in subsidy did not necessarily mean healthier finances for the company. Neither did rising attendance figures mean a lower deficit. Good housekeeping and dextrous exploitation of commercial opportunities were not rewarded, and this was compounded by the credibility gap. The RSC's skill in escaping from disastrous situations made each subsequent cry of imminent destruction less plausible, regardless of the truth. The better the RSC managed with what little it had, and in the process produced artistic successes, the harder it was to plead that the company needed more.

## New anxieties

In a foretaste of future difficulties, the strain of too much work was telling not only on Hall but also on most of the staff. There was widespread unease at the sacrifices being made in the constant crisis management of the company, and when overtime for the stage crew was cut by the greater simplicity of the new stage designs, there was the threat of a strike and pay rises had to be agreed. What seemed aesthetic and economic good sense did not encompass all those associated with the company. Hall's tiring schedule led to more remoteness from people who needed him to make decisions and to an increasing sense that he was letting more and more people down. In 1965 he took his first non-RSC job since taking charge at Stratford, directing (controversially) Schoenberg's opera *Moses and Aaron* at the Royal Opera House, Covent Garden, which in vain he hoped one day to transform as he had done Stratford. Though the RSC continued to teeter on the edge of financial ruin, the Stratford season was the most successful yet and was extended by three weeks. The year also turned out to be a good one for Hall the RSC director. His productions of the world première of Pinter's *The Homecoming* and *Hamlet* with David Warner, followed in early 1966 by *The Government Inspector* with Paul Scofield, sum up the RSC at its best: a 'relevant' and popular Shakespeare production, a bold new play, destined to become a standard, and a vigorous revival of a modern classic.

Hall's demanding diary included fractious meetings with Arts Council personnel when 'the Battle for London' was run again. The Labour government had appointed the first Minister of the Arts, Jennie Lee, who rationalised the system of allocating arts funding. Instead of the Arts Council chair negotiating with the Treasury – very much a close-knit affair among the like-minded 'old boys' network – the council now received its grant from the Arts Minister and disbursed it along lines agreed between the Minister and the Council. The 'arm's length' policy – the separation of the government and the Arts Council – had always been something of a fiction, as the Treasury's role in the RSC dispensation illustrated, and now it was further compromised. The new arrangement also gave the Arts Council chair greater power and Lee replaced Lord Cottesloe in that role with the newly ennobled Lord Goodman, her down-stairs neighbour and friend of press barons and gangsters alike. Bad blood between him and Hall went back to 1961 and Hall feared for the company's future in the capital.

The Arts Council offer for 1966/67 represented a rise of more than 50 per cent but was still £100,000 short of what the RSC wanted. The company hired a firm of business consultants, Production Engineering Ltd, to test its efficiency, and was told its operation could not make any major savings other than through cuts. The Arts Council refused to budge. Behind this manoeuvring lay Goodman's belief that London could not support two national theatre companies, although he was content with four orchestras and two opera companies; in Paris, the French government handsomely supported both the TNP and the Comédie Française. Goodman wanted to resurrect the idea of amalgamation with the National Theatre and thought the RSC should either leave the Aldwych in order to merge with the NT in London or that the NT should take over the lease of the Aldwych for six months of the year. The Arts Council drama panel, however, was unanimously opposed to Goodman's proposal. He dropped it but would not yield on the size of the grant. Flower believed the offer was the best the company was likely to get. In a rare incident of disagreement, Hall, who visited Goodman on only his second day in the job to argue for more money for the RSC, ignored Flower's advice and campaigned for a rise in grant. He threatened cutbacks across the board if more money were not forthcoming, to which Goodman replied that any reduction in work at Stratford would lead to a commensurate reduction in the grant.

The RSC's finance committee and Paddy Donnell pressed Hall to make drastic economies for the 1966 season in London. London was the cause of the mounting costs, but to make the cuts there would play into Goodman's hands and endanger the Aldwych further. Instead, Hall cut the number of Stratford productions to five, three of which were revivals. He cut the acting company by a third, closed the Studio, and cancelled touring plans. In London, he replaced some large-cast productions with smaller cast ones. The year ended with the company's smallest deficit and Goodman did not punish the company by reducing its grant.

Hall says the 1966 retreat was the year of his biggest mistake. It was the first time he had compromised in a defensive way. The programme of Stratford revivals, he felt later, was a humiliation and 'some of the life went out of the actors'.[17] Yet in London, even if leavened by a children's show at Christmas and a two-handed comedy, the repertoire was not designed to pander to comfortable tastes: plays by Peter Weiss, Sławomir Mrożek, Marguerite Duras, Friederich Dürrenmatt and David Mercer, as well the Brook-inspired, company-devised Vietnam War production US, was audacious programming by any standards. Indeed, in the midst of the cuts, Hall had again found the means to allow Brook the freedom to explore without guarantee of the result.

Brook had come to him without a text or cast yet a decision on whether to schedule a show was only to be taken ten weeks into the fourteen-week rehearsal period Hall had provided. It was to be the next stage for Brook of an exploration of 'relevance' that tested the limits of both topicality and resonance as well as the engagement between actor and audience. This was the period when politics fascinated Brook the most, and that year he had already staged Weiss's *The Investigation* in an act of solidarity with thirteen other European theatres, which were staging the play. He directed it with David Jones as a reading in order to avoid turning horror into a spectacle but discovered that he had simply made horror dull. In *US* he wanted to escape this problem and to put the Vietnam War on stage in a way that was as immediate and compelling as on television. There was considerable criticism of the eventual result, mostly from the right but also from the left, yet *US*, whatever its shortcomings, became another of the defining events in the RSC's history: a public examination of *the* decisive contemporary issue that put theatre at the centre of national debate. The RSC was certainly relevant now.

Inside the company, however, the situation was fraught. In 1966 Hall left the RSC for the second time, to direct *The Magic Flute* at the Royal Opera House. He had tried again to establish an associate director system (with John Barton, Clifford Williams and the newly arrived Trevor Nunn) and to inaugurate a similar system for designers (Sally Jacobs, Abdel Farrah and Ralph Koltai) under John Bury as head of design. But these had not bedded in and his absence caused increased anxieties within the RSC management about the problem of decision-making, a quandary that came to haunt the company in years to come. A tense situation was capped by the death from cancer of Fordham Flower. Hall was desolate, and he never fully engaged with the RSC again. Flower was the last of the brewing family to be chair and after him, although family members served as high-ranking governors and supported the subsequent chairs, Stratford lost the personal connection to this position.

In Hall's opinion his natural successor, Fordie's cousin Dennis Flower, would never be able to stand up to Goodman. Hall chose as the new RSC chairman George Farmer, 'a precise accountant, and no gambler'.[18] He was chair of the Rover car company as well as chair of the RSC's finance committee. He was critical of Hall's spending, especially the running down of the reserves, and pressed Hall not to gamble any more but rather to make more cuts. To Hall's annoyance, Donnell, the key to the administrative changes at the RSC and one of those increasingly irritated by Hall's absences, backed Farmer's point of view. Donnell had challenged Hall before, particularly over constraints on directors' budgets that did not apply to Hall, and when Hall reshuffled the administration in 1967 he moved Donnell to the 'long grass' of the Barbican project. An outsider, Derek Hornby, replaced him and became administrative director. He was a personnel and administration expert chosen disastrously from the British subsidiary of Texas Instruments by a top management selection firm. It was a clear signal that Hall and Farmer could see a time not very far away when the RSC would lose its founder, and the management skills of the private sector were thought to be required to ease the burden on Hall's successor.

Later that year Hall reached his decision to leave. A number of factors combined: Flower's death; consistent under-funding and the belief that subsidy was a tool for controlling the RSC; the stress of the Barbican venture, the opening of which had been delayed until 1972; recurrent illness – Hall had shingles again during rehearsals for *Macbeth*, his third serious collapse since founding the RSC; the disaster of *Macbeth*, Hall's first major failure at the RSC and the only RSC production he staged in 1967; and the pressures of filming (*Work is a Four Letter Word* and *A Midsummer Night's Dream*), which were affecting the RSC planning, especially at the Aldwych. The other important factor was that he had found his successor. He could have made a conservative choice yet Hall knew his successor had to come from the next generation and challenge what he and his colleagues had established. Thanks to a stunning production of Cyril Tourneur's *The Revenger's Tragedy*, which marked a distinctive aesthetic break with the RSC's style, Hall saw the future of the company in its director Trevor Nunn.[19]

## Trevor Nunn

Hall and Nunn shared a similar background. They both came from the upper working class, were East Anglian by birth and education, had attended Cambridge University where they were active in student theatre, and were in their late twenties when appointed to the senior RSC post. There the similarity ends. It had been necessary for Hall to dominate the institution in order to create a company out of a traditional and outdated theatre set-up, but it was also in his character. Hall the benevolent dictator seemed to come from a different era to Nunn. Hall had worked with 'sacred monsters' in the theatre at an early age and had been bloodied in the commercial system. Nunn had come from the growing regional theatre movement, and that only briefly. By his own admission he did not have the management experience that Hall had acquired before running Stratford. Nunn had only just learned to run a rehearsal, and had no idea about running anything larger. He had used somebody else's secretary to type letters, but had never chaired a meeting, could not read a balance sheet, and was totally unaccustomed to public speaking.[20] He was, perhaps as a consequence, more open to the company than Hall while being himself more private. He liked to be called Trevor, not Mr Nunn, and spent more time in the green room than had his predecessor. He did not seek the limelight and had none of Hall's PR antennae. He was a quick learner, and while he never seemed to enjoy the politicking as much as Hall, over his nearly two decades in charge of the RSC he came to be a seasoned campaigner and cajoler, skilfully developing and deploying the multifarious talents required to be a director in the rehearsal room and the leader of a major company. Indeed, by the 1980s he had come to be known for a particular piece of affable manipulation: to be 'trevved'. This overshadowed the loyalty he had inspired in guiding the RSC through the post-Hall years with sharp intelligence, impish sense of humour and apparently inexhaustible ability to talk at length without respite for breath or rumination.

After directing at Cambridge – and hearing Hall talk brilliantly to undergraduates there about the value of a company – Nunn had gone to the Belgrade Theatre, Coventry, on a television-sponsored trainee director scheme. The theatre being close to Stratford, Hall had found time to see Nunn's production there of *The Caucasian Chalk Circle*. Nunn rejected the offer that followed of an assistant director post, although he did subsequently accept the improved offer of becoming an associate, which, nevertheless, took some time to become a reality and involved interim assistant work at the RSC as well as solo productions. Nunn had a catastrophic first year at the RSC, which included the failure of an ambitious project on the General Strike designed to emulate the spirit of Theatre Workshop's *Oh! What a Lovely War*. The National Theatre had taken an option on a script written by David Wright and a Theatre

Workshop actor Clive Barker but had let it lapse. Hall wanted Nunn to develop the script of *Strike!* with the writers and the cast in much the way that Brook had created *US*. Nunn was to mount the show at the Aldwych using film, song and dance drawn from documentary sources. It became clear after a month of rehearsals that the project was bogged down through Nunn's lack of experience; consequently, the production was abandoned. The idea resurfaced in several incarnations, including a proposed manifestation in the Round House, which was to be turned into a fairground, but none was ever realised and the RSC never attempted anything like *Strike!* again.[21]

*The Revenger's Tragedy*, however, was a turning point in Nunn's life and that of the RSC. The brief last 'slot' in the reduced 1966 season of revivals had been a matter of much debate and speculation. Hall had planned a two-part adaptation by John Barton of medieval mystery plays but it was not ready. The alternative became the rarely seen Jacobean curiosity, chosen after a great deal of reading by Nunn and colleagues.[22] His solo debut at Stratford, the production was hurried into the schedule, given a negligible budget and forced to use the existing *Hamlet* set. It was a production of newcomers. Nunn introduced from his time at Coventry the designer Christopher Morley and, although Ian Richardson was by now an established RSC actor, several others of the main cast – Alan Howard, John Kane, Norman Rodway and Patrick Stewart – were also new to the company. At the dress run-through, Hall declared it the most exciting theatrical debut since his own, although privately, some sources say, it was not to his taste. He left Barton, who had helped adapt and edit the text, to see the production through its final stages and he disliked it, mainly for its rejection of RSC realism, the very thing that made it fresh. Nunn and Morley resisted the changes Barton was suggesting and were vindicated by the praise that greeted the production. It displayed the artistic energy and unity that had become the RSC's trademark but was of a different order. Focusing on social manners, the staging was simple but not neo-Brechtian, and the circle of bright light funnelled from above over the black and silver costumes gave the production a luminescent, decadent look. Like *The Comedy of Errors*, it was another of the RSC's emblematic triumphs in adversity. As Ronald Bryden wrote in *The Observer*: 'Every time the Arts Council tightens the screws . . . the RSC bounces back with some victory of sheer theatrical resource over economics, so brilliant as to suggest that it works best with its back to the wall.'[23]

In January 1968, after a year in which Nunn revived *The Revenger's Tragedy* in Stratford and then transferred it to London as well as successfully directing *The Taming of the Shrew* and a much-praised revival of

John Vanbrugh's *The Relapse*, Hall announced the changes in the leadership of the company. The RSC, he declared, was a team and Nunn, as part of that team, would hold the new post of artistic director and chief executive. There would be a directorate of Nunn, Hall, Brook, Scofield, Ashcroft and Hornby. Hall would cease to be managing director but would remain a director with special responsibilities for RSC film-making and supervising the Barbican project. Hornby was made administrative director immediately below Nunn. Barton and Terry Hands, who had joined to run Theatregoround, were made company directors for Stratford and London respectively and David Brierley was promoted from within to the post of general manager.

Continuity was seen as positive; it was not preservation but stretching back as well as reaching forward. It was important externally because the RSC brand had become international and was bigger than any one person. The marketplace needed to be reassured that the brand would not be devalued. It was also important internally for similar reasons: Hall had been the RSC. Without him, what would it be? However, he had chosen Nunn precisely to challenge what he had achieved. An RSC press release underlined stability: '[T]hese changes amount to a re-arrangement amongst the strong group of artists and executives who already head the RSC. Thus a continuity of the company's identity, as created by Peter Hall, is assured.'[24]

## Hall's legacy

Hall's legacy to Nunn was enormous. In statistical terms, he had doubled the number of theatres and tripled the audience figures. Artistically he had championed new plays, established a distinctive verse-speaking style and brought Shakespeare into the contemporary world. Most compelling, however – with all the mistakes and barely controlled chaos – was the nation's acceptance of the idea of a company, despite the fact that funding would never fall in line with the demands such a company, let alone an ensemble, might make.

The subsidy culture in Britain has made it virtually impossible to create a true ensemble, in the sense of a group with shared ideals that can work together over a sufficiently long period to develop a common understanding and empathy. The RSC had aspirations to this state at the outset, and in certain respects some of its achievements were akin to those of a skilled ensemble. But in choosing the description 'company', Hall had recognised that the size of his group, the scope of its ambition, the conditions of its existence and above all its pragmatism would disbar it from being an ensemble. Building a smaller ensemble might have been simpler but not to Hall, who believed it was easier to run two theatres than one. 'Company' was more flexible, less 'foreign' and allowed expediency its place. 'Company' happily suggested a retinue of retainers working together beyond the limits of a one-off show at a time when the presence of theatre – in the regions as well as in London – was socially important and derived from a cohesive engagement in what was considered a worthy cause.

While Hall was not interested in replicating the smaller, more idealistic and more sharply delineated ensembles such as the Living Theater in America or the Theatre Laboratory of Jerzy Grotowski in Poland, he did want the RSC to share a similar sense of belonging and purpose. He strove to imbue in each individual a responsibility for the company as a whole, to yoke the quality of personal work to the quality overall; a success for one was a success for all, but so was a failure. In building this shared aim, Stratford was critical. For all London's strategic importance, the crucible of the company remained Stratford, and Hall had been determined to make Stratford the place to be. Underpinned by his knack for publicity, its allure emanated from the quality of the work and the fashioning there of a company and a company style. The RSC's scale of operation and sense of being special helped mould the feeling of company, and in Stratford the collegiate style of life reinforced this.

'Campus' life at the Royal Staggers – or Shaggers, as it was affectionately known – developed intricate social structures from the epicentral activities in the Dirty Duck pub to company picnics, charity events and a nursery group. These were activities that would be repeated throughout the RSC's history. Over the years, a strong network emerged of RSC families – actors and staff and their children – who lived either in Stratford or in outlying villages and towns. The 1963 *Wars of the Roses* cricket match between the House of York and Lancaster in aid of World Freedom from Hunger summed up the peculiarly English appeal of the RSC. Len Hutton and Cyril Washbrook, the outstanding cricketers of their respective counties, led the two sides. Ian Holm (Richard III) played with his clubfoot and hunchback and used a runner. The author and local resident J.B. Priestley and leading cricket and music writer Neville Cardus acted as commentators. A then little-known actress Penelope Keith (various small parts) was the scorer and Leslie Caron gave the prizes. Umpires included John Barton dressed as Shakespeare and, in a convention prophetic of one-day cricket yet to be invented, the RSC wind band played a fanfare with every fall of a wicket and arrival of a new batter. The result was a draw.

Extensive extra-mural artistic events took on a life of their own and spread to London. Sometimes they came under the RSC umbrella – for example, *The Tremendous Ghost*, a programme of poems, broadsides, ballads and satire that ended the first week of Shakespeare's quater-centenary celebrations at the Royal Shakespeare Theatre. Mostly they were just supported by the RSC, as, for instance, in 1963, when about fifty actors appeared at St George's Church, Notting Hill and Southwark Cathedral in a new translation by company member Gordon Honeycombe of five mysteries called *The Miracles*. This type of activity expanded in the years to come from concerts and recitals into a rich assortment of youth festivals, children's plays, young writers pro-grammes, and an RSC fringe that became known as *Not the RSC*. Such initiatives overlapped with education work, RSC actors visiting secure institutions like Broadmoor, and exhibitions mounted by the RSC Gallery curator, who hosted artists in residence responding to company life. There were also links with Birmingham University's Shakespeare Institute, particularly during the RSC annual Summer School, and the Shakespeare Centre, which opened in 1964.

'Campus' life reached beyond enforced proximity – few people owned cars then and rail access was difficult – to create a communitarian feeling at odds with the hierarchies of West End theatre, which had been main-tained at Stratford during the 1950s. This feeling mitigated the hierarchies – of gender, colour, age, experience and status – that inevitably prevail in any company, depending on the social fashion, blend of per-sonalities and nature of the productions being rehearsed. In 1960, in Hall's first company in charge at Stratford, there was still a sense of 'nat-ural' order even if the grandeur of the past had been cast aside in public; Dame Peggy Ashcroft was not treated the same as 'spear carrier' Philip Voss. Even at university, when utopian ideals might seemingly be most freely expressed, Hall had used star billing in his productions. In public-ity for the 1960 season, actors were listed in three blocks, with different size typefaces reflecting the different status of each block. Alphabetical listing was introduced in 1963. Modern work helped redress the poor gender mix and distribution of parts of Shakespeare's plays, in addition to extending the range of plays on offer in an adventurous company that could turn young actors into names in their own right and give older actors a new lease of life.

The magnitude of the company paradoxically encouraged Hall and his immediate successors to keep the leadership small and to avoid over-rigid structures. Common sense and flexibility were key qualities. Communication was determined by a 'need to know' criterion while the issuing of memoranda – an art form in its own right within the RSC – proliferated. Bodies like the planning committee never met regularly and many of the important decisions were taken on the basis of individual relationships outside of formal meetings, which might be required to ratify or implement them. He surrounded himself with like-minded people and, as the organisation grew, relied increasingly on them for advice on bringing in newcomers. In such a context serendipity would inevitably play its part. Williams was a beneficiary of the chances thrown up by the sheer size of the undertaking, and, in a different way, so was Barton. Hall was disinclined to press Barton's departure following *The Taming of the Shrew* confrontation, but his refusal to go and his under-taking of a range of jobs – running verse classes, teaching and arranging fights, devising anthologies and adapting texts – were possible because of the scale and geography of the company.

The RSC's size also spawned or supported a range of roles new to the British theatre, such as casting director, literary manager and sound designer, and a plethora of different titles for evolving jobs, such as repertory manager, which became planning controller. The company played an important part in the 'professionalisation' of the wider theatre as the theatre world became more specialised and structured alongside the growth of arts management, marketing, sponsorship and education. Inside the RSC, Hall also introduced the notion of company-wide responsibility for different artistic disciplines. Iris Warren was in charge of voice production, Norman Ayrton movement, Denne Gilkes singing and Pauline Grant choreography. What this meant in practice differed from person to person and the needs of individual productions. Hall encouraged directors to be catholic in the choice of their artistic team and to bring in their own people – for example, Michael Elliott used the choreographer Litz Pisk. This could upset Stratford sensibilities, when, for instance, outside lighting designers were first used as this was not the Stratford tradition, which was for this to be undertaken 'in-house' by production staff.

Hall experimented with artistic associate systems as conditions changed, but these were marked by their improvisational nature. He made Bury head of design in order to keep him at the RSC, though he did not really play much of a role. He gave his thoughts to Hall and to other directors about design and designers, but he never hired or fired or censored work. He was there to help designers if they needed it, especially in relation to the workshops and the internal workings of the organisation, but his appointment did little to ease the problems of the pattern and rhythm of work given to the workshops and this remained true under subsequent heads of design. The biggest headache was requiring the head of the organisation not only to be a leading artist but also to be responsible for everything else, whether artistic or not. To become and remain a senior director requires constant practising of that skill and refining of associated personal qualities, from guide to gauleiter. The workload of running a mammoth institution is clearly an obstacle. Each RSC incumbent has handled the dilemma the best way they thought appropriate, but Hall was the only one who enjoyed the dual role, perhaps because he was creating not sustaining.

Hall had willingly shouldered the extra burdens he had heaped upon himself in creating such a large enterprise. By nature, he said, he was a 'night person' but in order to cope at the RSC, 'I turned myself into an early-morning person'.[25] He found time to read scripts and reply to playwrights, to a greater extent than his successors. The greatest need inside the company was for Hall to find time to plan, but that was always the first casualty because of the pressure of daily demands. He tried to make the institution as flexible as possible in order to meet all eventualities, to keep it open and critical while not losing the adamantine will to achieve his ambition. He enjoyed the cut-and-thrust of theatre life, which is supremely practical and collaborative, and has a habit of defeating well-made plans. He saw dynamism in crisis, and this was his adrenalin. Not surprisingly, the RSC as an institution had an unsettled, protean feel in its early years. As a transition from the old Stratford way of doing things, its sudden growth in scale and improvisatory nature would never be repeated. 'Early on,' he said, 'I had a sense that in starting the RSC I had created something that had a vitality and a will to grow which was unstoppable.'[26]

Not one of nature's lieutenants, he insists he is not power-mad, as he recklessly said to an interviewer once, but instead enjoys 'making things happen'.[27] To do that, he wielded the power in the RSC. Although the company ideal may appear to be egalitarian and possibly imply democratic involvement, Hall was interested in neither. In the face of the artistic director's power, there is inevitable scepticism from those on the receiving end, especially actors who resented being manipulated in his end-of-season 'surgeries' at which he assessed the work they had done and discussed the prospects of work to come.

Everyone who runs a theatre has to keep their own counsel and sometimes this is seen as duplicity. Perhaps it comes with the territory. You can't tell everybody everything all the time, particularly when you're dealing with the insecurities and vanities of talent. You try to avoid lying, but you sometimes have to withhold the truth, or some of it.[28]

Hall had his own share of vanity and insecurity, but his leadership had a sureness of touch that was shaped not by personal gain but by the desire to establish the RSC as a world-class company in 'the marketplace of Now'.

What was distinctive about Hall was not his opinions, nor even his directorial skill – considerable though that was – but his ability to implement the ideas, to pursue the interconnected elements as vital components of a single, unified notion. It was his entrepreneurial spirit driven by singular ambition, his political skills as an impresario in negotiating and exploiting the tensions and paradoxes of the situation in which he found himself, that gave the RSC its initial impetus. Brook wrote that Hall's aim was

> to create a living organism, where flexible imaginative conditions were related to flexible imaginative individuals in key positions. The new traditions of the new company were intelligence, youth and skill. . . . [Hall] calculated daringly, yet wisely, that unless his grand project was realised completely, the theatre would inevitably stagnate, and so it was better to spend the last penny today than save something for a future that would not be worth inheriting . . . a great deal of exciting and costly activity was the first constant on which he relied.[29]

The paradox at the heart of the project was the unavoidable tension between the ephemeral nature of theatre and the need to create a continuing network of collaborations – a company – in order to present the best theatre possible. The institution had to be stable enough to support the work yet flexible enough to be creative. As he left the RSC, Hall's observation on this tension between creativity and the institution was that the company and the associations it had built up were strong enough to make it last another five years.

# THREE

# THE AGE OF EXPANSION

Trevor Nunn faced a formidable task: the RSC was already world class –
how could he improve it? Peter Hall had stressed continuity, having
chosen Nunn precisely because he wanted him to challenge what he had
established. Nunn, on the other hand, needed the safety net and suste-
nance of continuity. He had no management experience and was thrust
into post with little time to prepare. Despite the RSC's achievements
under Hall, and precisely because they were associated with Hall, his
departure at a moment of financial calamity made the company highly
vulnerable. Would the Arts Council continue to support the RSC shorn of
the man who was synonymous with its very existence?

Yet in his first decade in office, Nunn succeeded not only in sustaining
the company's achievements but also in extending them, in bringing
greater depth and consistency to the company's work and greater variety
to the non-Shakespeare repertoire. His twin aims were to focus on the
actor and the audience. Relevance and popularity were crucial, but they
had to be questioned in order to be re-asserted, as did core notions of
ensemble and cross-fertilisation. 'I want an avowed and committed popular theatre,' he wrote later. 'I want a socially concerned theatre. A
politically aware theatre. In reality not in name.'[1] Nunn did what Hall
hoped he would. He followed Peter Brook's counsel that 'everything must
be re-examined and new solutions found. Anything is possible as long as
it serves one constant aim: the creating of conditions which make possible work of a certain quality.'[2] Nunn did not need to create a totally new

institution. He did need, however, to ensure its survival, to remake it again and to get it in better working order.

The bequeathed arrangement of artistic leadership did not last. Nunn says he believed he was acting as a caretaker and that Hall would return. Yet six weeks after handing over, Hall was gone. He did direct occasionally at the RSC until 1973 when, in an act of notable symbolism, he took over the NT. Brook, by now a brand himself, was loosening his RSC ties; he was busy filming and setting up his international theatre centre in Paris, though in 1970 he did return to Stratford and directed arguably the RSC's most celebrated production, *A Midsummer Night's Dream*, which only served to show what Britain and the RSC would be missing. Clifford Williams, who had been a possible successor to Hall, worked at the NT, in the commercial theatre and abroad, and maintained his relationship with the RSC but not as a central player. Scofield resigned from the directorate in April 1968 for personal reasons and was not to return to the company.

Ashcroft and Barton were the main links with the Hall years, and gave valuable guidance to Nunn. It was important for Nunn to have Ashcroft in his first company, just as it had been for Hall, and she played Queen Katherine in Nunn's production of *Henry VIII*. Barton served as Nunn's company director in Stratford and alongside him was Terry Hands, a graduate of Birmingham University and the Royal Academy of Dramatic Arts who had joined the RSC a year after Nunn and was almost exactly a year younger than Nunn. Hands had come from the Liverpool Everyman to run Theatregoround. In 1967 he had become an associate director and in 1968 had been given administrative responsibility for the London end. Nunn, however, pointed Hands toward Stratford and gave David Jones, an associate director since 1966, the Aldwych post. Nunn, Barton, Jones and Hands shaped artistic policy under Nunn's leadership. There was a good deal of tension in temperament and outlook within the group, particularly between Jones and Hands, but also a strong sense of commitment to the company.

Derek Hornby left in 1969 after a series of administrative bungles. The post of administrative director went with him and the general manager David Brierley became the senior administrative figure. Brierley had joined the RSC in 1961, having worked with Barton at Cambridge University and briefly been a teacher. He rose from assistant stage manager to general stage manager and administrative assistant to Hall; it was a valuable apprenticeship as he came to know the theatre inside out. He was to form a formidable team with the RSC's financial controller William Wilkinson, hired in 1968 by Hornby from the film world. Both

Brierley and Wilkinson were theatre devotees and believed in the company ideal. They maintained the civil service ministerial code that artistic policy was primary and not their business; their job was to find the most effective means to allow the artists to implement that policy. They were as wily as Sir Humphrey in *Yes, Minister* and steered the company adeptly through the vicissitudes of the next two decades.

Nunn needed their skills immediately as he inherited the company's most severe financial crisis, which, coincidentally, came in the wake of the 1967 devaluation of the pound. The RSC faced bankruptcy. Unfortunately for Nunn, the impending disappearance of the RSC was no longer news, as Hall had issued thunderous disaster calls in 1962 and 1966 and on both occasions the company had not only survived but also produced celebrated productions. During Nunn's first years in charge, when Britain was caught up in widespread recession, the company survived economically through improved box office performance, especially at the Aldwych where the 1971 season was the RSC's most successful, a reduction in company size, international tours – to the USA, Canada, Japan, Australia and mainland Europe, which consolidated the RSC as an international company – and deals with television and film companies.

Organisationally, these years were characterised by tackling the planning cycle, which shaped the company's ability to deliver its work. Nunn made the two-theatre operation more efficient, and that meant sorting out the relationship between Stratford and London as well as the management of the Aldwych, which was expensive to run, a planning nightmare and vulnerable still to challenge by the Arts Council, not to mention the RSC's own governors. The pattern and volume of transfers from Stratford to London (only seventeen out of forty-one productions from 1960–67) revealed an uneven spread throughout the London year as well as a lack of Shakespeare work for actors hired in London and a lack of modern work for actors from the Stratford end. A more coherent transfer policy would offer more efficient exploitation of productions and by reducing the number of new London productions would reduce London costs too. Nunn introduced a revised two-year model, which was to remain the norm for the RSC until the mid-1990s. He also gave London its own production manager and developed a more coherent set of backstage working routines, which facilitated the new operating model. This was based on two companies staying together for two years; the first year would be spent in Stratford and the second year would be spent in London, while a new company was formed in Stratford. The break between the end of the Stratford season and the beginning of the London one posed difficulties, but with the end of the World Theatre Season in

1973, space was created in the Aldwych schedule that allowed the easier rotation of companies and the Stratford season to be extended into January.

The RSC was like the proverbial tanker that cannot be turned round very quickly. With the exception of the 1972 *Romans* season, it was not until after 1974 that it became the habit for most of the Stratford productions to transfer, but even then it was rare for them all to make the journey. After this point, being denied a transfer was associated for directors and actors with the stigma of failure. The two-year system rationalised the production culture but at the same time reinforced the problem of 'factory' production, which had become apparent towards the end of Hall's regime. The issue was not the length of time a production stayed in the repertoire but the pressure to keep all productions in the work cycle in order to make it work efficiently. Added to this was the problem caused by dedication to the Shakespearean repertoire. The longer the RSC survived, the greater the difficulty as the plays kept coming round for production. The box office and history propel certain plays such as *Twelfth Night* and *A Midsummer Night's Dream* into production more frequently than plays such as *Titus Andronicus* or *Pericles*, and the very success of the RSC's own production of a particular play further complicates the assessment of when and under what conditions that play can be next seen.

Nunn's refinement of the two-year system meant abandoning the three-year contract, which had become as much of a burden as a prop for the company. Some actors took a 'year out' from the RSC, and a three-year commitment that involved one year's absence was no basis on which to develop long-term company relationships. Instead Nunn instituted a two-year contract (that is, two successive one-year agreements)[3] and made greater efforts to find new work in London to fit the company rather than the other way round. The changes meant it was easier for Nunn to build a core group of actors while he undertook the more drawn-out process of discovering his core group of directors. It also meant he could experiment with the idea of ensemble. In the early seasons, Nunn reduced the number of actors in the Stratford and London companies and made them more numerically balanced. This stringency meant greater sharing of roles in Stratford than usual and the development of a stronger sense of ensemble. All actors were stretched more and needed to contribute more but they encountered more opportunities, which were shared out more evenly. There was a renewed emphasis on classes, and voice work began to be taken in a new direction beyond technique into meaning. Physical and mental preparation of the actor was a noticeable trait of the company, and understudy work, always a contentious issue, was operating at an unprecedented high level.

## Break with the past

In reaction to Hall's signature style – a puritan realism accompanying a new public and political inquiry, which had been a response to the cloying richness of the enclosed late 1950s theatre – the company under Nunn kept the social backdrop in sight but turned to a more private and personal scrutiny, a more romantic speaking style and a sharper, more intensive use of colour. This move captured something of the love of display apparent at the time, especially among the young.

In 1969, Nunn's first season planned as director of the company and one of its most successful, the Stratford programme reinforced the break with Hall's aesthetic that had been evident in *The Revenger's Tragedy*. Known as the 'late play' season, it featured *Pericles*, *The Winter's Tale* and *Henry VIII* alongside a revival of *The Merry Wives of Windsor*, *Twelfth Night* and, as the RSC had done since 1965, a non-Shakespeare, Middleton's *Women Beware Women*. There was a boldness and simplicity in staging and an emphasis on theatrical gesture within a focused space, underpinned by striking use of light. There was, however, a continuation of the use of a generic set as the basis for the whole season, which had emerged for practical as well as aesthetic reasons under John Bury. A generic set was both economically more efficient and allowed greater flexibility through later decision-making. Nunn and his designer Christopher Morley varied the box format from season to season. The public highlight of its use was Brook's 1970 production of *A Midsummer Night's Dream* with Sally Jacob's gymnasium-like surround. Far from being the exception, Brook's luminescent production is exemplary of the RSC in this period.

Theatregoround (TGR) had outgrown its initial commando idea and was seen as the RSC itself instead of the 'warm up' act. Hands's TGR production of Dylan Thomas's *Under Milk Wood* was seen on the Aldwych stage in 1968 and *When Thou Art King* (adapted by Barton from *Henry IV, Parts 1* and *2*, and *Henry V*) was incorporated into the Stratford repertoire in 1969. The Arts Council, which did not recognise TGR as part of the RSC's core activity, accordingly never raised the company's grant to meet any of TGR's costs. These, therefore, had to be found by external funding or from within the RSC funds. By 1969 the costs were being primarily borne by the company and, against a backdrop of the acute financial problems, the governors threatened to close down TGR if the costs were not curtailed. In 1970, Nunn integrated TGR into the company's work. TGR productions rehearsed in parallel with the rest of the RSC rep and one TGR performance per week was added to the schedule at the Royal Shakespeare Theatre. In theory, the box office income from this extra show would support the entire TGR operation. These productions, which attracted a smaller budget than the other shows in the rep, maintained the TGR aesthetic of small casts, doubling, minimal scenery, props and technical demands to allow mobility and flexibility for visiting differing venues.

The value of TGR could be seen in its 1970 festival at the Round House in north London, which united the Peter Brook and the TGR threads of RSC life. Alongside TGR shows (*When Thou Art King, King John, Dr Faustus* and a new production designed for the festival, *Arden of Faversham*) were three Stratford productions: *Hamlet, Richard III* and *A Midsummer Night's Dream*. They were performed in rehearsal clothes and without décor, and were accompanied by demonstrations, including open rehearsals, and discussions with the audience. Brook's cast had experience of such exposure; it had already shown *A Midsummer Night's Dream* to children in the Stratford rehearsal room and at Birmingham's Midland Arts Centre as a way for Brook to engage the cast in self-reflection. The TGR festival was an attempt to do the same at a company level. Nunn said of the festival: 'It was the experience that gave me the greatest pleasure of the whole year, forgetting about design and presentation altogether.'[4] It also posed difficult questions about the future direction of TGR's work as the tensions between the educational and the artistic impulses were becoming unsustainable. Despite having added mainstream venues such as the Abbey Theatre, Dublin and the Oxford Playhouse to its itinerary to generate further income, TGR was closed in 1971 when the cost to the company could no longer be justified.

Nunn felt the RSC as a whole needed renewing and in 1971 did not direct but used the time to review the organisation. The following year he moved away from the radical ensemble approach and actor-focused simple staging and tried to make the company work on a different scale in a season of Shakespeare's Roman plays: *Coriolanus, Julius Caesar*, a revival of *The Comedy of Errors, Antony and Cleopatra* and *Titus Andronicus*. The four new productions were to be directed by Nunn with, in different combinations, co-directors Buzz Goodbody and Euan Smith (and John Barton on one production). Inevitably the project was compared to *The Wars of the Roses* but it was not to be a similarly bonding and defining company experience. Nunn believed the RSC needed new blood; the company size was increased and leading roles offered to newcomers. In fact this constant attraction of new actors alongside promotion of others through the company, accompanied by degrees of offence felt by those who believed themselves to be overlooked, was the norm at the RSC. It was a tribute to the strength of company sentiment engendered by Nunn that his plans caused such surprise and led to criticism from some who had formed the backbone of the company since he had taken over that the momentum of those years was being wasted.

There was also internal disapproval of money being lavished on new stage machinery, although the sums involved turned out to be modest in comparison to the rumours or the amounts an equivalent mainland European company would have spent. The stage and auditorium were extensively re-fashioned to Morley's design, which mixed his own interest in mechanics with an intention to duplicate the planned Barbican theatre. The stage was thrust further into auditorium in an attempt to create a single room, open stage area. Stalls seating was rearranged and overall capacity increased. Nunn's desire to paint an epic picture – each production began with a procession not requested by the text – was not served well by the new hydraulics. In fact, despite the season unfortunately being often remembered for the machinery, Nunn only used it to any great extent in the first two productions.

For the RSC, the Roman plays did not carry the resonance of the history plays. Since 1960, Stratford had not seen *Antony and Cleopatra* or *Titus Andronicus*, and had seen *Julius Caesar* twice and *Coriolanus* only once. They were not conceived as a group and in their distance from domestic narratives deal more openly than the history plays with political processes. For a London RSC audience, they also picked up on the company's 1970 production of Günter Grass's *The Plebeians Rehearse the Uprising*, which dramatised Brecht's ambivalent attitude to the workers' insurrection in Berlin while he was rehearsing his adaptation of *Coriolanus*. *The Romans* represented not just a stylistic change for Nunn – the choice to explore politics was also new. The Vietnam War and the revolutionary events of 1968 had shaken global politics. British social democracy was in crisis, the left and the trade unions were becoming increasingly active, and the post-war welfare state settlement was unravelling. The productions sounded a slightly apocalyptic note as they traced the trajectory from competing tribes through city, republic and empire to defeat by and ascendancy once more of hostile tribes. Yet on transfer to London, a sharper individual focus was evident – the mark of a company collectively continuing to explore over a period of time.

There was a mixed critical response with views changing, often fero-
ciously, when the productions came to London. Critics did not see the
productions as a group until then, when they were re-worked and scaled
down. Unlike the reception of *The Wars of the Roses* – which comprised
only three plays and more obviously linked – the critical emphasis with
*The Romans* was less on the collective accomplishment and more on individual performances: Janet Suzman as Cleopatra, John Wood as Brutus or
Nicol Williamson, who returned to the company as Coriolanus when the
season moved to London. Nunn was offered plaudits, though rarely for
the same production. As a director, his two main impulses – the human
scale of the actor and the social swirl of humanity – were not always rec-
onciled, yet he created moments of great power that displayed these two
qualities separately as well as some when both were in harmony. The
productions were clearly popular and generally acclaimed, and when
*Antony and Cleopatra* transferred to the small screen, it was regarded as
another breakthrough for televised Shakespeare. Irving Wardle in *The
Times*, despite initial concerns at directorial didacticism, described the
project as a 'monumental piece of work of a kind that defies the transitory
nature of stage performance'.5

*The Romans* represented a major achievement in Nunn's effort to be
popular and public on the big stage, but, as had happened in *The Wars of
the Roses*, the whole process took its toll on the architect and Nunn had to
rest because of extreme exhaustion. He was uncertain about the future of
the company and even the idea of amalgamation with the NT was resurrected once Hall had been identified as Olivier's successor, a move that in
itself added considerable pressure, coming as it did during *The Romans*
project. There was a sense of betrayal at the RSC and it caused a great deal
of pain.

Against a background of inflation rising faster than Arts Council
grants, the gap between the funding of the NT and RSC was widening.
However, the gap between their joint funding and the rest of the Council's
clients was also growing, and there was concomitantly mounting resentment, made most vocal by the emerging fringe theatre, at the share of the
cake going to the two national companies bracketed together now as the
theatre establishment. Luckily the delay to the Barbican project meant the
attack was directed mostly at the NT and its new home on the South
Bank, but it also gave ground to the idea of some kind of association
between the two organisations.

According to Hall, when he told Nunn that he was going to the NT,
Nunn said he could not continue to run the RSC for much longer and that
the company itself could not continue as it was. He talked of amalgamation

in order to make a strong NT. The idea seemed to be enhanced by the RSC's financial straits but the RSC's financial committee, Hall was told, was against the idea and suspected Hall of empire building again, which he denied. Olivier feared a takeover of the NT by the RSC – with Nunn as Hall's lieutenant – while the RSC chair feared a takeover by the NT. Hall proposed a slightly different idea, that until the Barbican was ready, the RSC could provide the Shakespeare on the South Bank and the two managements, which on the NT side contained several ex-RSC staff, would merge. A full amalgamation could result if desired at a later date. Nunn was, by Hall's account, unenthusiastic, particularly about the RSC giving up its non-Shakespeare repertoire to the NT, though he did agree to explore what might be possible. Olivier was sceptical and the Arts Council drama panel antagonistic about any association. Hall believed that Nunn's ambiguity about the direction of the RSC meant they were not in the best position to judge the merits of a merger. Both agreed to write to the Council saying that the mooted association had been abandoned but they hoped their respective grants would be sufficient to fund the two organisations as healthy, independent bodies. 'We can then duel on,' wrote Hall.[6]

For Nunn, although this was a relief, the major problem of what to do with the RSC remained. The unavailability of the Barbican, the panacea of Hall's dreams, meant his attention had urgently to be directed again at the structure of the company. In the 1960s the RSC's very size had generated excitement. In the 1970s, its scale was taken for granted. Nunn gave the example that towards the end of 1973, after it had hired The Place in north London for a second season, the company had opened twelve shows of classic and contemporary work in ten weeks at three theatres. The work for the most part was received enthusiastically, he pointed out, occasionally ecstatically, and box office records for the period were broken. 'But the collective achievement went unremarked,' he wrote.[7] That density of output was assumed to be the norm, which was a measure of the success of the RSC but also posed a problem because of the strain this expectation placed on the still evolving organisation. He believed the RSC had never got beyond the appearance of an ensemble working and had become 'a grouping of too many people doing too much less well than they are able'. He argued, nevertheless, that the RSC was better when it was doing ten things and getting eight right than doing two or three things perfectly. He promised contraction if the public showed they did not want what the RSC was offering. The re-organisation he chose centred on the opening in Stratford of The Other Place in 1974. It was a major step for the RSC to become a three-theatre operation, particularly in the midst of relative austerity, but it did not have to rent the space and could not have afforded to launch it in London.

## The Other Place

There was much discussion within the RSC in the early 1970s about opening a permanent third auditorium. Expansion was part of a coherent RSC view justified by making the company more available and fuelled by internal artistic need. Alongside an increase in extra-mural activity, the RSC held seasons at The Place in 1971 and 1973, which were reminiscent of the earlier Arts Theatre season but on a less ambitious scale.[8] The company found them artistically successful, though both had lost money. Nunn also wanted to build on the lessons of Theatregoround (TGR). It had taught the company how to extend the range and scope of its work by exploiting the RSC's resources and repertoire system, and it had initiated a lasting aesthetic for small-scale Shakespeare, for instance in John Barton's production of *Richard II* which became the prototype for his renowned 1973 'mirror image' version with Ian Richardson and Richard Pasco alternating the parts of the protagonists. The TGR aesthetic and collective work ethos had impressed Nunn and, although it had been overtaken by the innovation of the fringe, it showed along with the work at The Place that creativity in the company could be released outside the RSC's main theatres.[9]

Small theatres featured prominently in British theatre in the 1970s, not just for economic reasons but also for ideological ones. They were more than just venues or spaces; they were statements. In the spirit of Peter Brook's 'empty space', their neutral décor removed the distractions common to proscenium auditoria, where the typical gilt and ruby setting colours a production before it has had a chance to 'speak'. Studios reduced their own internal visibility by not hiding the structure and machinery of the theatre. They offered a play the chance to 'speak' on its own terms in a close, intense scrutiny suited to a fragmented, TV-dominated society. They expressed a classless and egalitarian approach, towards both the audience (who all paid one price) and the actors (no stars, everyone 'mucking in' for the common good). Ironically, in terms of seating capacity, they were by definition elitist. In an age when 'popular' became synonymous with audience numbers, they became less and less viable. Yet, prefiguring the trend in broadcasting for dedicated channels, they satisfied a range of 'minority' tastes and were much quicker to represent the breadth of society than the 'mainstream' theatres. For the RSC, the small theatre was also a public gesture of mitigation for the huge organisation it had become while, at the same time, adding to the company's size.

In the politicised atmosphere of the times, with the nation deeply divided by the failures of the post-war consensus, the pressure from actors and directors for new challenges continued unabated, reminiscent of the energy of the RSC in its early days. The Royal Court had already opened the Theatre Upstairs and the new NT on the South Bank was to have a flexible studio space. Nunn saw the possibilities of exploiting an RSC resource, the tin hut in Southern Lane that had been built for Saint-Denis's Studio and used by TGR as its headquarters. After a trial run as The Studio Theatre in June 1973, Nunn invited Buzz Goodbody, who had just worked with him on *The Romans*, to draw up recommendations for its further use. Goodbody was a feminist communist and co-founder of the Women's Street Theatre Group. She had joined the RSC in 1967, aged twenty, as John Barton's personal assistant and graduated from assistant and TGR work to 'full' repertoire productions. She was not the first woman to direct at Stratford; Irene Hentschel claimed that honour in 1939 followed by Dorothy Green in 1946. But she was the first since then and the first to survive the RSC obstacle course – periods of unemployment, waiting for something to turn up at the RSC and intense internal competition – and to establish a regular presence in the male-dominated company.

She believed the new theatre should be aimed at the public rather than provide an internal 'do your own thing' platform. Satisfying personal needs, especially of actors, would be a 'side effect of its primary concern – its development of a wider audience for classical theatre'.[10] For Goodbody, this was an artistic as well as a social imperative, a step towards crossing the barrier that lay between the RSC and the society that funded it. Echoing Hall's plan for a new London theatre, she saw cheap seats as a key factor. She did not view the size of the auditorium as a sign of elitism. It would only become exclusive if productions became consistently esoteric or too expensive. The new theatre would challenge the RSC's own proscenium traditions and allow the RSC to explore new methods of working as well as expanding its repertoire and reaching new audiences. This alternative status was captured in its name, a quotation from *Hamlet*.

The RSC planning committee gave the go-ahead, although the Arts Council was opposed and insisted that if a third auditorium were opened, the new venture had to be self-financing. In fact, while representing an extra gross cost, The Other Place over time would make a net contribution, not only from its own box office but also from income generated by successful productions that began their life there, like *Piaf* and *Les Liaisons Dangereuses*. With the help of actors, staff and management – in an informal arrangement that would not be possible in later years – The Other Place's administrator Jean Moore and Goodbody turned the tin hut into a rudimentary theatre with basic facilities in four months.

The first season comprised the following: two Shakespeare plays, *The Tempest* and *King Lear*, planned with teachers and shortened to give school students time to return home after the show and discussion that ensued; two new plays, *I Was Shakespeare's Double* by John Downie and Penny Gold, and *Babies Grow Old*, devised by Mike Leigh; a documentary play that went to schools, *The World Turned Upside Down* by David Holman; and two productions of revivals, *Afore Night Come* and *Uncle Vanya*. There were also workshops, seminars and Saturday morning open sessions that became a regular and popular feature of The Other Place life.

Significantly, a project that did not materialise was a festival in high season looking in a radical way at the classics, and at Shakespeare in particular, using other spaces in the town such as halls or gardens. Artists at The Other Place never experimented with form as Brook and Charles Marowitz had done at the RSC a decade before. For all the fine productions at The Other Place, it never established itself as a centre for aesthetic innovation in classical theatre, a lack that contributed to the RSC's decline in the 1990s as a cultural force.

Its second season opened in April 1975 with Goodbody's stunning production of *Hamlet* but was overshadowed by her suicide four days later. Nunn returned from Los Angeles where he was on tour with his RSC production of *Hedda Gabler* to take *Hamlet* through its run. Moore kept the theatre running as Barry Kyle took over direction of the remainder of the season. Goodbody's death was a tremendous shock to the company as well as to Nunn personally and it affected the company for many years to come. She was a pioneering figure who opened the company up to new ways of thinking and working and provided the impetus for the rejuvenation of the RSC in the mid-1970s. Far from jeopardising the future of The Other Place, her death seemed to have the opposite effect and resulted in renewed commitment to the RSC's small-scale work. Under Kyle's instigation, a permanent auditorium seating 180 designed by Chris Dyer, John Napier and Dermot Hayes was installed for the 1976 season, although Kyle decided he did not want to continue to run The Other Place. Nunn took over for that season before handing over to Ron Daniels, who ran the theatre until it was demolished in 1989 and replaced by a new building.

The Other Place had its own aura, and retained its sense of being like a shed, a place where things were made. It was cold in winter and hot in summer; the audience queued in the elements and, until a van was provided, had no interval refreshments. It induced camaraderie both within its casts, who had to share primitive facilities, and between cast and audience, who not only sat close to the actors but for whom the amenities were likewise so basic that a strong identification arose. The Other Place was everything the larger theatre could not be in terms of such an association.

Within the confines of the repertoire system, directors experimented with staging at The Other Place, which enjoyed a tremendous record of production across the range. It acted as an internal commentator, like the fool at court, which is particularly useful when there is a strong continuity between regimes or one artistic director stays in position for a long time. It could offer direct juxtaposition, for example *King Lear* in the Royal Shakespeare Theatre and Bond's *Lear* at The Other Place, or a comparison of styles and approaches by attracting a new group of directors, designers and actors from the fringe who disputed the RSC's values and acted as a regenerative force. Its village hall licence restricted the number of public performances it could give but allowed educational work to be undertaken and increased its availability for workshops. This developmental strand of work made it important for company reasons, a litmus test for the internal health of the RSC.

## Rich vein

Opening The Other Place had been a typically bold RSC move in the midst of another financial crisis, which was so severe that the following year, 1975, Nunn had to cut back at Stratford the number of productions at the Royal Shakespeare Theatre to four – three new productions and one revival. This reduction represented a greater retreat than Hall's in 1966, and, remarkably, the number was the smallest since the first Shakespeare theatre had been founded on that site nearly a hundred years before. The Aldwych – which had been thriving under David Jones with Pinter premières, popular shows like Boucicault's *London Assurance* and Jones's own productions, such as O'Casey's *The Silver Tassie* and a series of Gorky plays – ceased temporarily to perform in repertoire. As if to underline the depth of the crisis, a centenary appeal was launched commemorating the founding of the Shakespeare Memorial Association by Charles Flower. Enforced restraint, which was embraced ideologically at The Other Place and had its counterpoint at the Royal Shakespeare Theatre in a rich minimalism, once again seemed to lead to productive artistic results. The company entered an extraordinary period of artistic creativity and virtuosity in an unparalleled range of classical and contemporary plays that lasted through to the beginning of the next decade.

The signature note of RSC big stage Shakespeare for this period came from Terry Hands and the designer Farrah. In 1975 Hands took over from Barton as Stratford company director and directed all four Royal Shakespeare Theatre productions, *Henry V*, *Henry IV Parts 1* and *2* and a revival of *The Merry Wives of Windsor,* the first time a single director had been responsible for a whole season. Defying chronology, Hands opened out of sequence with *Henry V* in order to let the Chorus provide a prologue to the whole enterprise with his appeal to 'imaginary puissance' and the 'brightest heaven of invention'. The cast, about half the number of *The Wars of the Roses*, achieved a high degree of ensemble playing on the raked stage reminiscent of the deck of an aircraft carrier. He not only undercut the bombast and pageantry but also, using the play's internal dialectic of debate, questioned the notion of heroism and the meaning of nation. Yet, unlike the contemporary plays at The Other Place, Hands ultimately invoked an idealised 'one nation' sensibility at this moment of national anxiety, and that was the tenor of his subsequent history work, which stressed poetic rather than political consonance through sweeping theatrical authority. With Alan Howard at the head of the company, Hands and Farrah essayed each of the three parts of *Henry VI* in 1977, confident that there was an audience for them now and did not need condensing as Hall and Barton had done. They were rehearsed as one production and opened on consecutive evenings without the usual break in between. They emerged as more complex and ambiguous than the heavily editorialised Hall/Barton version and were praised as revelatory, with Hands's fluent staging receiving particular credit. The same team's fine run continued that year with *Coriolanus*, which toured Europe to much acclaim. In 1980 the team completed the history cycle with the pairing of *Richard II* and *Richard III*.

Nunn's work at The Other Place unlocked him as a director and resulted in a string of notable productions in both the RSC's large and small spaces: *Macbeth, The Comedy of Errors, The Alchemist, Three Sisters, Once in a Lifetime, Nicholas Nickleby, Juno and the Paycock, All's Well That Ends Well.*[11] His dexterity mirrored the company's own newfound agility and wide-ranging expertise which moved in the small spaces from new plays such as *Destiny* and *Piaf* and revivals like *Bingo* and *Timon of Athens* to popular hits in the Aldwych such as *Travesties, Wild Oats* and *Privates on Parade.* In this period, the last half of the 1970s, the RSC flourished as it expanded. It not only opened The Other Place, but also established its annual residency in Newcastle upon Tyne, initiated The Warehouse in London and launched its annual small-scale tour. The company even planned to open a third auditorium in Stratford, which was thwarted only through lack of finance.

The Other Place's existence allowed the RSC to overcome its habitual dissatisfaction with traditional touring and reach a wider audience through regular visits of a different kind to the Northeast. Following an ambitious 1962 tour offering the full range of the company's work, the RSC had wanted to tour the north every year but the money was not available. The company did continue large venue touring but not on the same scale as the 1962 tour, either in terms of the number of productions taken or the number of venues visited. This type of touring was very expensive and not artistically very satisfying; the receiving theatres were not always appropriate in dimensions and staffing to cope with the RSC's demands and it was difficult to establish links with the audience. These drawbacks had convinced Hall to set up TGR but when it was closed down in 1971, the company became vulnerable to criticism because of the extensive touring undertaken by minimally funded fringe companies. The founding of The Other Place made it possible to offer the full variety of the RSC once again beyond Stratford and London. In March 1977, the company took four productions from the Royal Shakespeare Theatre to the Theatre Royal in Newcastle and four Other Place productions to the nearby Gulbenkian Studio in the University Theatre. 'Campus Stratford' came to town for a five-week season, during which the RSC also held special activities, sometimes in other venues, from open theatre days and schools' workshops to lunchtime and late-night entertainments, anthology performances and after-show discussions.

Four months later the RSC expanded further by opening The Warehouse in London's Covent Garden to make sense of the two-year cycle. As soon as The Other Place had opened, the question of taking the productions to London arose. From the first season, *Lear* played at The Place and from the second *Hamlet* was seen at the Round House. A regular venue was desirable and Howard Davies, who had first directed at the RSC in The Other Place's opening season in 1974, was appointed artistic director of the fourth RSC theatre before the space had been found. After studying on a directors' course at Bristol University and being a stage manager, Davies had become artistic director of the Bristol Old Vic Studio and had directed several shows for Avon Touring. Goodbody persuaded Davies, who was initially hostile to the clique running the RSC, to join the 'enemy' and fight within the institution for what he wanted. He brought with him a group of artists who formed the core of much of the company's new work in the 1970s. The policy of Davies's theatre was to present new British plays alongside transfers from The Other Place.

The Arts Council as ever was wary of RSC expansion and senior RSC personnel also needed persuading: it was harder to be self-financing in London than Stratford because of the rent in a volatile central London property market, the cost of converting a building into a theatre and equipping it, however minimally, the need to contract out the making of sets and costumes as the RSC did not have workshops in London, and the higher overheads. The second London auditorium had to succeed fast. After much searching and false starts, the RSC returned to a site it had used for rehearsals and part of the *Theatre of Cruelty* season. Known as the Donmar (an amalgamation of the first names of theatre manager Donald Albery and Margot Fonteyn for whom he bought it), the RSC turned it into a theatre called The Warehouse. The first performance went up half an hour late because the electricity had only just been turned on and the front concrete steps, which had to be rebuilt because they had fallen two feet short, had still not set.

The new plays in the first season were chosen from a nine-month back-log of scripts and comprised Howard Barker's *That Good Between Us*, C.P. Taylor's *Bandits*, James Robson's *Factory Birds*, Barrie Keeffe's *Frozen Assets* and Edward Bond's *The Bundle*, written specially for the occasion. Interleaved with these new productions were transfers of *Schweyk in the Second World War*, *Macbeth*, *Bingo* and Charles Wood's *Dingo*. It was altogether an extraordinary opening programme and brought a new edge to the RSC profile in the capital.

In the following year, 1978, Nunn took the commitment to reaching new audiences further and complemented the residency in Newcastle by launching what became known as the small-scale tour and later the regional tour. In the spirit of TGR, it arose directly from The Other Place. Jean Moore administered the tour on loan from The Other Place, a third of the company had worked on Nunn's Other Place production of *Macbeth*, Nunn directed one of the productions and Ian McKellen, who had played Macbeth, led the tour. Backing came from the Arts Council's touring department and, presciently, the RSC won sponsorship from the US firm Hallmark Cards. The tour was aimed at locations off the beaten theatrical track, and took with it a simple, specially designed, platform stage. It comprised *Three Sisters*, *Twelfth Night* and an anthologised enquiry into Englishness *And Is There Honey Still For Tea?* devised by company member Roger Rees. It also provided morning workshops for schools. There was insufficient time to check out all twenty-six venues properly, and most proved to be too large as well as already being a part of an established theatrical life. This mismatch between aim and implementation was a result of Arts Council pressure on the RSC to play middle-scale theatres which the Council was funding.

The company refined its operation with the second tour, in 1979. It took its own flexible seating, which on average coped with between 400 and 470 people, as well as technical equipment and a stage, making the company independent of the venues. There were tussles over the choice of plays, with the company keen to present itself as a cross-fertilising theatre. Some venues resisted new plays and only wanted Shakespeare; some did not want Shakespeare at all and only new plays; some even cancelled when they discovered there were no stars in the cast. Except for a couple of years when funding was not forthcoming, the tour became a regular feature of RSC life and the company settled into a routine of usually taking two Shakespeare productions. Although there were always problems achieving an even geographical spread, it helped meet the company's obligation to the taxpayers who part-funded the RSC, and, for many audiences, the tour was their first experience of the company's work.

During this period of expansion when the company's output approximately doubled, the RSC showed that a labour-intensive industry like the theatre could increase productivity. Up to a certain point, the RSC became more efficient the more it did; broadly speaking, the same number of people worked harder for little or no extra cost. With two theatres it had proved difficult to increase the number of performances, and even achieving full capacity, which was an objective upper limit, would not have put the company in profit. But in four theatres the same number of RSC personnel could present more performances to more spectators as the small theatres used up spare capacity. Highly complex internal accounting allowed for budgetary ingenuity and the RSC's survival, although primarily artistic, owes a great deal to creative accountancy.

The new structure, however, brought new problems in the planning and casting processes. Production 'slots' were now spread across two theatres each, and the repertory system meant cross-casting had to become highly sophisticated in order to balance the needs of the productions and those of the actors, who were to appear in a line of parts in the different spaces. It became difficult to drop poor productions because the length of runs was not that flexible – depending on how many, if any, productions in a season could play against each other – and yet the company could not always exploit a good show to the maximum. This particularly affected new plays that began in London, such as Bond's *The Bundle*, which received a pitiful number of performances relative to its artistic merits.

Nevertheless, for the first time, cross-fertilisation had become a continuous practical reality. The four-theatre structure enriched the company by extending the repertoire possibilities and attracting a new generation of artists, who were to become the backbone of the company and led to successes such as *The Life and Adventures of Nicholas Nickleby*. The new structure allowed the company to bring on young directors, such as Bill Alexander and John Caird, a process that both the RSC and NT had found difficult to achieve. In choosing Davies to run The Warehouse, Nunn broke new ground by appointing as an associate a director who had no interest (at the time) in directing Shakespeare.

Despite greater delegation, the four-theatre operation also meant a greater burden for Nunn to carry and in 1977, as the fourth theatre was being introduced, this pressure was increased as he faced a leadership crisis. David Jones was appointed producer of BBC TV's *Play of the Month* and Terry Hands accepted an offer from Peter Hall to join the NT to run an ensemble in the Olivier Theatre. Nunn felt he could not let Hands go and the only offer he could make to match Hall's was to make him joint artistic director. Hands took up the post the following year and the future direction of the RSC became yoked to this sibling relationship, mixing comradeship, rivalry and mutual irritation within a shared and deep commitment to the company that had shaped their professional lives.

## Financial crisis

The financial situation they faced was deteriorating badly. In 1979 – the election year of a Conservative government dedicated to rolling back the role of the state in the arts as elsewhere – the Arts Council, in addition to sections of the press, called for the RSC to economise by closing The Warehouse, which was targeted because of its socially oriented new play repertoire. Ironically, shutting the theatre would have saved little money, and Nunn was opposed to closing it as a gesture because of the artistic and ideological surrender that would represent. He said provocatively that he would rather close the Aldwych, an option that was seriously considered and would at least have had a significant economic effect. In the end neither happened, but it foreshadowed battles to come. The Council believed that the disparity between its grant to the RSC and the company's expenditure was growing dangerously out of line. The RSC believed the Council was doing nothing to save it from going broke.

Yet, as the new decade dawned and the prospect of moving to the Barbican became at last a reality, out of this economic crisis the RSC fashioned a typical riposte: John Barton's three-play marathon *The Greeks* and the two-part adaptation by David Edgar of *The Life and Adventures of Nicholas Nickleby*, directed by Trevor Nunn and John Caird using the whole company. These two epic projects at the Aldwych proved to be the culmination of the extraordinary sequence of RSC productions that stretched back to the mid-1970s and stood as testimony to the company's health under Nunn's leadership before the Aldwych was swapped for a new theatre in the City of London.

*Nicholas Nickleby*, in particular, showed the RSC's refusal to be bowed by adversity as well as its recurring knack of imaginative improvisation. Instead of closing the Aldwych after the Stratford transfers had finished their runs, Nunn decided to stage one production that could involve all the actors. Through necessity he broke the tyranny of the production schedule and found the result a liberation.

Prompted by a recent visit to the Soviet Union, where, he had discovered, it was common to adapt Dickens for the stage, he decided this would meet the RSC's current calamitous situation and chose *Nickleby* as the source book. When it came to asking the actors to recontract for London after the Newcastle season, Nunn had no text and no parts to offer, only a project. The actors were asked to make a total commitment from the outset, which caused some upset and was modified to allow the opportunity of dropping out after five weeks of rehearsal. Remarkably, all but a handful accepted and together with the artistic team they embarked on a creative process the RSC had never undertaken before.[12] Out of their collective explorations, Edgar created a new text that was remoulded as the process unfolded and the project developed into what became – despite initially low-key responses from some critics – one of the RSC's outstanding productions. This was popular theatre with a bustling flourish; actors merged with the audience in the aisles and by way of a platform from the stage through the middle of the stalls and a catwalk along the front of the dress circle. Action moved swiftly and fluently as detailed characterisation jostled with broad theatrical brush strokes in a swirl of energy. It triumphed on Broadway and was recreated successfully for the small screen. *Nicholas Nickleby* laid a marker for Nunn's subsequent big stage work and symbolised his belief in and affirmation of the value of company.

# FOUR

# BARBICAN BOUND

Despite artistic success, the RSC under Trevor Nunn and Terry Hands entered the 1980s, when the chill wind of monetarism was gathering speed, technically insolvent and haviing to borrow at increasingly high interest rates. The annual rise in the Arts Council grant was less than the company's deficit and yet, ironically, the company paid the government in VAT and National Insurance more than its annual grant. Fortunately, it negotiated a good deal with the City for its occupancy of the Barbican, which was set for 1982. Nunn decided the new theatre, designed to RSC specifications and boasting supposedly the most advanced technical facilities available, should have productions to match the ambition of the building. He believed, following a visit to the US, that the technical accomplishment and standards of production were higher on Broadway than in London and introduced in 1981 a policy of enhancing physical presentation as a means of changing that situation and keeping the RSC's big stage work popular.

It was an apparent reversal of the anti-decorative, actor-based approach associated with the RSC's best work as well as a response both to the minimalism of previous seasons and to the growing assertion by designers of their presence and contribution. They felt the company was too text-centred and had not kept up with continental scenography. The introduction of the policy also coincided with Nunn's foray into the commercial theatre with the designer John Napier on the Andrew Lloyd Webber musical *Cats*, which was to change Nunn's life. By accident he wrote the lyrics for 'Memory', one of the show's hit songs, which, along with his earnings as the director and subsequent income from *Starlight Express*, *Les Misérables* and a string of successful musicals, made him very rich. The aesthetic trend this represented chimed with the spread of individualism and the worship of money in a society that was losing its collective life.

While the new approach at the RSC produced some strong designs, it also had some disastrous consequences. The human scale of theatre was lost and on occasion the purpose of a play was skewed. Hands, for example, working in the new Barbican theatre misconceived Peter Nichols' *Poppy* as a lavish musical instead of a tatty one. *Peter Pan*, which followed it, went badly over budget and came to symbolise an unfortunate habit at the Barbican of performances being cancelled because of technical problems both on and off stage. Although in the case of *Peter Pan* there was the mitigating factor of the Barbican being unfamiliar, the emphasis on design led the ambition of artists there regularly to collide with economic reality. Due to financial pressures, the RSC allotted too little preparation time to mount shows of the complexity in which it was now engaged, and the resulting loss of performances damaged its relationship with its audience. Performances had been cancelled at the Aldwych but the public effect was different at the Barbican where expectations were altered by the fact of the theatre's modernity. Defenders of the 'designer' policy, nevertheless, could challenge this assessment by pointing to a rise in audience figures as vindication.[1]

## The Barbican

The move to the Barbican itself caused palpable nervousness in the RSC. The understandable anxiety of leaving the Aldwych, a theatre the company had occupied for more than two decades, for an unknown building and an uncharted as well as unprecedented relationship with a local authority landlord was overlaid with deeper concerns arising from the traumatic experience of the National Theatre's occupation of its new home on the South Bank in the mid-1970s. Debilitating internal labour disputes followed much public criticism of the cost of the building. The RSC did not want to be trapped in a white elephant that devoured its finances, nor to become institutionalised as an establishment theatre umbilically associated with City financiers. Although it was seen as the theatrical establishment, it had managed to renew itself constantly and resist ossification. In the context of national organisations, its image was still remarkably radical, thanks to its popular verve and contemporary work. Given the company's financial vulnerability, however, the threat to its identity was even more serious.

The Barbican itself was a mixed blessing and did not live up to Hall's original assessment of the proposed move as the most important development for the company since the first Stratford theatre was built. It was to have laid to rest any lingering arguments about the RSC's presence in London, yet it precipitated a revival of those arguments that eventually led to the company's voluntary withdrawal from a permanent presence in the capital. Hall's commitment to cheaper seats and a youth policy was lost in his enthusiasm for RSC growth. Although he admired the main theatre, when the centre finally opened in 1982 he described the result as offering 'an inhuman environment like a second-rate airport'.[2]

Senior RSC personnel – Peter Hall, John Bury and Paddy Donnell – were directly involved in the design and others, like Peter Brook and Michel Saint-Denis, contributed their thoughts. Inspired by the Total Theatre ideas of Walter Gropius and Erwin Piscator and the practical reality of the Mermaid Theatre – also situated in the City – the team under architect Peter Chamberlain came up with an auditorium seating just over 1,000 in a single, huge, wide room. There was no proscenium, although a flexible proscenium was added. Hall insisted on the centrality of the actor speaking to, and not at, the audience from a single point of command. No seat was more than 65 ft from this point, which can be found 8 ft from the front edge of the stage. The off-stage areas were cavernous. There was a single raked stalls area with aisles only at either end of the seats, each row having its own door, and three narrow, overhanging balconies stacked one above the other, which curve back in towards the stage. In a sign of the times, the opening night audience applauded as the doors running along the sides of the stalls, which had been held open by electromagnets, closed simultaneously. In other design terms, both externally and internally, what was seen as advanced in 1965 had lost its special character by 1982. Acoustic trouble, related to sound being sucked up into the fly tower, caused problems for actors and audience alike. There were also difficulties with the technology, mainly to do with the fly system and lighting, and in the crucial area of transfers from Stratford, the stage did not match that of the Royal Shakespeare Theatre as it was supposed to, and transfers remained problematic.

A studio theatre called The Pit, seating up to 200, had been added to the original plan to replace The Warehouse and had to be paid for by the RSC. The black box was built below sea level in what was to have been a rehearsal room, and as a result displayed a maze of pipes and a large air duct in the middle of the low ceiling that sloped to match the rake in the larger auditorium above. Soundproofing was never wholly satisfactory. In contrast to The Warehouse, The Pit never established its own identity, despite the good work that was often seen there, and it became just another RSC space. It was pulled in several directions. Some of the new plays would have been better received at a fringe venue like the Bush Theatre in west London, while other shows harboured production ambitions beyond the capability of the space or the budgets allocated to them. Expectations aroused by the prices charged caused public dissatisfaction with the levels of comfort and put pressure on the type of repertoire and production on offer. There was no dedicated publicity to raise The Pit's profile, and the tortuous public access by way of lifts or stairs did not inspire audience affection. Schemes were advanced to reconfigure and rename The Pit but they proved too expensive, and then leaving the Barbican took the company's energy elsewhere.

Despite breaking RSC London box office records there, the company could not overcome the problems of the Barbican centre, which became the stuff of legend. The Barbican was isolated not only from 'theatre land' (which is true also of the Royal Court in Sloane Square) but also from a sense of life in the evening. There was no 'passing trade' and scarcely a passing taxi. Audiences were not in the best frame of mind when the show started. Signposting from the local tube stations was poor and the un-prepossessing car parks echoed the centre's dated 1960s look. There was not a great choice of restaurants nearby, and on-site food was limited in range and quality but costly (though it improved under Searcy's at the upper end of the market). The complex, which included a concert hall, a cinema, an art gallery, a sculpture court, a library and a conservatory, lacked a focal entrance point. A £10 million attempt to create one by installing golden muses above, and hanging mirrors below, the front awning aroused derision, which affected the RSC by default. The next Barbican director removed the offending objects but the damage had been done.

Once inside the centre, static was a menace and the floor numberings and internal directions were bewildering. Twenty years and several schemes after the opening, money was still being spent on trying to sort out this problem. Also, it was not easy to find out what was playing. RSC 'visibility' was a problem, both for productions at the Barbican and more so for any being presented at another London venue. This drawback was compounded by trouble with the box office. Barbican staff sold the RSC's tickets because Stratford's box office system was not compatible with the Barbican's, yet they often had little knowledge or understanding of the company's work. There was no sense of ownership for the RSC and little opportunity to change the 'feel' of the centre, to leave the company's mark before the audience entered the theatres. Although the Aldwych was also rented, because the RSC was the sole tenant, it had seemed as if it did belong to the company, whereas at the Barbican the RSC was clearly just one attraction among several others.

The company's public image as well as identification with its audience suffered. Technical problems and cancelled performances in the main theatre added to scepticism at the benefits of civic modernity, while the introduction of a Patrons' Subscription Scheme on the elitist Covent Garden model underlined the distance the RSC had travelled since the idealistic early days of the company and the democratic impulse of the RSC Club. The scheme, which eased the company's cash-flow problems by bringing in money up-front, had been started in 1980 at the Aldwych just prior to the Barbican move; for a certain level of donation, individuals or companies could name a seat and join the priority-booking scheme ahead of RSC mailing list members. The scheme was developed to attract corporate members, with its own hierarchy of status from silver members through gold to benefactor level. There were associated privileges at the Barbican, like the use of a patrons' bar, which subtly affected the culture of RSC theatre-going.

While actors and RSC staff admired aspects of the theatres, especially the combination of epic and intimate in the larger theatre, they were frustrated with the centre itself and the backstage arrangements, however spacious compared to the Aldwych. An actor who started work at 10am for a rehearsal and finished at 11pm after a production might never see natural light. Attempts were made to improve the windowless rehearsal rooms but in 1987 the RSC decided that the volume of rehearsal work and the conditions at the Barbican made it necessary to rent a separate rehearsal space, a move that widened the gap between actors and administration. (Even the three rooms in this former cinema in Clapham, south London, were not sufficient to cope with the workload, and extra spaces had to be hired elsewhere.) Actors and staff also suffered from what became known as 'sick building throat', an under-the-weather feeling many believed was caused by an 'airless' working environment and its unhealthy air circulation system. In the offices, which were also windowless – though a few had glass-ceiling panels – rewiring or other technical repairs and maintenance frequently interrupted work. The walls of the narrow corridors seemed to be scrubbed endlessly to remove moisture staining from above. Improvements to the centre made after John Tusa became managing director in 1995 came too late for the RSC. It had already lost something that could never be recaptured and could not yet discover a way of starting again.

## Financial scrutiny

A year after the RSC's move to the Barbican, the Prime Minister's Efficiency Unit put the company's standing as national institution to its severest test. The unit's chief of staff Clive Priestley, a punctilious civil servant in the Prime Minister's private office, led a financial scrutiny of both the Royal Opera House and the RSC. The age of the statistic had arrived, dominated by obsession with measurement and determining value by 'outcomes'. Yet, much to the chagrin of the monetarists who believed that art had enjoyed a free ride for far too long, Priestley judged both organisations to be under-funded, generally reliable in their financial management and worthy of continued and, indeed, increased support. However, he found the Opera House appealed only to a tiny section of the nation, was inefficient in several areas and needed to make considerable economies. In contrast, he praised the RSC for its productivity and breadth of national appeal. It was 'one of the most efficient and effective bodies I have come across'.[3] The RSC served the public and the theatrical profession well (in terms of employment, range of opportunities and training) and – in the critical phrase of the times – was good value for money.

Priestley had only one major criticism: lateness in planning and hence in the production process, which caused the troughs and peaks in production departments and the resulting disproportionate amount of overtime. He made recommendations concerning the management of shows into performance, and renegotiating the working conventions in stage operating at the Barbican. He also recommended extending the planning cycle, with budgets set three years in advance, and repertoire planning to be completed earlier to allow designs to be completed earlier, which in turn should smooth out the aforementioned peaks and troughs. He suggested greater visibility of senior artistic and administrative management in Stratford departments, closer involvement of heads of department in planning in order to make even more efficient use of staff, and costs to be allocated to each of the theatres on the basis of resources consumed. His main proposal, however, was more government money for the RSC to allow all the above to happen. It was a stunning vindication of the institution.

He later wrote that the RSC had won its argument and that the scrutiny had shown the enervating and wasteful effect of gross uncertainty in the relationship between a company and the funding authority. He rebutted claims that he had been enchanted by the company, yet on the production side there is evidence to suggest he was won over by the excellence and skill of the design and manufacture, which meant he did not always challenge all the costings properly. He became a governor of the company after the report was issued. The company made certain housekeeping changes (such as limiting telephone and taxi use) and took steps to reorganise internally to allow greater flow of communication. The government response was to give with one hand and take away with the other. The Arts Council's regional development policy cut the funding of many groups, particularly those considered subversive, while the RSC was rewarded with an adequate grant rise (to £4.9 million). Government also accepted that this new level would establish a satisfactory baseline for future operations. In fact, in the subsequent years, nothing of the sort materialised. Using the Priestley formula to calculate what the RSC should have received, by 1987/88 there was a shortfall of nearly £1.3 million, rising the following year to £2.2 million.

The continuing crisis in RSC funding led the company to innovation not just in the artistic field but also in the financial field, particularly in sponsorship. The crucial figure was Kenneth Cork, chartered accountant, insolvency specialist and later Lord Mayor of London. He had succeeded George Farmer as chair of governors in 1975 and remained in post for a decade. Ever since becoming a governor in 1967, he had been apprehensive about the RSC's financial viability. As RSC confidence in the Arts Council's ability to deliver a satisfactory solution ebbed, he argued in the traditional Stratford mode for the implementation of self-reliance measures. The year he joined, he established and chaired the Royal Shakespeare Theatre Trust.[4] He says in his memoirs that the main reason for setting up the Trust was to prevent insolvency in case the company became bankrupt due to an inadequate Arts Council award.

The Trust was a charitable body, the funds of which could not be taken directly into account by the Arts Council when negotiating the grant to the company. In practice, the existence of private RSC funds did influence the Arts Council's attitude to the company, as it had in Hall's day when he pursued a policy of running down the reserves in order to remove any obstacle to receiving state money. There is little evidence to suggest, however, that the RSC would have received better treatment from the Arts Council had the Trust not existed. The Trust raised money for immediate RSC needs and, through investment, ensured the independent supply of longer-term funds from which grants could be made to the company, for instance to equip The Pit. It organised an annual Lord Mayor's gala at the Barbican from 1985 on.

In the spirit of the RSC Club but on a more manageable scale, a support organisation called Friends of the RSC was formed in 1983. Supplemented by Friends of The Other Place, and supported by the Trust, it kept alive the notions of the early Club and also raised money for the company as well as organising social and educational events.

Despairing of Britain's ability to protect one of its prime national institutions, Cork also directed the RSC towards the USA, a course it would increasingly follow. Americans had a long history of support for Stratford – and Benson's Stratford company had toured the US as long ago as 1913. Cork built on these connections in setting up a US fund and, in a symbolic linkage, selling a square foot of Stratford soil to the Americans – an echo of the quasi-religious gesture in 1936 when water from the River Avon was sent in a box made of the charred wood from the burnt Stratford theatre to consecrate a replica Globe theatre in Dallas at the Great Texas Exhibition. Cork recruited Geoffrey Cass, a management consultant and later chief executive of Cambridge University Press, as a founder Trust member, and on Cork's elevation to the chair of governors, Cass became chair of the Trust and the powerful finance and general purposes committee. He succeeded Cork as chair of governors in 1985, and Cork succeeded Harold Wilson as president.

Before sponsorship became a necessary element in British theatre funding, the RSC had proved an innovative force in gaining business backing for its activities. *The Sunday Telegraph* and the Midland Red Bus Company had helped Theatregoround, and the *Daily Telegraph* had sponsored the World Theatre Season. In 1978, Hallmark Cards donated £12,000 to the RSC's inaugural small-scale regional tour, and without private patronage, the RSC would not have been able to extend its audience reach during the ensuing years, whether through large, middle or small-scale touring. In 1979, the company gained sponsorship for five Stratford productions and for the Warehouse season while some firms offered sponsorship in kind – seats, paint or photocopying the company's archive. For a number it was their first taste of arts support.

In the 1980s, the RSC brokered groundbreaking sponsorship agreements, first with Royal Insurance and then with Allied Lyons, later called Allied Domecq. The RI relationship – two sets of three-year deals – helped the company through a very difficult financial period but also carried with it the danger of increased vulnerability. Once the relationship came to an end, how would the RSC be able to replicate it and with what leverage? Indeed, the gap between money running out from that deal and the beginning of the next was perilously small and severe cutbacks were only just avoided. To Allied Lyons, with profits of £505 million, paying

£1.1 million a year for three years was, according to one journalist, a bargain price for 'cultural credibility and one of the world's most up-market calling cards'.[5] There were auxiliary benefits too: the RSC helped train the firm's managers while the multinational helped the RSC re-organise its box office and exploit its trade mark overseas.

The staggering upsurge in sponsorship revenue (rising from 1984/85–88/89 by 307 per cent) dwarfed the increase in income from transfers, television and tours (29.3 per cent) as well as the growth in box office receipts (51.9 per cent). Company members, however, were not always happy with the consequences. Unease grew among the acting companies at the contrived nature of the audiences for corporate evenings, when evidently many were present for the alcohol not the art, at having to undertake supplementary PR work to please sponsors and their guests, at the branding of productions – a car company *Hamlet*, for example – and occasionally at the political ramifications, for instance when a tobacco company might be involved. Sheila Hancock, who was leading the 1983 small-scale tour, questioned sponsorship of a visit to Workington in Cumbria by British Nuclear Fuels Ltd. If the sponsorship were rejected, seat prices would rise beyond the reach of many local people in an area of high unemployment, thereby negating the purpose of the visit. But if accepted, the owners of Windscale, or Sellafeld as its nuclear plant had become known, would garner much-needed publicity as benign local benefactors. The actors fulfilled their commitment after it was agreed they could perform at the plant a new play, *Derek* by Edward Bond, and say in any interviews they undertook whatever they wished about their sponsors.[6] In 1986 Jonathan Pryce led an internal campaign against sponsorship by Barclays Bank of the forthcoming production of *Macbeth*, in which he played the eponymous king, because of the bank's complicity in the South African apartheid economy. The RSC was forced to ask the bank to withdraw.

Internal disquiet was also evident at the expansion of the sponsorship department in relation to others and a tendency for the value of projects deemed worthy of backing to be judged by status and the size of their budget. The department found raising small amounts of money difficult – for example, to support experimental new work or children's plays – and spent much of its energies administering the large sponsorship deals the company had entered into. A general antipathy to the government's privatisation programme informed some of the antagonistic reaction to the encroachment of sponsorship, though dealing with the commercial business sector did challenge a precious quality within the theatre and paradoxically broke down its isolation from the surrounding society. The sponsors themselves resented the core role government was forcing them to play and wanted government to maintain its funding of the organisations they were keen to exploit. On a different level, the RSC ran into trouble with the Arts Council when it was denied acknowledgement on a programme because the sponsor had been given sole right in that respect. Private sponsors frequently received more exposure in RSC material than the public funding bodies, regardless of the differences in economic contribution. There were sundry reasons, most importantly the historic tensions arising from the insufficiency of the Arts Council's grant as well as specific publicity demanded made by sponsors.

## Loss of focus

With the move to the Barbican, the adjustment to the RSC's identity highlighted a more general predicament over the company's direction. Productions were still earning high praise – in 1983, for instance, *King Lear*, Adrian Noble's debut large-stage RSC Shakespeare, Terry Hands's productions of *Much Ado About Nothing* and *Cyrano de Bergerac*, and David Edgar's new play *Maydays* – but questions were being asked about the effects on the company of the joint directorship and the level of energy being dedicated to addressing structural problems.

Driven by expansion, the RSC had become locked into the cultural equivalent of 'Fordism', an industrialisation of art in which volume of output had become an end product in its own right and was now taken as the norm. Relentless turnover lay at the centre of the process, which was given public cohesion by the potency of the RSC brand name. Yet, at the same time, the process was undermining the individual creativity that sustained the brand. The iron grip of the production schedule was reinforced by various attitudes and practices that had aggregated over time in response to this constraint. Years of invention to circumvent problems had caught up with the company. Despite cloistered weekend sessions of senior personnel, administrative modifications and recourse to management consultants, longevity of leadership made significant change harder to implement.

Arriving at decisions was necessarily a process of negotiation in which hierarchies of power and influence constantly clashed and competed, yet decision-making had become unnecessarily serpentine, especially in choosing the repertoire and the artists who were to realise it in practice. Expansion had turned planning and casting into a seemingly endless series of attenuated and exasperating procedures. Preparations for a new season of Stratford productions, which might number fifteen and have to last in the repertoire for up to two years, would overlap with planning tours, West End transfers and new productions in London. The overall balance of a season was not only hard to find but difficult to sustain. The company was looking for balance between Stratford and London, between Shakespeare, new plays and other work, between productions perceived to be good box office and less popular ones, and between each of the theatres as well as within the programme of each theatre. The delicate balance would alter when a decision affecting one of its elements was taken, either provisionally or 'finally' – and by whether 'final' actually remained absolute.

Inevitably the artistic needs of the company vied with individual artistic considerations, and striking that balance was the exhausting task of the artistic director or company director in charge of a season. In contrast to Hall, who tended to approach directors individually with a request to undertake a particular production, Nunn had instituted a bidding system, which gave rise to intense internal competition and reinforced the complexity of the process. The RSC system encouraged directors, especially those without much experience of theatre elsewhere, to change their minds frequently and to defer making binding decisions until the last possible moment in order to maximise the chances of finding a better solution. The end result frequently was late offers being made to outside directors, giving them insufficient time for preparation, and frustration among the actors who were being courted in the intricate planning dance.

Both 'sides' used whatever leverage they had. At the RSC end, there was understandably much contestation among a season's directors to agree on which actors to approach – seeking the right mix of continuity and fresh faces – and on which parts to offer. For actors their availability was a key bargaining chip in responding to the initial line of parts and to its subsequent revisions in addition to being an issue in its own right, given the different working patterns of theatre, film and television. Like the RSC, the actor would most likely want to delay making a decision until the latest possible moment, in case an appealing film or television role came along. The RSC, however, would need to resolve the issue sooner rather than later in order to better proceed with the remainder of the planning, yet actors often complained that the RSC made offers and then made no more contact with the actor or delayed confirming a decision until forced to.[7]

Such issues were not peculiar to the RSC but were amplified by the company's particular system and much dissatisfaction was predictably blamed on the artistic directors. The distinctly different tastes, approaches and personalities of Nunn and Hands represented a strength artistically but in terms of leading the company had become a problem. Hands exuded confidence, charm and ambition, and seemed to be at ease with his verbal and intellectual fluency but also with his condescension. He did not have Nunn's analytical eye for detail when it came to running the organisation and inspired less loyalty among company members than did his senior partner. The differences between them were such that the company divided into Nunn's camp and Hands's camp, to the point where loyalties were detected, however inaccurately, by which taxi driver one chose to use. In the hurly-burly of company life, one artistic director was played off against the other and when both became more remote in the 1980s as the rehearsal workload, caring for the company and escalating administrative duties made increasingly incompatible demands on their time, the organisation began to experience the frustrations of Hall's last years.

The problem was exacerbated when, after more than decade and a half at the RSC, Nunn took work outside the company, which he was entitled to do, first in 1981 to direct *Cats* and later in 1984 to direct *Starlight Express*. It was unfortunate timing for the company, which needed strong and direct leadership, especially as on the former occasion the transfer to the Barbican was imminent. There was much internal disquiet about Nunn's inaccessibility – encapsulated in the legend that the acting company wrote to television's *Jim'll Fix It* programme to arrange a meeting with him. Nunn's relationship to the company and its personnel had changed and Hands was unable to compensate.[8]

Nunn made two more lasting contributions to the company before he finally left in 1986 to become a freelance director. His production with John Caird in 1985 of *Les Misérables* was to earn the company regular and indispensable injections of money from its extraordinary West End run and completed his own RSC journey toward popular musical theatre that had begun when he first arrived at the company twenty years before and added lyrics to Robert Bolt's children's play *The Thwarting of Baron Bolligrew*. His second contribution was to oversee the opening in 1986 of the RSC's fifth auditorium, the Swan Theatre, which had been announced in the late 1970s and postponed through lack of finance.

## The Swan

Several factors combined to make Nunn look for a third Stratford auditorium. None of the RSC's theatres in Stratford or London reproduced the internal shape of an Elizabethan or Jacobean playhouse and, despite recurring experiments by the company in general and Nunn in particular to fashion such a setting on the Royal Shakespeare Theatre stage, none offered a permanent solution. The company also wanted to extend its interest in plays by Shakespeare's contemporaries. Past efforts had been very successful in the smaller spaces but had played to too few people, whereas in the larger spaces they were often over-stretched and exposed. Finally, the annual renewal of the licence for The Other Place was becoming increasingly fraught and unlikely to be granted much longer, and the space itself could no longer satisfy the aspirations of a group of directors who had formed the core of the RSC for nearly a decade. A new theatre would allow the further exploration of the sixteenth- and seventeenth-century canon and give the company a much-needed shot in the arm.

The site chosen was the so-called Conference Hall – a curious mix of a space that was both disregarded as mundane and workaday because the daily business of rehearsal took place there and revered for many a stunning run-through of a production that lost its spark when transferred to the big stage. The hall was housed in the rear of the theatre, which had survived the fire of 1926. It was opened in 1933 as part of the new building and was available to hire for events like meetings or dances. After the war, when the Stratford season expanded, it was used as a rehearsal room and in the early 1960s for the Studio's end-of-season 'flare ups' as well. Anthony Quayle had drawn up plans in 1949 for a Stratford theatre to be built along the lines of an Elizabethan public playhouse but they proved to be too expensive. Ironically, he had rejected the governors' idea of converting the Conference Hall because he needed the rehearsal space. Money would be a problem again, particularly as the Arts Council, adhering firmly to its tradition with the RSC, would not fund such an innovation, although it did not oppose the move. The company demonstrated that the extra costs would be containable within the Swan's own revenue and did not therefore require additional Arts Council funding. The US oil company Amoco had agreed to finance the building until forced to withdraw by the cost of an oil spillage at sea by one of its huge tankers. Nunn and the RSC's president, the former Prime Minister Harold Wilson, could not find replacement funding, despite a trip to the US. It is entirely in keeping with the romantic feel of the theatre itself that it was rescued by chance, and by an anonymous donor at that. An American millionaire saw the model on display in the RSC's Gallery and on discovering its history, offered to pay for the project to be realised. The name of Frederick Koch was not revealed until the Queen officially opened the theatre in November 1986.

Several inspirations lay behind the design of architects Michael Reardon and Tim Furby. The most practical were experiences of chamber classics at The Other Place and, more particularly, the timber setting for the Royal Shakespeare Theatre's 1976 season designed by John Napier and Chris Dyer, which The Other Place had influenced. This setting attempted to turn the Royal Shakespeare Theatre into an approximation of an Elizabethan inn yard theatre; a three-sided forestage thrust into the auditorium and the circle and balcony tiers appeared to continue through the proscenium as galleries where audience could sit. Napier did the initial drawings for the Swan conversion. Other influences were the RSC's small-scale tour visit in 1977 to the arts centre at Christ's Hospital, Horsham – an exciting intimate space co-designed by Bill Howell, who was also responsible for the Young Vic space used by the company as a third London venue – and Johannes de Witt's 1596 sketch of the Swan Theatre. The swan was a potent symbol in Stratford, the centrepiece of the RSC's first logo, and was the name chosen for the new theatre.

Seating 430, the theatre has a stage that thrusts like a tongue into the audience, which surrounds the stage on three sides in a horseshoe shape, rising from the stalls through three sets of galleries. A gallery runs across the back of and above the stage for musicians or action, or both. Actors, who can enter and exit on the different levels, also use a walkway wrapped around the back of the stalls, which takes the audience to their seats. This enhances the sense of identification between actor and audience sharing the same space. The audience enters either through the neo-Gothic Picture Gallery entrance, a remaining symbol of the original theatre, or from a gravel area abutting the riverside lawn. The audience effortlessly crosses from picturesque Stratford to a warm theatrical sanctuary inside, a theatre within a theatre, linking two 'golden' eras of national 'greatness' and 'prosperity' – the Victorian and the Elizabethan – from which many potent images of Englishness are derived.

In many ways the Swan is the quintessential RSC theatre, emblematic of what the company had become: celebratory, wistful, questioning, irreverent even, but without transgression. The demeanour of the space and the radiance of the interior – light brick walls, light stone and, overwhelmingly, light wood – were welcoming, informal and liberal, a comforting escape from the concrete harshness of the Barbican and an antidote to its cold modernity. The Swan makes a statement and imposes itself on whatever production it houses as much as on the audience. The immediacy of the auditorium is more engaging than the distance between audience and stage in the Royal Shakespeare Theatre and less threatening than the intimacy of The Other Place – a 'human' proportion that makes it satisfying to so many people. The design of the theatre places the actor and performance at its heart. No one is more than 30 ft away from the action. The audience can see each other, like a secular congregation,

enjoying its own communion and community in a world that has produced an increased sense of isolation and alienation. The Swan opened at
a time of social disintegration when radical Conservative politics were
cloaked in the colours of spurious national pride. In the face of that, the
theatre is a vibrant space that evokes a 'never never land' of honest,
decent, non-sophistication, a blend of the warmly domestic and sani-
tised rustic, far away from the grime of the contemporary grimy world.

Its initial purpose was to explore the plays of Shakespeare's contemporaries and those coming just afterwards, and in this it has a proud
record. It added classics from different cultures and periods and, with less
frequency, new plays as well as plays by Shakespeare himself. Opening up
the context of Shakespeare is a reminder that he was not alone but part of
a thriving theatrical culture as well as fulfilment of Hall's ambition to
recapture the earlier Elizabethan moment. The language of historical
retrieval – rescuing lost plays – bolstered the public service ethos of the
company but also underpinned a tendency found in the Royal
Shakespeare Theatre to view the past as provider of transcendental value,
thereby losing the specificity of plays in a generalised aesthetic. This feeling is inherent in the project itself, which 'rescued' a theatre from the shell
of one that had been destroyed. There was a commonality of feeling that
spread from many of the early signature productions, such as *The Fair
Maid of the West*, the production that played at the official opening,
through *The Rover* and *The New Inn* to later shows such as *Eastward Ho!*
and even *The Malcontent*, the latter no longer shocking but amusingly
familiar, as if to say 'nothing changes'. The audience was made to feel safe
in the presence of highly disparate plays from centuries past, and was
offered a unifying aesthetic reassurance in the face of both the theatre's
and the audience's shared sense of social ineffectualness. The past plays a
crucial, sanctifying role in the space. The first modern play to be staged
there, *Restoration* by Edward Bond, was used as a counterpoint in a season
of Restoration plays and the first new play, *Singer* by Peter Flannery, con-
sciously evoked Jacobean conventions in his cutting fable of post-war
rapaciousness.

The enforced simplicity of the Swan's staging and promotion of the
actor harks back to the RSC spirit of the 1970s, a welcome relief from the
policy of visual extravagance on the larger stages, which was running out
of steam in the mid-1980s. The promontory stage invites a muscular,
front foot delivery, and, because the area in front of the back wall is relatively weak, action tends to come down towards the audience and
encourages movement rather than stillness. There is an openness about
the space that requires flurry rather than reflection. Various approaches

have been used to counter the 'feel good' inclinations of the space and not all productions succumb. Max Stafford-Clark challenged the accepted approach and brought an explicitly modern sensibility to Richard Brome's 1641 comedy *A Jovial Crew*, not by costume or setting but by using a contemporary dramatist Stephen Jeffreys to adapt it and Ian Dury to write new music and lyrics. Deborah Warner in *Titus Andronicus* used contemporary references – an aluminium ladder, a light bulb, a Disney song – to counterpoint the absence of ethical intrusion in her postmodern exploration of male power. Directors have wanted to 'roughen up' the space but the repertory system makes anything radical very difficult. Michael Boyd was able to alter the auditorium and darken its colour for his productions of *Henry VI, Parts 1, 2* and *3*, but this was possible because the three plays were running in their own self-contained repertory.[9]

The Swan has offered a stylistic critique of productions in the Royal Shakespeare Theatre, as The Other Place had done the decade before, and as a theatre it seems like one of the RSC's 'other' spaces. Unlike The Other Place, the Swan is not physically separate from the parent theatre and, indeed, they share dressing rooms, offices and green room, and yet to the audience the space seems quite distinct, reinforcing the feeling of independence from what was now perceived as the overblown originating organisation. Yet the Swan is cemented into the RSC's production and value system, and is necessary to the RSC's overall financial health in a way that The Other Place and The Warehouse were not. This critical role in the company's finances placed a burden on the choice of plays and style of production. Like The Other Place, it followed a similar course of expanding ambition and costs. The use of stock costumes and props was quickly superseded by its own requirements. As productions became more lavish and demanding, the workshops were not able to cope and work was contracted out.

Inevitably the Swan altered the role of The Other Place. Its very flexibility, and success, had tempted artists to keep pushing its limits, testing it beyond its own capacity, with the result of more technically demanding shows and larger expenditure. The initial energy of establishing the theatre had been transformed into supporting its own kind of production line. Audience expectations changed too; seating became numbered and comfort became an issue, perhaps unsurprisingly as shows began to seem like auditions for a grander environment. The existence of the Swan encouraged these ambitions. Many artists working at The Other Place in the late 1980s seemed to want to produce Swan shows but did not have the production capacity, staffing or budgets to cope. The Other Place may still have been interesting but it ceased to offer an internal critique of RSC style. The cost of renovating the old building to meet required standards was too high and thought was given to constructing a new Other Place. Once the Swan had been established, the inevitable happened. The company closed The Other Place in 1989 in order to replace it with a custom-built and better-equipped building, designed by the Swan's architects and housing not only a theatre and a front-of-house area that offered refreshment and shelter but also offices, two rehearsal rooms (named after Michel Saint-Denis and Buzz Goodbody) and other improved backstage facilities.

The Swan's success also caused the unravelling of the company. The burden of extra work generated by the Swan pushed the RSC to breaking point. Efficiency and size fell out of kilter. Despite extensive searches and several plans that eventually failed to materialise, there was no long-term London equivalent. There was no money to build one or hire one permanently. Every season there was a massive planning headache of how to accommodate the Swan shows in the London season. Some productions were scaled down to fit The Pit and some scaled up to fit the Barbican. The results were costly and frequently, but not always, bore the scars of the surgery. Artistic standards were compromised. Sometimes shows were taken to other theatres, such as the Mermaid and the Young Vic, which entailed their own costs. Not only were the numbers of actors and shows becoming ludicrous, but also workshops and wardrobe departments were unable to cope with the extra demands, which inevitably could not be rationed evenly during the year, and this raised production and stage operating costs.

## Terry Hands

When Nunn left the organisation after twenty-one years' remarkable service, he left Hands an almighty mess. Hands, who himself had been with the company for twenty years and had been joint artistic director for a decade, could offer nothing new. Problems that had been accumulating gained new visibility. The company's position in the profession had declined and it had lost wider support without properly noticing. It was over-extended and the internal structure was not able to cope, and projects were taken on without adequate time and support being given to them. While associate directors jockeyed for position in the succession, arcane and clumsy decision-making processes were exposed under the pressure of the new company workloads. Believing in the importance of a monastic dedication to art and the purifying power of crisis, it is not surprising the RSC drifted further off course in these confusing times. Unevenness of productions, particularly on the main stage of the Barbican, and indecisiveness meant Hands's judgement was called into question and what might have been hailed as imaginative if better executed either failed to materialise or came across as muddled.

Hands held on to a romantic belief in the company that derived from the impulses and scale of the 1960s and was not in accord with the current reality. He preferred the word 'investment' to 'subsidy' and insisted the RSC was a private organisation because only a third of its funding came from the state. He viewed the National Theatre as the 'official' British theatrical institution and wanted the RSC to be the irreverent rebel. Yet projects that might have staked such a claim foundered. He planned to stage all Jean Genet's plays in new translations; *The Screens* would finally be presented by the RSC, this time in the Barbican's sculpture court lit by braziers; and Wole Soyinka would direct in The Pit his specially commissioned version of *The Blacks*. Soyinka pulled out when he saw the set-up at the Barbican and an attempt to replace him with Charles Marowitz collapsed. The project was abandoned with the only survivors a tired revival in 1987 by Hands of *The Balcony*, which he had directed sixteen years before at the Aldwych, and a double bill of *Deathwatch* and an all-male *The Maids* in new adaptations by David Rudkin directed by Gerard Murphy and Ultz. A revival of Lionel Bart's musical *Blitz!* with some new songs and a new book by Tony Marchant was also planned but later dropped. Hands did support the RSC's catholic new play policy – it was no surprise to find work by Edward Bond or Howard Barker at The Pit – and he championed modern and new plays on the large Barbican stage too, like *Moscow Gold*, an epic about Mikhail Gorbachev written by Howard Brenton and Tariq Ali, and productions of his own such as *Red Noses* by Peter Barnes and *Singer* by Peter Flannery.

Hands's own Shakespeare work had lost its authority, yet he opened the company up to new directors, such as Nicholas Hytner, but without forging a new identity for the company. Deborah Warner's brief yet celebrated association with the company is revealing in this respect. She had set up her own Kick Theatre Company in 1980 as a response to what she saw as the RSC's shortcomings and had gained sufficient attention by 1987 to be asked by Hands to direct *Titus Andronicus* at the Swan. He had not seen her work but others in senior management had; Brian Cox, already cast as Titus, had mentioned her name to Hands after several directors had declined the job. There was one week to go before rehearsals began but she accepted because she knew the play and Kick was in abeyance due to lack of funding. Her production of *Titus Andronicus* was garlanded in

Britain and abroad, and she looked set to fulfil the regenerative role within the RSC of previous radical outsiders. *King John* and *Electra* followed in 1988 and 1989 to much acclaim, the latter beginning what would become a long-term working relationship with the actress Fiona Shaw but one that was not to be conducted at the RSC. The company did not offer her the conditions she required and allowed her to be wooed by the NT.

The RSC still attracted artists because of the resources, expertise and opportunities it offered but less and less because of its work or what the work stood for. The excellence of individual productions was being seen increasingly as just that, the result of individual rather than company accomplishment. The RSC's eclecticism and outbreaks of theatrical 'camp' had stretched the company's individuality to a dangerously vulnerable degree. Antony Sher's performance in 1984 of Richard III on crutches had marked a return to individual bravura, which not only stood in shattering opposition to the RSC's previous approach but also heralded a stylistic free-for-all that had undermined the company's distinctiveness. The number of actors had trebled since the RSC's first season and had reached a point at which connections between artists and shared beliefs were ever harder to discern. Without radical action, the RSC could no longer be sustained as a company in anything but name.

Changes in the profession had made recruiting and retaining actors harder. Artistic innovation was happening elsewhere and, with few exceptions, was not being nurtured by the company. Complacency, sometimes smugness, stemming from a belief that the RSC was the best, cut the company off from developments outside. The hubris of the 1988 disaster of the musical *Carrie* summed up the company's situation. Directed by Hands, it did not lose the RSC any money because of the guarantees agreed with the co-producer, but it did irredeemably tarnish Hands's reputation and severely damage the RSC's standing.

The media took *Carrie* as a cue for attack. Hands reasserted company coherence by giving Adrian Noble the 1988 Stratford season to run, and Noble's success with *The Plantagenets* that year was divined as the shape of things to come. For Hands, however, the strain increased. Under tremendous pressure from within and without, he announced he would resign in 1991. His successor was indeed Adrian Noble. He would have a year as artistic director designate, starting in March 1990, and during that year Hands and the RSC suffered an unprecedented blow. Despite record contributions to the coffers from *Les Misérables*, a City grant of £500,000 and a three-year sponsorship deal with Royal Insurance, the largest of its kind in British arts history, the accumulated deficit had reached just over £2 million. The consequence was closure of the Barbican Theatre and The Pit in the autumn of 1990 for nearly five months. The bubble had finally burst. The breach in the London operation, threatened ever since Hall made the historic move into the capital, had finally occurred. The writing was on the wall, not only for the future of the RSC in London but also for the future of the RSC itself. The company would never be the same again.

# FIVE

# CRISIS AND MODERNISATION

Adrian Noble became artistic director in 1991, coincidentally the year Peggy Ashcroft died. He began a transformation of the RSC that was more radical than any undertaken since Hall had created the company with Ashcroft at its head. At first Noble tried to revive the monster, then to transform it into a different animal altogether. All the while the thread he held on to that linked him to the past of Hall's RSC was that of 'company', but good intentions collapsed under the pressure of ill-prepared plans and the reality contradicted the rhetoric. The clash between the demands of monetarism and the desires of public service that was played out across society in the 1990s finally defeated him.

His elevation was firmly in the RSC tradition: continuity with change. As with Nunn when he had been appointed, Noble had no experience of running an organisation and little knowledge of the theatre outside the RSC. Trained at Bristol University and the Drama Centre in London, he flirted with the left but decided after working briefly in community theatre in Birmingham to abandon any political role for his theatrical efforts because the priorities of the working class lay elsewhere. As he put it, he need not worry why he directed plays.[1] He went to the Bristol Old Vic under a director's bursary from 1976 to 79 and then worked at the Royal Exchange, Manchester until 1980 when his production of *The Duchess of Malfi*, with its imagistic flourishes reminiscent of Hands's style, caught the eye of the RSC and he was invited to join the company. In a reversal of the role in which Hall found himself, Noble was welcomed as a classicist with little interest in new plays, although in his first years at the RSC in the 1980s he was praised for a string of productions such as *The Forest, A Doll's House, King Lear* and *Antony and Cleopatra*, which ranged from the modern to the Shakespearean repertoire. At the RSC, he set himself apart from his peers but was not alone in coveting the RSC throne. His ambition for the prize was given headway in 1988 when Hands conferred on him the responsibility for that year's Stratford season. He staged his version of Shakespeare's Wars of the Roses under the title *The Plantagenets* and, after a year away from the company, won the crown.

With the traumatic closure of the Barbican, the underlying tensions within the company between its creativity and institutional forms had reached breaking point. A major review of the state of the company was imperative, despite a favourable Arts Council report on the RSC's activities. The report noted the continuing extraordinary statistics of the institution:

> [I]t provides 7% of the productions, 15% of the performances, 21% of the attendances and 33% of the box office income of all subsidised building based drama companies in England . . . There can be no doubt whatever that the RSC has given the nation value for money.[2]

The achievement, however, masked many internal problems.

Noble began with a boyish energy and a sound analysis: the company's practice of expanding its way out of financial trouble had led the RSC to try to be all things to all people and thereby to lose focus. In response, he declared: 'My aim is that we should be the best classical theatre company in the English-speaking world. It's as simple as that.'[3] He issued a personal manifesto to the company called 'Why We Do What We Do' based on an interview he had given to *The Times*, in which he said the company should continue to present new plays 'not because they're new . . . but because they excite and amaze people, because they make them emotionally literate'. In a shift from previous RSC attitudes, he said new plays would be defined in relation to the core of the RSC, which was classical work. In practice this meant a demotion for the role of the contemporary playwright, even though the company continued to present excellent new plays. Noble expressed an interest in storytelling and described the central function of the RSC as to 'make living the experience that poetic drama can give'.

The audience was to be the fulcrum of his approach. No one space was to have priority; rather quality was to be the priority and would be emphasised throughout. There would be a new stress on the values of the company, which would be properly trained and artistically renewed. But what was meant by 'quality' and what would the company be trained for? His appeal to 'the spirit and the heart' and creating 'mighty experiences' was fresh and invigorating but the results of his philosophy ultimately turned out to be regressive. While he still believed, as Hall had, that Shakespearean production should be publicly funded because Shakespeare was good for the nation, the crusade now was not to challenge and to question but to defend. The RSC was to embrace more passionately the role of the repository of Shakespearean language and virtue. In an understandable desire to refocus the profile of the company and to adjust the organisation to the new realities of both the screen-dominated acting profession and a rapidly changing social context, Noble defined the RSC in contradistinction to the NT: the RSC was the classical company and the National Theatre was not. His insistence on the primacy of the classical, however, led to its etiolation. The contrast with the NT became an unfortunate one, that of being eclipsed.

There were good signs at the start: the return of Robert Stephens to the classical stage at the head of a revitalised company; the opening of a new Other Place to replace the old tin hut; a new tenancy agreement at the Barbican; and a generous grant from the City of London to match an award from a newly created, state-supported Enhancement Fund to help the total subsidy rise by just over 50 per cent. This rise put the company back more or less where the Priestley Report had wanted it to be, but as happened immediately following the report, not for long. For the bulk of the 1990s the RSC was on standstill grants and by 2002, Noble's last full year in post, the cumulative losses had risen to an unsupportable £2.4 million.

Like his predecessors, Noble had to deal with problems on several interlocking fronts. His repeated experiments with the Royal Shakespeare Theatre's environment set what became a familiar pattern in other areas of the company's life. He tried a brick wall surround, the audience on stage, Japanese walkways, altering the length and angle of the rake, raising the height of the stage, and taking the forestage into the auditorium like the prow of ship. His quest was brought to a head by the realisation following a buildings review that new health, safety and disabled access regulations, which would come into force in 2004, could not be met without substantial reconstruction. His solution was the most drastic: to demolish the theatre. He faced clashes with sections of the theatrical profession, who recalled the many historic triumphs to which the theatre had played host, and, more vociferously, with the heritage lobby, who sought to preserve the Grade II listed building (if not its interior) as one of the most prominent examples of public architecture by a woman, Elizabeth Scott. There were even demonstrations outside the theatre.

As he searched for ways to square the institutional circle and reform the company as a whole, the changes he made and the way they were made aggravated rather than quelled the problems. It was a bumpy process that led him, as with the Royal Shakespeare Theatre, to propose a radical answer: to demolish the RSC as it had hitherto been known.

## Modernisation

There had been much internal discussion at the highest echelons about changing the way the company was run. The first public sign of innovation was the RSC joining the modern world by advertising the post of artistic director and subjecting the selected candidates to interview. This method of appointment meant not only a different relationship between the successful candidate and the chairman of governors but also gave greater scope to the governors to implement changes they wanted to see. Hands as the outgoing artistic director and chief executive had suggested that the administrative burden had become so encumbering that it had to be shared and Noble's selection was accompanied by the creation of the new post of executive producer. This position went to Michael Attenborough, artistic director of Hampstead Theatre in north London. Genista McIntosh was elevated from within the company, having served as casting director, planning controller and senior administrator, to become associate producer as the third member of a management triumvirate.

Further change came in the dramatic ending of the contracts of the associate directors and the introduction of a freelance system of hiring directors. Some commentators put this down to the removal of erstwhile rivals, but it was also a response to the inability of the company to renew itself in this area. The new structure for the senior artistic and administrative management of the company was completed by changes made to the governing body through the creation of groups dealing with such matters as fundraising, budgeting, membership, marketing and legal affairs. In 2000, this process was taken further by the slimming and restructuring of the governing body and its subsidiary boards and committees.[4] The whole modernisation process and future direction of the RSC in the 1990s was a product of the relationship between Noble and

Geoffrey Cass, the chair of governors and former management consultant who was responsible for the reorganisation of Cambridge University Press.

Removal of the associates, however, did not lead to the expected liberation because the institutional ideology remained entrenched and no consistent alternative was on offer. With the removal went a great deal of accumulated expertise in Shakespeare production and the bulwark of artistic continuity, which now resided with Noble. The coherence of the company disappeared. The old system was hardly equitable; hierarchies held sway, with the artistic director at the top, yet sacrifices were made and rewards gained overwhelmingly in the service of the collective name. Belonging to the company could mitigate the competitive nature of theatre but now even this alleviation had been removed and it was more difficult to appeal to a spirit of compromise. Freelance artists lacked the same commitment to the RSC as associates, and, in a ruthless profession, were understandably only concerned with their own show. Freelance directors were not paid enough to follow their productions through the two-year cycle. Their terms of employment encouraged them to move on quickly to their next engagement and to leave the RSC production to the good offices of the stage management team once it had opened rather than see it through its run.

The freelance system also placed greater strain on building the acting company at a time when attracting actors to Stratford was getting harder. Freelance directors had less time to give to the drawn-out, collective casting process, which was already made more problematic by the understandable lack of consensus on what constituted good acting – or, indeed, what constituted 'theatre' itself. There was less common knowledge of actors in general, and not always much acquaintance with actors who had already worked for the RSC. There was, therefore, less agreement on which actors should be asked to join the company. Moreover, while it was healthy to have a good supply of new faces, many were unprepared for the rigours of the RSC repertoire. Noble was a unifying force through his own productions, but found it difficult to give sufficient attention to the productions of others, an even greater need than previously because of the context of the freelance arrangements. Company verse classes aimed to offer a communal as well as a learning experience but the needs of individual productions often undermined these attempts at ensemble fusion. A healthy heterogeneity became a disparate collection of isolated statements. While 'company' was proclaimed in the oratory and given a more elaborate façade complete with a 'mission statement', the conditions for it were being diluted at the level of the work.

Undoubtedly the company was still enjoying public success. Noble's own sequence of large stage Shakespeare productions in his first seasons – *Henry IV Parts 1* and *2*, *The Winter's Tale*, *Hamlet*, *King Lear*, *A Midsummer Night's Dream* – was praised alongside Swan and The Other Place productions by a range of directors new to the company who had markedly different styles – Michael Attenborough, Michael Boyd, Sam Mendes, Katie Mitchell, Steven Pimlott, David Thacker – and veterans such as John Barton. What was lacking was what the RSC stood for. The brand name was still strong but becoming worryingly blurred. Reactive adjustments to the freelance system, such as making some directors like David Thacker and Max Stafford-Clark resident directors, did not tackle the root problem and were superseded by a return to an associate group five years into Noble's reign. Attenborough became principal associate director alongside Michael Boyd, Katie Mitchell and Steven Pimlott as associate directors. Gregory Doran later joined the group.

Another vital facet of Noble's modernisation was a new managerialism. Under-funding of the expansion in the 1980s, and the inadequacy of internal support for this growth, had consolidated the endemic problems and extra costs of over-pressurised and protracted planning and decision-making. Advances in health, safety, labour and fire regulations added to this liability while advances in technology led to greater complexity, not greater fleetness. In the 1960s, for example, the RSC might have been able to run a dress rehearsal for a large theatre production on a Sunday afternoon and open the production the following evening; but this was not possible now. In response, Noble expanded middle and senior management, which came to be the company's driving force. Bodies such as the planning committee were renamed and enlarged to include so many people that meetings had to be moved to the town hall to accommodate the numbers. Its role, however, was reduced to a gesture of involvement.

Central to the new managerialism was the producer system, which came to the fore when McIntosh left the company in 1991 to join the NT as executive director. The system was in particular a reaction to the historic failure to establish an effective head of design post and was intended to make the organisation in relation to productions work better and internal contacts flow more easily. Efforts to gain time and to plan more efficiently the enormous and increasingly sophisticated off-stage endeavour required to deliver and maintain the RSC repertoire often ran counter to creativity. For the RSC's large theatres, a five-month lead-in time for design plans was requested, three months before rehearsals might begin. This constrained discovery in the rehearsal period, a growing emphasis of the most creative directors and designers, many of whom had developed their crafts on the less restrictive fringe. Other physical and resource problems – such as storage or the matching of generic budgets and scenery space allocation (established before productions are known) to the needs of the actual productions – inspired great ingenuity in their resolution. But, although collective solutions such as the use of a permanent basic set for a season could help, the often fierce negotiations involved did not always produce results entirely in line with the original creative impulses that lay behind the productions. Producers, it was hoped, could tip the balance back towards the artists.

Communication, consultation and participation also needed to be improved to bring the administrative capacity of the company in line with its workload. While in the 1980s there had been an increase in RSC jobs in non-theatre areas such as marketing, sponsorship and education and the number of 'support' staff had risen to nearly 500, the size of the senior management had remained relatively small. The disadvantage of a closely knit, highly expert and long-serving top administration was a lack of transparency about decision-making – rarely straightforward in any case – and a concomitant sense of frustration felt by those who were not part of the inner circle. Poor communication within and between different departments and the absence of a sense of ownership of the company's work had become major problems that producers aimed to tackle.

Each production was assigned to one of the producers, who oversaw that production's budget and worked closely with the production managers of the auditoria concerned and with the artists engendering the production. The producers helped put artistic teams together and stood in for them in departmental or casting meetings if they were absent, which under the freelance system happened frequently. The producers had to adjudicate between a series of individual demands that were connected only by the sharing of physical facilities and actors. Being new to the company, the producers did not carry the baggage of traditional RSC practices. However, as many of the artists they were dealing with were also new to the company – a prime reason for having producers in the first place – this advantage was not always consolidated. The producers added another layer of administration and did not always have the detailed knowledge of, or technical expertise in, all the parts of the process over which they were in charge, and this could cause tensions with those who did.

Producers eased Noble's administrative load – unlike Hall he did not relish this side of the job – and provided him with feedback that he was missing from the loss of the associates. Although he started with a determination to avoid the remoteness that had come to bedevil Nunn's last years, the producer system removed him further from the company outside of his own productions and made him seem more distant. Producers carried the authority of the artistic director but could not escape from being seen in the role of messenger and were not always able to carry through their tasks when the intervention of the artistic director was still required. This was often the case when they had to deal with directors and designers at their most vulnerable moments, either at the point of initial preparation for a production or in preview when changes needed to be made. A producer might make a reasonable suggestion to improve a production but the artists concerned might take no action unless the artistic director were personally involved. Another drawback was the number of productions they had to oversee, which made it hard for them to do the job thoroughly. The producer system, which was subsequently modified – budgets, for example, were given back to production managers – gave a much-needed jolt to the languorous RSC leviathan, but it was not a long-term solution and added other problems to the institutional burden.

Managerialism was extended to the running of a theatre. Noble put Tony Hill, then head of education, in charge of the new Other Place, which was the first time a company theatre was run by an administrator and not by an artist. Hill was given a projects brief and a producer's role. The usual five production slots were reduced to three, and this diminished the collective impact of any one season. Hosting corporate promotion events eroded the theatre's radical image while the projects organised there, which were of high quality and linked to training and development, suffered the usual problem of how their discoveries could be fed back into the rehearsal rooms and the company's public work. The very excitement of this internal work contrasted unfavourably with the routine nature of much of the RSC's offerings.

Noble recognised the limitations of his first years' experiments and his return to an associate system saw a director back in charge of The Other Place. Noble wanted The Other Place to regain artistic credibility by appointing Phyllida Lloyd and Katie Mitchell to run the theatre, but this plan collapsed over the persistent problem of casting. Noble did not want the Lloyd/Mitchell company to be autonomous and isolated, and Mitchell took over alone in 1996. Her appointment and her work at The Other Place signalled that the company had not stopped asking important questions. But in order to ask them, she felt obliged to create the very island Noble had feared and her leaving after three years encapsulated the RSC's artistic quandary.

As artistic director of The Other Place, Katie Mitchell subjected the theatre – décor, performance space, front of house – to thorough re-examination. The new building aimed to recapture the dynamics of the old theatre, in terms of stage space and audience relationship, and had many advantages over the tin hut, but could not provide the found quality that made the first theatre so distinctive. Mitchell wanted to transcend the modest but assertive functionality of The Other Place Mark 2, which bore the brick look of a new town supermarket. She oversaw a radical reassessment of what the theatre should be. In physical terms, this involved changes to the front-of-house area, which was made more welcoming, and to the auditorium, including removal of the gallery to improve sightlines – though her preferred solution had to be compromised as the reduction in seating it required was rejected by management.

Mitchell returned to Buzz Goodbody's vision and resurrected the community and youth dimensions, though only with limited success. Like Goodbody, she linked the RSC to new artistic forces and introduced other media, such as a video facility, exhibitions and installations. Like Goodbody, she also paid great attention to the preparation of the actor and encouraged actor development (for example, Alexander technique, capella work and physical training).

In her first season, Mitchell won a measure of independence in the casting and, as with Brook's companies of the past, hers was cut off from the actors working down the road at the Royal Shakespeare Theatre. She was unhappy with her production of *The Mysteries* and took the opportunity afforded by the transfer process to London to rewrite and restage the piece – an opportunity often cited as an advantage of the two-year cycle but which was rarely used for creative reworking. Pressures of the institution were such that little new could be done beyond putting in a replacement actor because there was neither time in the schedule nor money in the budget. The emphasis was on technical adjustments, because the London and Stratford theatres were not compatible. Her efforts to rework *The Mysteries* met management resistance and even resulted in a leaflet being issued to the audience implying a distance from the production.

Mitchell was exhausted by the battles over casting and the performance space. She felt her brief to provoke and challenge was not supported institutionally. For example, her suggestion that certain performances at The Other Place should be free to encourage greater access was dismissed as romantic earnestness. She found she had to become confrontational in order to achieve her goals. However, by the time a resolution was reached with management, she had moved on from – or forgotten – the inspiration behind the original aim.

Mitchell resigned in 1998 in order to gain more artistic freedom and Steven Pimlott took over the space, which was transformed again. In his first season a white box design by David Fielding stripped the space back to its outer walls. Curiously, this was a throwback stylistically to the 1960s but it had the effect of once again making the work at The Other Place achieve its own coherence. Pimlott's production of *Richard II* with Sam West led directly into their collaboration on *Hamlet*, taking with them from the small to the large space an arresting, spare and lucid style. Mitchell and Pimlott had restored The Other Place's critical role within the RSC but any chance of sustaining this was ended when the theatre was closed in 2002 as part of Noble's redevelopment plans. It became the rehearsal home of the first production (in the Swan) of the Academy, comprising actors recruited from drama school graduation.

## New working model

The closure of The Other Place came at the end of a process of alterations to the RSC pattern of working that Noble had begun nearly a decade before. Early on, he had tinkered with the scheduling in order to counter the tyranny of the production factory line. In 1993, he tried to relieve the massive pressures on the opening productions of the Stratford season, which were often forced to make the biggest compromises on casting and were usually late in starting rehearsals, still not fully cast. In the first 'slot' that covered the Royal Shakespeare Theatre and the Swan, he presented straight runs of productions that already existed and were high profile: in the Royal Shakespeare Theatre Kenneth Branagh in *Hamlet* playing against Simon Russell Beale as Richard III in the Swan. But after two more seasons, Noble realised that more drastic change was required. He introduced what became known as the new access operating model: leaving the Barbican for six months of the year, touring more and adding to the residency in Newcastle a second in Plymouth.

David Brierley's imminent retirement as general manager after twenty-eight years in post was the cue for an administrative rethink as part of this realignment alongside the return to an associate director system, in which Attenborough became principal associate director. His role as executive producer was taken by one of the RSC's producers, Lynda Farran, a new post of development director was introduced (and filled by Jonathan Pope, who had looked set to take over from Brierley) and a new general manager, William Weston, was appointed from outside, having been executive director and the driving force behind the creation of the West Yorkshire Playhouse.

The new model was hastily announced and ill thought through. It began a damaging process that was badly managed and led to greater uncertainty both within the company and, from outside, about the company.

The model had two main purposes. One was aimed at the theatrical profession, for which the allure of the RSC had faded; actors' agents were becoming increasingly reluctant to advise clients to sign up. Criticism of the RSC's early empire building in the 1960s, especially from underfunded artists active outside London, had been balanced by the widespread sense of excitement at the ambition of the new project. Now, joining the RSC had become just another acting job. The company was not embracing new methods of working or welcoming enough innovators. It was perceived as arrogant, isolated and run by a clique. Perhaps this is inevitable when a strongly defined company profile is being achieved, but the company no longer enjoyed such a profile. A specific, practical problem relating to actors had also arisen at the London end of the operation. An actor's contract in the two-year cycle was initially for sixty weeks, which took his or her engagement to the end of the Newcastle tour. (Until the establishment of the Newcastle residency, the initial period had been fifty-two weeks; it was extended by eight weeks to cover Newcastle.) The contract was renewed for London on the basis of transfers there as well as new work to be offered. Over time it became apparent that many actors were leaving in the autumn when the transfers had completed their runs. This meant hiring virtually a new company for the final six months of the cycle, and, in terms of cost, time and the integrity of the company, such an extra encumbrance became unsustainable. The new model was designed to make the RSC more flexible and therefore more attractive to actors by allowing them shorter contracts, the opposite of the appeal under Peter Hall. There would be less cross-casting, and therefore less cross-fertilisation between the classic and the modern. The basis for building a company was being removed at source.

The other main aim was to make the RSC a 'theatre for the nation', a title it had claimed since Hall's days. A year after the model's launch, chairman Geoffrey Cass declared the RSC to be 'a truly national Company with 80% of the population able to see a performance by the Company within an hour's drive'.[5] The issue of how geographical spread might be reflected in the repertoire and style of the RSC, or of what the nation in the 1990s meant, was not addressed because it was taken for granted that Shakespeare was universal and that people wanted to see the RSC perform his plays.

Under the new access model, following a short season to bridge the old and the new schedules, the Stratford season was to run from November–

August instead of March–January and the visit to Newcastle would occur in September, not February. Opening a new season in the cold and dark of November was not well received and had deleterious consequences later when, due to change-overs between seasons, the Stratford theatres were 'dark' in the summer at the height of the tourist influx. In 1998 there were two Stratford seasons with no cross-casting and in 1999 a Stratford festival season reverted to opening in March, followed by a winter season beginning in November. Audiences as well as RSC personnel were confused and the company's identity was fragmenting rapidly.

Despite the hullabaloo surrounding the Plymouth residency – thirteen places had asked to be chosen – it was quietly dropped after only two visits through insufficient local support and difficulties in raising adequate finance.[6] The RSC's gaze turned towards the USA and the first residencies in Brooklyn and Washington. More international touring and a new stress on the RSC's ambassadorial role as a major flagship abroad accompanied this move. An RSC agent was appointed in the US and a five-year partnership announced with the University of Michigan, to begin in 2000. The former residencies were not sustained, and the latter relationship required productions to be scheduled at a time suitable to Michigan that could also be exploited elsewhere to make them viable, thereby restricting the much-vaunted flexibility of the RSC's ever-changing new arrangements. In 2001 a support organisation RSC America, with an American board, was launched. Collaborations with the Massachusetts Institute of Technology and Columbia University were also developed but to what extent artistic benefit would ensue from such connections was difficult to judge. The dismal production of Salman Rushdie's *Midnight's Children* in 2003, produced with US support, was not a hopeful sign and suggested the thinking behind the international RSC brand needed revising alongside a new evaluation of what being a 'theatre for the nation' involved.

The press turned against Noble, as it had done against Hands, and the off-stage problems overshadowed achievements on stage. Noble's defiant response was to intensify the organisational changes. Another new operating model called Project Fleet, to be introduced progressively over a two-year period, was announced in 2001. Building on the earlier model and taking it further, the aim was laudable and necessary: to make the RSC structure serve the productions and not the other way round. It was designed to make Stratford a more attractive place to work for artists by shortening the contracts and by allowing them space to experiment and innovate. It would involve more stand-alone productions and still less cross-casting and was intended to make the RSC 'more agile' and 'less institutionalised'.[7] It meant the complete withdrawal from the Barbican when the company's operating agreement ended in May 2002.

Ever since Noble had become artistic director he had wanted to leave the Barbican. Now, a decade later, he was to realise his wish. This abandonment of a London base was the utter reversal of Hall's plan but by this time the RSC had three theatres in Stratford in which to show the range of its work – though soon to be reduced to two – and Stratford was no longer a stranger to experiment or the radical new play. Noble argued that a London presence would be sustained through commercial deals and at a wider range of venues than the Barbican offered. How well equipped the RSC was to realise this aim was open to question. Its first forays in London to benefit from the new flexibility were not encouraging. A West End transfer of two routine Shakespearean productions was badly advertised, a season at a refurbished Round House was artistically uneven, poorly costed and lost money, and the RSC's return to the Barbican with the lacklustre *Midnight's Children* revealed the isolation of the company. The type of international productions the Barbican had presented in its BITE seasons since the RSC's partial pulling out – work ranging from Complicite to Robert Wilson – demonstrated how far the company had been stranded artistically. Tellingly, the RSC did achieve success with a transfer from the Swan to the West End in 2003 of an entire season of seventeenth-century plays performed by an ensemble, suggesting that company work was popular and still worth pursuing.

The company's abandonment of the Barbican placed renewed focus on Stratford. This should have been welcomed there but it only added to the widespread consternation. Plans for the RSC's buildings were unclear; the proposal to demolish the Royal Shakespeare Theatre had been accompanied by a plan to establish an education centre at The Other Place and create a new theatre – or theatres – in a 'theatre village' by the River Avon. However, with finance a major issue and the fate of the large theatre uncertain, the details were hazy.

Low staff morale at Stratford plunged to new depths with the announcement that the latest operating model would necessitate new contractual arrangements and large-scale redundancies, including long-serving people with Stratford family connections to the theatre. The changes affected all sections of the workforce but were most fiercely resisted by the stage production departments, the most labour-intensive and expensive in terms of overtime. The problem of sorting out working methods and pay differentials between departments had been left unresolved for too long and was seemingly beyond negotiation. The Priestley Report had made obvious points but nothing had been done because the price of change in human terms was considered too high. Now the staff, with their trust in senior management seriously undermined, could not understand why a system that had worked for three decades was suddenly no longer viable. They were not going to negotiate the end of their livelihoods, and change by fiat was the outcome. Many of those who did escape the axe faced the prospect of becoming peripatetic, thereby losing any consistency in their work, or having to apply for different jobs to stay in RSC employment – a situation seen either as the company circumventing labour law or, more generously, as forming a new beginning. A fixer called Gary Smith, who had helped the Thatcher government frame anti-union legislation and see off the miners, was hired to oversee employee relations. Moreover, the changes were rushed through to beat a European deadline affecting labour legislation on the need for consultation on redundancies.[8] A strike in opposition to the plans by technical and production staff supported by the acting company was only just averted but the damage to the company's standing could not be easily or quickly repaired.

While the company had decided by withdrawing from the Barbican to forego its grant from the City – which, overall, had treated the RSC well and come to its rescue on more than one occasion – the savings from the move could be set against this loss, and the Arts Council had pledged to maintain the level of its patronage.[9] Yet, while the Arts Council supported the direction the RSC was taking, it also believed its only comparator, the National Theatre, had coped better in adjusting to the 1990s freeze in public funding. Adverse comparisons were made between the good housekeeping of the NT and the weaknesses of financial and administrative control within the RSC. The Arts Council provided a one-off additional grant to the RSC in 1999 followed by a generously funded Lottery stabilisation programme, so that the company could examine its budgetary and production systems and plan for redevelopment. There was also an 'in principle' commitment from the Arts Council to contribute £50 million of Lottery money, to be match funded, for the wholesale redesign of the Stratford theatres and facilities. The Arts Council was locked into the RSC's development plan, which was being steered by the RSC's new chair, the leading QC and former chair of the Nat West Bank Lord Alexander of Weedon, who took over in 2000. Although it was costing the Arts Council a great deal to bail out the company, which was committed to further reducing reliance on the state, it had achieved what it historically had always wanted – the RSC as a single-base Stratford company.

The partial withdrawal from the Barbican had been badly managed from a public relations and internal staff point of view, but this later phase of the RSC revolution was an even bigger disaster. General manager William Weston, who left in 1999 after making little impact, was replaced the following year from industry by Chris Foy, a former chief executive and chair of the giant Unilever firm and non-executive chair of a specialist consultancy practice serving the cultural sector. He was given the new role of managing director, a telling choice of business nomenclature and its first use by the RSC since Hall had held the title as head of the RSC's artistic triumvirate in 1962. It signalled a break from the David Brierley days of the administration serving the artists and suggested a new battle for power and control between the two. Foy's lack of theatre experience showed in a muddled description he issued of the new operating model while addressing the Stratford company. In so doing, he managed to insult all the actors present by explaining the new model was required in order to attract better actors. There was also a suspicion among the actors that this approach meant making the RSC more attractive to 'stars', always a contentious issue. One consequence of the difficulty in attracting actors to the RSC was the recourse to one-part offers or a foreshortened commitment, both running counter to company philosophy. The RSC rarely agreed at the outset to an actor taking only one role, although occasional dispensation might be made for a 'star' actor who had a strong association with the RSC and who might use celebrity to help the company. The new dispensation appeared to be institutionalising what had previously been understandable if regrettable pragmatism.

To offset some of these criticisms, the shorter, more flexible contracts were accompanied by a continuing and greater emphasis on training and development because it had become harder to cast the high number of productions at adequate levels. But joining the company for a short burst offered an actor little or no time to be involved in training and failed to address the issue of how to raise the general level of company skill. There were related concerns about the repertoire, not only in trying to find new life in the Shakespeare productions but also in regard to the vulnerable place of new plays and the severing of already frayed links with living playwrights.

Noble's latest plan dismayed many inside and outside the profession. It became known that the governors had not been consulted about the changes before they had been announced. Terry Hands resigned from the RSC advisory directorate and Sir John Mortimer resigned as governor. Unfavourable media coverage of the plan itself, of its handling and of Noble's desire to demolish the Royal Shakespeare Theatre in favour of a much-derided Shakespeare village, added to the sense of chaos at the RSC. There was even muttering that the redevelopment plans were being kept obscure because of their effect on Stratford land prices. The RSC was a major landowner and some senior personnel also owned properties that might be affected.

In the midst of overseeing these complex changes, Noble announced in May 2002 that he was to resign the following year. The timing of the announcement shocked Stratford. It came just after he had successfully opened the West End musical *Chitty Chitty Bang Bang*. He was hurt, he said, by constant criticism, not just from the media but also from within the profession and the company, especially over his absences to prepare the lucrative musical at the crucial moment in his own plan when the redundancies took place and the new structure for the company was being established. Yet his decision cleared the way for a new figure, Michael Boyd, to bring a fresh eye to the problems. Belfast born, trained in Moscow and having run the exciting Tron Theatre in Glasgow for a decade before joining the RSC in 1996, Boyd brought a welcome non-English perspective to the company. Departing from the RSC tradition of leading from the rehearsal floor, he decided to spend the first year of his regime thinking through the issues facing the company. As two of the remaining three associate directors, Michael Attenborough and Steven Pimlott, left in 2002 and only Gregory Doran remained, Boyd could build a new artistic team with few impediments.

Boyd's appointment was a reminder that good work had been achieved amidst all the turmoil and was often overlooked or quickly forgotten because of the company's disarray. The RSC had regained artistic ground with its millennium project, *This England: the Histories*, comprising Shakespeare's history cycle of eight plays beginning with *Richard II* and ending with *Richard III*. The project had no star names and had diversity of viewpoint built into the way it was organised. Unlike the singular vision of previous versions, these productions were divided up among four directors and took place in the company's three different Stratford spaces. Boyd won an Olivier award for his contribution, the *Henry VI* trilogy and *Richard III*, all of which opened in the Swan.

## Turning back the clock

A sense of community, even if a fractious one, had disappeared under Noble's stewardship. Notions of security and service influenced by the experience of or proximity to world war still held sway in the 1960s but had been buried by the 1990s and the rule of so-called free market philosophy. RSC corporatism replaced the critical loyalty of before, which had been based on the dedication of individual expertise to the company. Attempts by the institution to remain flexible within an ever-changing and more constrained world became increasingly centralised and, paradoxically, RSC modernisation condemned the company to remain old-fashioned for longer than was necessary. In certain practical areas – for example, catering, both for the company and for the public, or the introduction of the electronic revolution for internal communication – the RSC was slow to move. In the adoption of managerial practices from industry – for instance, in creating a 'human resources' department – it moved inappropriately. The bureaucratic theatre Hall had wanted to avoid had slowly been taking hold and now it had arrived, not on the back of inflated state subsidy but, through its insufficiency, on the need to survive in the marketplace. 'Birtism' at the BBC had come to the RSC when the qualities theatre had given to management theory – self-motivation of small groups of multi-skilled workers – were abandoned for an inappropriate 'top down' model.[10] Noble tried to rectify this in his final plan but by this period the necessary internal cohesion to bind the different groups together had gone. In the process the company had lost a sense of its own history.

There was the telling insistence regardless of reality that the company had never been in better shape and would be in even ruder health in the future if everyone pulled together. The new managerialism, intended to improve efficiency and communication, did not, however, provide structures to make the company more democratic or open, and when the amount and number of salaries in the upper administrative range were first made public in 1995, their scale and extent further undermined any residual feeling of company among the poorly paid majority. Nor was the new bureaucracy necessarily more 'user friendly' than the old system – producers, for example, could be as devious and remote from the individual needs of artists and staff as any director and middle management as unresponsive. Instead of welcoming debate, the internal culture was now one of acquiesce or leave, and a dangerous gap had opened up between the management and the art.

The RSC flag under Noble had become in his words a 'quite reactionary' one.[11] His defence of Shakespeare's language and downgrading of new plays placed him on the high ground of conservative cultural populism, which aimed in vain to bind the nation together again. The RSC was promoting itself as articulate, and articulating, on behalf of those who were not and could not be. But who was listening? While simultaneously trying to modernise the institution to meet the demands of the new social order, Noble took Stratford back to where it had been in the 1950s and reinforced the company's distance from its rapidly changing society.

PART TWO

# Staying Alive

# SIX

# BEYOND THE BARD

In examining the tension between the creativity of the RSC and the company as an institution, the central terrain is the quality and meaning of the work that appears on stage, the nature of the repertoire and, broadly speaking, the worldview it may be said to express. Whether or not the company has legitimacy as a national and international institution is ultimately decided here. By any yardstick, the RSC has been an enormously protean and inventive company in this regard, reinventing and re-energising itself over four decades despite inadequate state support and providing some of the outstanding theatrical experiences of the latter part of the twentieth century.

At the heart of the RSC's stage work lies its relationship to the playwright whose name the company bears and the modern production of whose plays the company rejuvenated and transformed, setting an international benchmark. No other artist carries the historical and global baggage that Shakespeare does and, equally, no other offers the limitless opportunities for artistic exploitation. Neither Chekhov nor Brecht, the playwrights at the core of two of the other great European companies that inspired the founding of the RSC, carry such impact. In return, the RSC has been committed to an unprecedented level, range and depth of inquiry into his plays in a variety of styles and spaces as a living, changing dialogue with contemporary society.

The RSC has always had to confront the myth of 'Shakespeare', the collective label that encapsulates all the accumulated mediations of and accretions to the playwright's name, whether in the different versions of the texts, the countless productions or the films, theories, commentaries and merchandising. Neither the RSC nor 'Shakespeare' stays static. The vast output and impact of the RSC – along with a swirling mix of other influences ranging from the British education system, Hollywood and huge developments in Shakespeare studies to rapid social changes – add to the definition of 'Shakespeare', and this, in turn, also has its effect on the RSC. Despite sustained attacks, 'Shakespeare' has retained his special place in British and world culture: 'Shakespeare' has remained national and international, particular and universal, esoteric and transcendental – the globalising myth, in which everyone's history seems to be written, the more so as his own biography is very thin. Without the popularity of 'Shakespeare' there would have been no RSC in the first place. And while the RSC would never challenge the heart of the myth – the unparalleled greatness of the plays – there has been a struggle in riding the myth to balance authority with innovation, to use the myth rather than to be used by it.

Inheriting custody of the shrine brought the double burden of privilege and responsibility, a unique but contested position within the complex maze of Shakespeare's global contemporary presence. The company had to satisfy a national and international audience and be both local and general. It had to represent authenticity and continuity and yet continually be new and embody change. To reassess iconic Shakespeare dynamically meant challenging the very inheritance that gave the company its claim to legitimacy. For Hall, the pressure of the heritage industry was felt on the stage. The baggage of bardolatry was carried by actors, audience, academics and critics alike, a formidable alliance that not only demanded Shakespeare be produced 'properly' but was prepared to police productions deemed to fall beyond the pale.

Although bardolatry was anathema to Hall and his colleagues, it no doubt contributed to the box office and, thanks to the success of the RSC, became an even bigger business and therefore an even bigger burden to the RSC in questioning conventional interpretations. Hall played the 'bard card' astutely; for example, he revived the tradition of a Shakespeare birthday production, arranging the 'first night' to occur on Shakespeare's presumed birthday. But as time passed and the 'doublet and hose' orthodoxy he fought was replaced by the postmodern prescription of a-social eclecticism, the company rejoined the bardolators' camp in its commercial embrace of bard merchandising and tourism. Certain productions ironically exploited yet reflected this bardolatry, such as *Twelfth Night* (1994), in which Tudor Stratford was represented on stage, whereas others from an earlier time had explicitly debunked it. In The Other Place's 1974 opening season, *I Was Shakespeare's Double* by John Downie and Penny Gold challenged the idea that visiting Stratford would aid an understanding of Shakespeare's plays and in 1976 Edward Bond's *Bingo* undermined the stereotype of the transcendent humanist Shakespeare. By the turn of the new century, however, the attacks had become neutered; the production of Peter Barnes's *Jubilee* in 2001 revealed nothing more scornful in its look at the origins of Stratford bardolatry than the safe irreverence of a cheeky, end-of-term revue.

Compounding the problem of bardolatry for the RSC was the anomalous position Shakespeare occupies in the British cultural landscape of being caught between the popular and the esoteric, a division itself overlaid by the 'high' and 'low' art separation. Shakespeare's plays, which – uncomfortably for some – contain both high and low, have been ushered into the pantheon of Art for the delectation of the elite and yet they retain their popularity. The RSC set out to challenge this separation, but as the space between high and low diminished and the rest of the culture echoed the transience of theatre by celebrating the disposable, the old private club that sequestered Shakespeare did not disappear. Against a background of social fragmentation and a decline in Shakespeare production by the reps and touring companies, it was not surprising that it was left to the mass medium of film to return Shakespeare to mass popularity. This was both good and bad for the RSC. It gave a point of access while making the task more difficult, especially in relation to the young. Even as the battle was being joined to maintain Shakespeare's privileged position in the education system, there was a declining amount of live Shakespeare for the school students to see. The obligation to study Shakespeare implied that his plays belonged to everyone. Yet the lack of live experience of Shakespeare, taken together with a number of other factors – such as the financing of school theatre visits, the way the plays are taught for examinations, and the increasing remoteness of the language – combined to keep Shakespeare the preserve of the few. This cultural division of ownership replicated and reinforced the social division, and renewed the pressure on the RSC to reconnect its Shakespeare work to its society.

Peter Brook, the theatrical magician whose critical spirit floats over post-war Stratford production, summed up the Shakespeare problem as 'deadly theatre'.[1] Overthrowing it was the key to unlocking the rest of the company's work:

Year after year, bands of sincere and dedicated people go about doing these plays as best they can, and yet the one thing that everyone wants – which is for the play . . . to reach an audience with a maximum power – takes a quite opposite form. This respect and this love turn into set routines, patterns and conventions, which gradually creep into every single department, and so well-meaning people present their favourite dramatist in a way that is the complete betrayal of what they themselves set out to do. Now this is the root problem and branches out towards other forms of theatre, other plays.[2]

Brook wanted to escape the prevalent idea that modern plays required 'real' acting and Shakespeare a heightened form. 'All involve search for truth, truth of emotion, of ideas, of character – all separate but interwoven.'[3] In his preface to the English edition of Jan Kott's *Shakespeare Our Contemporary*, Brook identifies the problem for those producing Shakespeare as how to relate the plays to 'our lives'. He writes that the young actors who are aware of 'the deadly issues at this moment at stake in the world' tended to shy away from Shakespeare. It was no accident that at rehearsals they found plotting, fights and violent ends 'easy' – they had the clichés ready to deal with these situations, which they did not question. But, he writes, they were deeply vexed by problems of speech and style, which though essential, 'can only take their true place if the impulse to use words and images relates to experience of life'.[4]

Hall posed the question slightly differently; he asked how the company could make a bridge between what it honestly thought Shakespeare's intentions were and the contemporary audience. He wanted to honour the truths of those texts as perceived four centuries later without pretending they were easily accessible or uniformly gripping. 'Relevance' became the litmus test for the RSC and the crucial site for interpretive battles in a society ever more eager for meaning and interpretation. How far should the plays be manipulated in order to satisfy a current need? Hall acknowledged there was risk in interpreting Shakespeare but believed that once a director had decided to undertake a production of a particular play, interpretation had already begun. 'Interpretation is not a sin but a necessity', he wrote and 'the risk must be taken if our performances are to have meaning'.[5] It was a measure of the company's openness and consistency in exploring this territory that, for instance, Hall's production of *Hamlet* and Brook's of *Marat/Sade*, offering diametrically different views of the role of language and social interaction, could happily sit in the same season together.

Cross-fertilisation with contemporary work, especially new plays, was also a crucial part of the RSC's attempt to 'have meaning' and its Shakespeare work needs to be seen in the context of the repertoire as a whole. Sometimes this link was explored directly, although the results were uneven. On one occasion, Howard Davies's 1983 production of *Henry VIII*, a playwright – David Edgar – was used as a dramaturg; and on another occasion Charles Wood was commissioned to write the adaptations of the *Henry VI* plays that formed the first two parts of *The Plantagenets* directed by Adrian Noble in 1988. Although Wood's text was not finally used, his vision of the plays informed the production's narrative sweep. In the millennium project *This England: The Histories*, the connections to society were not only inscribed in aspects of the productions themselves, such as the jumble of noise drawn from different periods and sections of English society that opened *Richard II*, but the company presented in London the responses of playwrights who had been asked to react to the overall theme.

Before the existence of the RSC, an obvious sign of Shakespeare's 'relevance' or 'applicability' had been the use of contemporary dress.[6] RSC orthodoxy spurned this practice as too limiting. A few directors earned notoriety this way – for instance, Robin Phillips with a bikini-clad version of *The Two Gentlemen of Verona* complete with swimming pool – while some directors, like Bill Alexander in his 1950s account of *The Merry Wives of Windsor*, garnered high praise and for one of the company's chief visiting directors, Michael Bogdanov, it was a trademark. The RSC tried to see Shakespeare's plays as new plays, which they were when he wrote them, and regarded their geographical and chronological setting as a matter of imaginative preference rather than historical authenticity. Design played an important role in freeing productions from unnecessary historical as well as physical encumbrance. RSC scenography reflected the desire for fluid movement in spare, a-historical environments. Period accuracy was generally seen by the RSC as being just as restrictive and reductive as a production completely in modern dress. Costumes in particular, the company thought, should not tell too much history the audience did not need to know. The early RSC ideal was for costumes to be 'worn' enough to be human, historical enough to suggest period connections and contemporary enough to free the bodies of actors as well as the minds of the audience.

This sceptical attitude to authenticity lay behind the cool response of the RSC to the Globe Theatre project, which was first announced in 1964. It was a logical impossibility to recreate the conditions of Shakespeare's day, the company believed, and furthermore society had outgrown the original theatres. In reply, the Globe asked if that were the case, why had society not outgrown the plays as well? Leaving aside the RSC's proprietorial resistance to competition and its desire to build its own theatre in London, there was at root a reluctance to cede authority to the past rather than secure legitimacy through the present. Interestingly, the company later turned avidly to the Swan Theatre, which represented a different meeting of past and present. While not slavishly attempting to reproduce the dimensions and materials of the Elizabethan playhouses in the modern Swan, the company honoured them as its inspiration.

How and where a play is set in a production, and how the actors look, move and speak, says a great deal about the view of the world being presented. While there was no company doctrine, and each director was highly individual, RSC productions often exhibited certain familiar qualities, such as muscularity of style and fluidity of action. What characteristics they shared would mostly be more evident than the differences, and a season at the RSC would represent a different Shakespeare to the one on offer at the replica Globe. A welcome desire to communicate rather than obfuscate, however, often led to literalness in RSC productions in which the director places quotation marks around whole scenes, if not the entire play itself (and in the process extends the running time, occasionally to unsustainable lengths). The actor likewise adds quotation marks to selected passages or actions – most commonly, a covert textual reference to the male sexual organ is accompanied by descriptive arm gesture – in order to ensure the audience understands the point. As an extension of the RSC's direct style of performance, this can simplify a play even in the demonstration or celebration of its internal oppositions and incongruities.

Informing much of the RSC's Shakespeare has been an a-historicism that stressed similarities between the present and the past, placing the audience in a line of continuity within history, rather than emphasising the differences and drawing attention to the possibilities of change. Embracing a multitude of explanatory codes as if they are of equal merit reinforces this inclination. For instance, having disposed of the verities of the 1950s, the modern Shakespeare of ambiguity and contradiction nevertheless offered similar reassurance to the audiences of the 1960s. Both versions confirmed that Shakespeare was transcendent. For all the telling images provided by the RSC, its rich focus on the individual, its refusal to treat Shakespeare solemnly or with too much reverence, its productions have been littered with a ragbag of stage clichés produced by such an approach every bit as limiting as the 'doublet and hose' the RSC sought to overturn: prostitutes sit with their legs wide apart, emphasised cleavage is used as if conveying historical authority, clowns speak with a 'provincial' accent, kings with Received Pronunciation, and the uneducated crowd in yokels' 'mummerset'. Such a 'theatricalisation' of social relationships underpins a view that sees within history an unchanging core beyond and indifferent to class or other distinctions. Whole productions buttress this view by reaffirming a social cohesion that only exists in the world of the artefact, regardless of the volatility laid bare in the play itself. At its most conservative, this places Shakespeare in the camp of heritage tourism. Exceptions to this approach – for example, three directors of *The Taming of the Shrew*: Michael Bogdanov, who built de-construction into his aesthetic, Di Trevis who linked gender power to class power, and Jonathan Miller, who assumed a Renaissance vantage point – represent a minority, and were rarely to be found on the full-time staff.

Where the RSC positions itself in relation to Shakespeare – claimed as the exemplar of both universality and diversity – is an important social question, particularly when the idea of a universal culture is increasingly being challenged in an increasingly diverse society. Shakespeare's role in the making of the nation, his function in the former empire as a conduit of English moral superiority and his place in the educational system ensure that his plays remain a key site of ideological and cultural debate. A questioning, sceptical Shakespeare is as much a representation of the nation as a patriotic one. In the RSC's treatment of the history plays, which has come to be emblematic of the company, the balance has tilted towards the former. The 1972 *Romans* season presaged the theme of the 1974 general election 'Who runs Britain?' It also asked 'What is Britain?', thus fulfilling one of the critical obligations of a national institution.

There was a distinct whiff of F.R. Leavis's lost organic society about many RSC productions, which also seemed to reflect the view of George Orwell, who, when writing about British comedians, opined that: 'They remind one how closely knit the civilisation of England is, and how much it resembles a family, in spite of its out-of-date class distinctions.'[7] RSC productions would often tap into a stream of English middle-class regret at industrialisation and the advent of mass society in which a mythically classless, stoic gentry is presented as emblematic of an England that is inherently conservative rather than progressive. Shakespeare, the major source of justifying quotations by politicians of every hue, lends himself to being dragooned as symbolic of an essential English-ness, but context colours the interpretation. In the 1950s, English-ness was usually portrayed as a hegemonic notion that occluded other national and cultural identities; yet, as society shifted, it gradually cracked under the strains of history. Shakespeare, nevertheless, was still being corralled into service by those who continued to define English-ness against the standard of an imaginary 'real' England now apparently lost or debased beyond recognition. RSC productions that echoed such nostalgia played into the hands of these conservative forces while productions that challenged this view undermined those forces and offered succour to their opponents.

As Peter Hall said: 'There is no final Shakespeare'.[8] This was not the orthodoxy of the time but has become so. By the end of the twentieth century it was commonplace to talk of many Shakespeares – for instance, the feminist, the colonialist, the Tudor apologist or the gay. Multiplicity became the key to the RSC's long-term relationship to Shakespeare and even the paradoxes within such readings could be accommodated: Shakespeare could be misogynist as well as feminist, colonialist and liberationist, the patriot and the internationalist, the elitist and the populist, the quintessential English artist and the transcendent universalist. The inexhaustible variety of versions is the source of the company's veneration of his work, and reinforces his iconic status both nationally and internationally. Shakespeare is thereby seen yet again to prefigure all our futures by having nothing constant to say about any of them but always something pertinent. There are limits to the RSC's elasticity, however. It has followed prevailing notions of character-based linear narrative and avoided radical formal experiment. There has been no all-male Shakespeare, or transgression the other way with women playing male roles such as Richard II or Lear. Nor has there been a wholly gay version of any Shakespeare play or a 'non-white' interpretation.

The fecundity of interpretation both feeds the high rate of turnover and provides the necessary novelty demanded by the RSC's production line, reflecting the role of the new in, and the increasing tempo of, a restless society. The instability of meaning in the relativist whirlpool favours, and subsequently relies on, the dominance of directorial flourishes, which thrive precisely because the huge array of options makes the authority of the director paramount. While the RSC has rewardingly explored the tension between text and performance, it has also fallen victim to invention for its own sake as an answer to staleness. Its promiscuity of interpretation could only be sustained, paradoxically, by cohesion of the RSC 'brand' and its reliance on the importance of and care for the text, an insistence buttressed by every manipulation of and departure from it. As Hall was fond of saying, if one paints a moustache on the Mona Lisa, it is there for good, whereas the text of a Shakespeare play remains whatever happens in a particular production.[9]

The RSC brand was not an automatic gift from the previous regime, although the Stratford location and Stratford's ascendancy over the Old Vic gave the new company a good start in its bid to establish its trademark. Indeed, after the absorption of the Old Vic into the National Theatre, the RSC exerted a formidable and dominant grip, becoming the 'market leader'. Its very existence promoted the idea that Shakespeare was special and that the RSC was indispensable to an understanding of him. Deploying Shakespeare successfully in all five differently configured RSC theatres further underlined this essential role. The company redefined the plays and their reception, collapsing old notions of 'difficult' or 'marginal' texts as successful production rendered any and all 'accessible' and 'popular'. In 1977 the RSC completed the staging of what was at the time regarded as the complete Shakespeare canon when it presented *Henry VI, Parts 1, 2* and *3*. In 1986 it added *Two Noble Kinsmen*, attributed to Shakespeare and Fletcher, in a production that coincided with the play's inclusion in a volume of Shakespeare's *Complete Works*, and, having given a reading during the millennium histories project, in 2002 it presented *Edward III* as written solely by Shakespeare. The company underlined its authority with attendant proprietorial attitudes and practices. The BBC TV series of Shakespeare productions begun in 1978, the only comparable body of work to stand alongside the RSC output, was judged against standards set by the RSC, albeit in a different medium. Ironically, when Hall took over the NT and discussed planning co-operation with Trevor Nunn, his chosen successor at the RSC, he remembers with mild pique Nunn behaving as if 'in effect the 37 plays of Shakespeare belonged to the RSC' – a situation he himself, more than anyone else, had engineered.[10]

This sense of the RSC owning Shakespeare was reinforced by its concern for textual scrutiny as its touchstone. Stratford had a history of usually brief attempts to restore Shakespeare production to full texts, dating back to Frank Benson, who staged an uncut *Hamlet* in 1899. A search for veracity through the texts, however, did not mean the texts were sacrosanct. Brook had already led the way in his pre-RSC Stratford productions through textual adaptation, a major weapon in the armoury of 'directors' theatre'. Before it became a cliché of academic and critical writing, Brook was no longer treating the classics as untouchable vessels of a single truth waiting to be revealed through diligent rehearsal but as material to be reworked by the director-author. Paradoxically, he approached the radical task in the conservative spirit of grave respect for the playwright, and edited the text to suit his interpretation of the purpose of the play. As he had done with *Romeo and Juliet* in 1947, Brook removed references to reconciliation in *King Lear*; he staged the blinding of Gloucester in full light and in place of Shakespeare's portrayal of the servants' concern for him, Brook had the sightless earl stagger off, banging into them. Brook tailored the text to make Edmund comprehensively the 'bad guy' by cutting the line 'But Edmund was beloved' and Edmund's line 'Some good I mean to do'. As if to emphasise this point, he gave Albany's closing lines of the play – 'We that are young Shall never see so much, nor live so long' – to Edmund's brother Edgar. It was no accident that the production became dubbed Brook's *Lear*, and a section of scholars joined certain critics to pillory him for his textual depredations. Although Brook encouraged Charles Marowitz, who lacked Brook's respect for Shakespeare, to experiment in the *Theatre of Cruelty* workshop with more radical textual alterations, Brook never followed Marowitz's path of producing collage Shakespeare. RSC directors, likewise, did not engage in the wholesale reordering of texts to fit a psychoanalytical approach but, for directorial emphasis, decisive speeches were often strategically relocated and extracts from other texts interpolated.

The mandarins of textual rectitude believed that the RSC had a solemn duty to present the plays in approved ways and, in the apparent absence of internal company constraint, felt they were called upon to police the police. *The Wars of the Roses*, for example, the defining moment of Hall's time at the RSC, represented a heinous dereliction of duty, though the crime was mitigated by the relative unfamiliarity of the *Henry VI* plays compared to *King Lear*, an acknowledged masterpiece of European culture.[11] By drastically adapting the *Henry VI* plays, the keepers of the flame turned out to be the deepest traitors; John Barton rather than Shakespeare wrote 1,444 of the 7,450 lines. Barton, who wanted to be a writer, saw himself in a British theatrical tradition stretching back to the middle ages of editing texts to suit contemporary circumstance. It was, after all, what Shakespeare had done to Holinshed, Bocaccio and others, and what had happened to Shakespeare's texts themselves over the centuries. Hall and Barton later disagreed in their assessment of the propriety of the project, Hall calling it 'reprehensible'.[12] In a newspaper debate with hostile critics, Barton argued that while scholars had gone to great lengths to establish exactly what Shakespeare wrote, ironically the more that was discovered, the more it became clear how amended the texts were. Such delving, he wrote, challenged the notion of an untouchable text, of a text that represents with certainty Shakespeare's own 'complete and preferred version'.[13] The nub of his, and the RSC's, belief was that only production could make a play theatrically viable. This was not an anti-academic position, however. He believed that the more theatres were in touch with scholarship, and the more scholars were in touch with the theatre, the better it would be for Shakespearean production.

The RSC has enjoyed a unique and fruitful as well as occasionally hostile interaction with scholarship, which built on the earlier relationship of Stratford under Anthony Quayle and Glen Byam Shaw with the

*Shakespeare Survey* and *Shakespeare Quarterly*. As theatre studies increasingly embraced performance and the academic apparatus provided durability to the ephemera of theatre, the two camps had a mutual interest in each other's activities. They both reinforced ideas of theatrical tradition that confer seminal status on past productions and assess the innovation of the present within that tradition. The RSC owed a great deal to the scholarly background of its directors. This encouraged the authoritative and distinctive image of the RSC and led to the practice of RSC directors undertaking their own research and textual emendations. Scholars, however, have helped the company in research and the preparation of acting as well as published play texts, thereby supplementing the work of the literary manager and the directors themselves. The influential Shakespeare editor Stanley Wells became the company's vice-chairman in 1990 having served as a governor since the mid-1970s.

Despite the branch of academe, represented by Harold Bloom, that prefers its own private and cerebral affair with the texts to any living embodiment, the RSC's productions have become the object of much academic analysis and contributed importantly to the development of trends within Shakespeare studies. Critical 'schools', such as the cultural materialists, often found themselves deploying arguments in their appraisal of the RSC that were promoted by the RSC itself. When semiotics and its successors triumphed over literary criticism in the universities, however, the gap between the company and academe grew. The scholarly challenge to universalist notions of culture together with attacks on author-centred narrative theatre, which suggested Shakespeare was not only elitist but also representative of a redundant art form, widened the gap, and the lack of invention in the company's Shakespeare work made the RSC a less interesting focus for erudite examination.

No amount of textual work can replace vitality on stage, and that was justifiably the RSC's main concern. Fluidity of staging based on close textual reading in a social context with an acknowledgement of the presence of the audience was the early RSC trademark.[14] Textual rows abated even though textual adaptations constantly recurred. 'Relevance' was redefined as times changed and the radicalism of Hall's era became the orthodoxy that needed challenging. Some directors collapsed relevance entirely into aesthetics while others tried to explore social and political meanings in new ways. Whereas the norm had been to explore cause and effect, it became the fashion to look just at effect without the cause. This could be formally interesting but 'why' had been lost and replaced with 'how'.

The company was regenerated from within by both the lavish and the puritan minimalism of its 1970s Shakespeare work; however in the 1980s and 1990s the 'deadly' theatre of the 1950s began to make its comeback. Possible external sources of renewal were ignored. After Hall, the impact of continental Europe disappeared, despite the French connections of Terry Hands who worked at the Comédie Française. Avant-garde performance experiments were ignored. While this reflected an understandable shift towards indigenous new playwriting and a healthy disdain for the immoderation of 'director's theatre', it also expressed a self-defeating insularity, haughtiness and fear of rivalry. On the question of not inviting non-English speaking directors, it was said without evidence that celebrity figures such as Patrice Chéreau, Peter Stein or Giorgio Strehler would be too expensive. Another major excuse was language. Michel Saint-Denis had not wanted to direct Shakespeare in England because of this problem and unhappy experiences with Franco Zeffirelli (*Othello* in 1961) and Karolos Koun (*Romeo and Juliet* in 1967) suggested caution would definitely be the wisest policy. Robert Lepage's mud-splattered production of *A Midsummer Night's Dream* at the NT in 1992 confirmed RSC directors in their prejudice. When a foreign director – Yukio Ninagawa in 1999 – did eventually work for the company again, the choice seemed to rely as much on the availability of Japanese funding as on his artistic suitability. A combined creative and producing team (as well as a combined sponsorship team), resulted in an unhappy ragbag of styles and many a disconsolate actor. The production of King Lear, which opened first in Tokyo and then in Stratford, proved a box office success but an isolated experiment in crossing cultures.

Although there were many bright RSC performances, by the company's own high standards, much of the work had become honourable but routine, and most of it was unexceptional. The ability to reflect and comment on society in anything but an ironic way was being lost in the drive for technical bravura. The RSC's subsidy was insufficient to free the company from its commercial imperatives and the production of Shakespeare had become just a custom. A domestic, country-house *Hamlet* in 1997 that deliberately eschewed the play's political dimension was a symptom of this over-production and perpetual quest to surmount the deadening effects of familiarity. The company had been asking itself for many years how it could be 'relevant' five times a year and when certain titles reappear with the regularity of a merry-go-round? The director of the production Matthew Warchus acknowledged the problem by suggesting, only slightly tongue in cheek, that the company institute a moratorium on Shakespeare. For all the company's expert and distinctive work on Shakespeare over four decades, the battle to revivify the plays of this dead, white, male, European, Christian versifier would – as ever – have to be fought all over again.

## Non-Shakespearean work

Central to Hall's reform of Stratford was the company's performance of non-Shakespearean plays. Indeed, for most of the RSC's life, the company performed more of this work than Shakespeare, even though it lacked the latter's singular focus and high profile. There was a precedent for the presentation of non-Shakespearean work, going back to the early 1900s and particularly in the 1940s when plays by Sheridan, Jonson and Marlowe were seen at Stratford.[15] Hall's first endeavour beyond Shakespeare signalled the company's interest in the world of which Shakespeare was a part, though Hall himself was not to direct any plays by Shakespeare's contemporaries. He chose to open the RSC's account at the Aldwych with Webster's *The Duchess of Malfi* – a choice that shocked critics; one wrote that it stemmed from a university-based, English Literature notion of drama and that audiences would prefer 'Shakespeare's wealth' to the 'small change of second-rate Jacobeans'.[16] It was true that this small change was the currency of the Cambridge University Marlowe Society but it was also to be found in the artistic pockets of Joan Littlewood at Stratford East and Bernard Miles at the Mermaid Theatre. Hall's choice of director, Donald McWhinnie, fresh from success with the première of *The Caretaker*, underlined the company's thinking. McWhinnie believed Webster was closer to *Waiting for Godot* than *Othello*, an attitude that permeated the company's extensive exploration of Shakespeare's contemporaries. This proved to be a rich vein of future work, which helped to define current notions of Jacobean drama and allowed the RSC to counter effectively the museum image of a classical theatre company.

Following *Women Beware Women* in the 1962 Arts Theatre season and the 1964 Aldwych production of Marlowe's *The Jew of Malta*, which transferred to the Royal Shakespeare Theatre in 1965, the critical moment came in 1966 with the success of *The Revenger's Tragedy*. Unknown to audiences but celebrated by T.S. Eliot after a long period in the critical wilderness – and reputedly only one professional production since its debut – Nunn produced the play as a succulent excoriation of decadence that seemed closer not to Beckett but to Joe Orton and *Marat/Sade* than to Shakespeare. Such revivals did not carry the dead hand of past productions or the ingrained expectations or the 'authenticity' problem and,

being little known, tapped into a sense of relevance in its widest interpretation through the surprise of discovering a body of plays that still
spoke across the centuries. As other theatres, such as The Citizens' in
Glasgow, began to present Renaissance plays regularly, the RSC expanded
its focus through the opportunities afforded by the studio space of The
Other Place, in productions such as *The Witch of Edmonton* by Dekker,
Ford and Rowley and George Farquhar's *The Twin Rivals*.

While there was a waning of the RSC's large-scale work in this area,
which was subject to enormous box office pressures and 'competition'
from Shakespeare, the company's enthusiasm for the re-evaluation of
seventeenth-century drama and its evident popularity gave rise to the
opening of the Swan. It was originally created to explore the plays of
Shakespeare's contemporaries and those who came soon after him. This
led to a re-examination of plays by the better known of his peers, such as
Ben Jonson and Christopher Marlowe, as well as to the 'discovery' of still
performable plays by generally unfamiliar authors such as James Shirley
and Thomas Shadwell. The RSC invoked its public service remit. It was
fulfilling a national responsibility in raiding a vast and dusty dungeon full
of lost treasure. The echo of heritage – we arise from the past and still to
some extent live in it – was reinforced by the Swan's dominant architecture and the theatre's growing importance in the economics and profile of
the RSC. Comfort was found in the playwrights of the past, who, like
Shakespeare, were mined for a transcendental message, even – and perhaps especially if – depicting a society in moral chaos. An exception like
Max Stafford-Clark's 1992 production of Richard Brome's *A Jovial Crew*
ruffled feathers in the RSC because of the liberties he took with the text.
He was not alone, however. John Barton regularly adapted works he was
directing, such as Aphra Behn's *The Rover*. Stafford-Clark believed he
was liberating a hidden text whereas Barton believed he was saving plays
from their shortcomings.

The enduring popularity of this area of work was shown by the success
of the 2002 Swan season of five seventeenth-century plays, which transferred to the West End and won an Olivier award for the outstanding
achievement of the year. Although not suffering the acute production
line problems of the Shakespeare output, some titles, such as *The Duchess
of Malfi*, *Women Beware Women*, *The Changeling* and *The White Devil*,
became familiar to artists and regular theatre-goers and through this
incorporation seemed to lose the transgressive power of their strangeness.
*The Revenger's Tragedy*, for example, was given a new production by the
RSC in 1987 as a recognised classic, studied not only at university level
but also now at 'A' level too.

Alongside *The Duchess of Malfi* in the opening Aldwych season was a range of plays that foreshadowed the pattern of the RSC's other non-Shakespearean repertoire, an eclectic mix of new plays, British premières and established plays from other cultures: two British premières – Jean Giraudoux's *Ondine* and Jean Anouilh's *Becket* – were accompanied by the world première of John Whiting's *The Devils* and a distinguished revival of *The Cherry Orchard*. This European bias could be seen in the following season with the inclusion of *The Caucasian Chalk Circle*, the first Brecht play to be seen in a West End theatre and at the time a bold choice, even though Hall disagreed with the Brechtian production style of its director William Gaskill. The RSC was clearly positioning itself within and as part of continental European theatre: in 1963 its British première of Friedrich Dürrenmatt's *The Physicists* came the season after its first appearance in Zurich and was won because of the company's ensemble reputation, and the production of Rolf Hochhuth's *The Representative* was seen in the same year as its debut in Berlin. This emphasis was both a matter of outlook in the leadership of the company and a result of Hall using as a play adviser the Hungarian-born Martin Esslin, who was well connected in mainland Europe. The inauguration of the World Theatre Season in 1964 was the most public affirmation of this proclivity and the staged reading of Peter Weiss's *The Investigation* in 1966 on the same evening as other European theatres the most symbolic declaration. This interest could be seen in the influence of Brecht and Artaud on the company and in its presentation of plays by, among others, Roger Vitrac, Sławomir Mrożek, Marguerite Duras, Günter Grass, Jean Genet and, in 1964, the only RSC production of a full-length Beckett play, *Endgame*. Directed by Donald McWhinnie under Beckett's supervision, it was not critically successful but achieved a remarkable unity of expression. Peter Brook described it as 'the greatest event in the English theatre for many years'.[17]

Beckett did not provide the large-cast, full-bloodied plays the RSC was looking for to satisfy its company needs; these were exemplified by the string of excellent David Jones's productions of Gorky plays in the 1970s. With the demise of the World Theatre Season in 1975, the year its director Peter Daubeny died, the European connection declined. Fewer contemporary European plays were presented as new British plays took precedence. Having done a great deal to break the isolation of British theatre, the RSC gradually retreated into a lofty remoteness from the contemporary theatre of its neighbours, despite an occasional foray with an older play by Botho Strauss or Bernard-Marie Koltès. The European dimension, nevertheless, was understandably at the centre of the company's examination of plays from other cultures, which conformed to its approach of finding meaning in the past. John Barton adapted ancient Greek material in *The Greeks* and *Tantalus* to support his sceptical view of life and his belief that all stories have been told already. Noble took a more spiritual approach in his quest for the poetic when he staged the Sophocles trilogy *The Thebans* and two new plays, Timberlake Wertenbaker's *The Love of the Nightingale* and Howard Barker's *The Bite of the Night*, explored the legacy of Greek myth. The company, however, has avoided ancient comedy – for example, Aristophanes and Plautus, which, given the latter's relationship to Shakespeare, seems remiss. As might be expected of a national theatre, the lineage of European drama was well represented, if not religiously covered: the Spanish 'golden age', though no Lope de Vega, Molière though not Racine or Corneille, and a little Strindberg but not the historical plays, along with much else from Goldoni and the German enlightenment through to nineteenth-century Russians and Ibsen.[18]

Occasionally selection was based on a theme, such as the medieval season at The Other Place and the Restoration season at the Swan, which comprised three late seventeenth-century plays and, as a counterpoint, Bond's *Restoration*. A linked pairing, for example running Molière's *Tartuffe* alongside Bulgakov's *Molière* or *Antony and Cleopatra* alongside *Tamburlaine the Great*, might also shape selection. There was less of this deliberate juxtaposing than might have been imagined partly because of the complexities of the planning process and partly because of a resistance to what might be interpreted as university programming. It was also apparent that reviewers rarely commented on the intended counterpoint. Nevertheless, choices did mostly stem from intellectual curiosity, like widening the focus on Shakespeare's contemporaries to another country, as with Tirso de Molina, whose Spanish play *The Last Days of Don Juan* is the earliest major treatment of this key European character. Sometimes the attraction lay in exploring a lesser-known work by celebrated names such as Ibsen, for example *The Pretenders*, alongside what have become the stock plays in the western dramatic canon by him or Chekhov, which have ceased to seem 'foreign'. The RSC frequently commissioned new translations in order to see an old text afresh through the prism of a contemporary playwright's imagination and use of language, but this offended certain translators – and multilingual playwrights – when the chosen playwright could not read or speak the language of the original. In such cases, the RSC, like other companies, would employ an underpaid yet vital 'literal' translator, whose work is often undervalued or ignored. The RSC did credit translators, and on occasion established a healthy and 'more equal' relationship between the linguistic expert and the stage wordsmith.

Naturally enough, interwoven into this repertoire was a regular exam-ination of British and Irish drama, from the mystery plays, through Restoration plays to the likes of Harley Granville-Barker and T.S. Eliot – though not Noël Coward – Sean O'Casey and Brendan Behan, though little Shaw. An interest in contemporary American plays began in 1967 with Jules Feiffer's *Little Murders* but subsided after Albee's *All Over* (1972) until it resurfaced in the 1980s and 1990s around an association with Richard Nelson that extended to nine plays along with productions of plays by Bernard Pomerance, Sam Shepard and Naomi Wallace. The company also dipped into American popular drama, from William Gillette's *Sherlock Holmes* and *Once in a Lifetime* by Moss Hart and George Kaufman to the Sam and Bella Spewack/Cole Porter musical *Kiss Me Kate*.

After Hall left, the RSC under Nunn more actively pursued a popular dimension to its repertoire alongside its other strands of work. A run of productions, beginning with Dion Boucicault's 1841 comedy *London Assurance* (1970) and including Tom Stoppard's *Travesties* and John O'Keeffe's 1791 comedy *Wild Oats* culminated artistically (via Nunn's musical version of *The Comedy of Errors*) in *The Life and Adventures of Nicholas Nickleby* (1980). After the move to the Barbican, this strand of work continued with productions such as *Poppy* but became subsumed in the issue of what to present at Christmas, a problem the company had wrestled with since producing Robert Bolt's children's play *The Thwarting of Baron Bolligrew* in 1965. At the Barbican, as an alternative to the com-mercial theatre's worn-out pantomimes packed with minor television personalities, the RSC pioneered the family show that appealed to adults as well as children, such as the new text version of *Peter Pan*. The RSC Christmas show, however, became a tired and unimaginative formula in the 1990s (for instance *A Christmas Carol*), which, as a reaction, resulted in slick but curiously cold productions (for instance *The Lion, the Witch and the Wardrobe* and *Alice in Wonderland*) instead of a rethink.[19]

The search for the popular show outside of the Christmas slot also brought its artistic disasters, notably *Carrie*, but also its successes, like *Les Misérables*. Nunn refused to acknowledge the false distinction between 'high' and 'low' art and attacked the snobbery that would deny a produc-tion like *Les Misérables* its place in the programme of a company like the RSC. However, the balance of work within the company shifted in the 1990s. Whereas *Les Misérables* in 1985 had running alongside it in The Pit a season of three spiky Howard Barker plays – one of the defining moments in contemporary British playwriting – by the time of *The Lion, the Witch and the Wardrobe* in 1998, such a combination was absent because the role of new plays, the chief element of the RSC's non-Shakespearean work, had been demoted.

## New plays

The 'new play' only took on its special, contemporary meaning in the post-war years when the epithet 'new' came to carry the force of 'original' and the quality of not having been seen before became much sought after. It gained this potency at the same time as the role of the playwright was advanced in the non-commercial world of the Royal Court under George Devine, whose 'right to fail' became a rallying cry against commercialism. 'New' came to stand for a significant, meaningful text that had 'relevance' and new plays became the central platform in the emerging theatre of national significance. The Royal Court opened up the prospect of being a playwright beyond the confines of the privileged few and public subsidy gave writers commissions and supported a network of theatres that made a career as a playwright an attractive proposition. As the number of professional playwrights grew, a greater premium was placed on 'newness' and at the RSC there was the added edge of being the essential partner in the dialogue with the classical repertoire.

Not surprisingly, as a director who was pledged to the text as much in classical as in contemporary work, Hall placed himself in the Devine camp rather than that of, say, Joan Littlewood, who valued writers as part of a team but not as the prime source of meaning. The commitment to a writer rather than merely to a particular text was part of Hall's ensemble philosophy and was inscribed in the company's name through the inclusion there of a playwright. His belief in cross-pollination as essential to the creativity of the institution and how it represented the society it was serving involved living playwrights participating actively and centrally in the work of the company and not only in presenting their plays. Hall saw the RSC as part of a community of theatres, however diverse, generating a plethora of playwrights reminiscent of the proliferation in Shakespeare's day and it was thanks to him that until the 1990s any aspiring RSC director was expected to demonstrate a commitment to new plays. This commitment, however trimmed and trammelled, led to important long-term relationships with a number of playwrights such as Howard Barker, Peter Barnes, Edward Bond, Howard Brenton, Nick Darke, Nick Dear, David Edgar, Peter Flannery, Pam Gems, Christopher Hampton, Robert Holman, David Mercer, Adrian Mitchell, Richard Nelson, Harold Pinter, Stephen Poliakoff, David Rudkin, Timberlake Wertenbaker, Peter Whelan and Charles

Wood. Relationships were occasionally formalised, for example through writer-in-residence schemes (funded by television companies, with the money being paid to the RSC not the playwright), and, in the case of Edgar, Nelson and Whelan, as RSC Honorary Associate Artists.

New plays brought their own problems for the fledgling company in terms of casting: could a group of actors assembled initially to perform Shakespeare also meet the particular and different needs of new plays? At first the response was makeshift, allied to an attempt to address the issue on a longer-term basis through training and experiment in the Studio. The problem remained, however, and was a factor in the expansion of the RSC, which made a wider pool of actors available and increased the flexibility of the company. In general, unless economics or a particular circumstance dictated otherwise, the RSC turned down scripts that would have required the hiring of actors from outside the existing company.

It was always a struggle to find new plays and there was never a 'golden' period. Hall commissioned from the outset. From his initial contracts, however, only *The Devils* by John Whiting came through and was performed.[20] Hall was deliberately cautious in the first season and all the new plays were historical 'costume' dramas, although *The Devils* broke from the stereotype and proved a success. David Rudkin's *Afore Night Come*, originally seen in the 1962 Arts Theatre season and then transferred to the Aldwych, was the first RSC play that dealt directly with contemporary life to make a public impact. It confirmed the RSC as a company with bite. It was revived in the 1974 opening season at The Other Place following a RSC production at The Place the previous year of his *Cries from Casement as His Bones are Brought to Dublin*. Rudkin became the unofficial 'house' dramatist at The Other Place in a creative relationship with its artistic director, Ron Daniels. Harold Pinter, whose work defined the importance of the writer at the early RSC through his partnership with Hall and his own involvement with the company as a director as well as a playwright, shared Rudkin's strong sense of form and language.[21] Their plays were complex, distinctive and disturbing but exhilarating and they became iconic of RSC new writing.

The institutional cornerstone of the relationship between the RSC and the playwright was the commission. Although the RSC received more than 1,000 unsolicited scripts a year, all of which were read (until a policy change in 1997 abandoned this practice), this was not the most likely route to a production. A commission was, and a commission was offered only in the expectation that a production would ensue. The company had to commission enough writers in order to meet the demands of the available 'slots' without over-commissioning and having a surplus of scripts that it could not produce. There was never any budgetary obstacle. Ahead of the NT, the RSC set a standard for payment of writers following the introduction of a minimum contract, for which the RSC, ironically, was indirectly responsible. A dispute in 1972 between the RSC and John Arden and Margaretta D'Arcy over their play *The Island of the Mighty* became a focal point in the creation of the Theatre Writers' Union, the moving force behind the establishment of such a contract.[22] Writers were guaranteed a certain level of protection, affecting changes to the script, key casting decisions and attendance at rehearsal, for which they would be paid.

A commission was a gesture of good faith as well as a legally binding document, and it was a rarity in the 1970s and 1980s for it not to be honoured by a production. The company followed a writer-centred approach established by Hall, in which support of the playwright was as important as the production of any particular play. The timing of a commission in terms of a writer's work and development was important. Critics greet new plays at the RSC with different expectations to other theatres; exposure at the wrong moment or with the wrong play can be highly damaging to a writer. A commission might help a miniaturist expand, an established writer depart from the familiar, or a blocked writer find a way out of the impasse. Using such an approach, the company might offer a writer a commission to translate or adapt a play, either as a way of keeping in touch with the company when a new play did not seem likely or even as an introduction to the company – as was the case with Christopher Hampton. The RSC staged his version of *Tartuffe* and this led to a commission that turned out to be *Les Liaisons Dangereuses*. The RSC also revived important modern work, for example Charles Wood's *Dingo*, Edward Bond's *Bingo*, Trevor Griffiths' *The Party* and Howard Brenton's *The Churchill Play*. This was a service to the writer, who might not find another theatre willing or able to restage the play, as well as to the public, which might otherwise have not had the chance to see it. The RSC could also confer status on a play, which helped both national and international recognition, and some – *Destiny*, for instance – became that hybrid of the age of novelty, the 'modern classic', without requiring the subsequent production life associated with such a description.

It is in the nature of the company–playwright relationship to be tense and problematic as well as creative, and it was by no means an easy or smooth relationship. As with casting, institutional as well as inter-personal questions had to be negotiated in order to secure a production and many factors come into play – which director, which space, which actors, and how the 'slot' relates to other 'slots' in the same season, for instance.

There was no automatic right to production, even with a commission. Personal commitment by a director was the usual deciding feature, as when Peter Hall overrode the planning committee and proceeded with a production of Pinter's *The Homecoming* against the majority view. He was, of course, the boss, but the approach remained after he left the company. For example, Ron Daniels decided to direct *Destiny* by David Edgar at The Other Place, where he was artistic director, even though the company had already rejected it. In fact, it had been commissioned and rejected by Nottingham Playhouse and, reworked, vetoed by the board of the Birmingham Rep where Edgar was playwright in residence. Despite occasional rumblings from governors, especially in the early days, the RSC unlike the NT – or Birmingham Rep – did not tolerate direct interference from its board on repertoire matters. Writer–director relationships, such as between Hall and Pinter, Jones and Mercer, Daniels and Rudkin and Edgar, or Alexander and Whelan, were able to flourish or not under their own momentum.

The opening of the small theatres in the mid-1970s changed the RSC's relationship to playwrights. Being on the economic margins meant these spaces had restored the 'right to fail', which had proved increasingly hard to sustain at the Aldwych. This liberated the writer's imagination to respond to and exploit what the RSC could do best for writers – offer support through the whole process from inception to production as well as exceptional resources, notably a large group of actors who work together across the repertoire, becoming skilled in meeting the demands of intricate and individual language. This situation offered the RSC opportunities for sustained involvement with a greater number of writers beyond those who had a particular relationship with an RSC director. Playwrights were more able to write for and even, on occasion, with the company. For example, Robert Holman spent the early part of the 1984 Stratford season watching and relaxing with the actors and then wrote *Today* for a specific group who performed it later that season. Writers became involved in the full range of RSC extra-mural activities, in workshops and fringe events, and were able to see all the company's productions free of charge.

With the launch of The Warehouse under Howard Davies in 1977 as a theatre originating new plays, the RSC's focus shifted from continental Europe and the USA to Britain, in response to the abundance of indigenous talent thriving especially on the fringe. Davies and his generation were sceptical of the RSC and of what was perceived to be commercial new plays by writers such as David Hare or Christopher Hampton, who might have seemed obvious candidates for the company. At The Warehouse, the work was politically conscious, both utopian and pragmatic, and much fantastical and brutal imagery as well as visceral and metaphorical vocabulary – an apt reflection of a complex society in decline. This post-censorship drama debunked the myths of Englishness in plays like *Bingo* (Shakespeare the asocial artist), *Dingo* (the heroism of World War II that shaped post-war society) and *The Churchill Play* (the totemic wartime leader). Alongside the engaged play, such as David Edgar's *The Jail Diary of Albie Sachs*, there was also a body of work, exemplified by Peter Flannery's *Savage Amusement*, that linked social and political realism in a sombre view of an alienated society, in which the people have been robbed of the responsibility for their own lives.

With The Other Place increasingly featuring new work – and demolishing the fable that the Stratford audience could not cope with such heady stuff – it was possible for more new plays to have longer runs by being seen during the residency in Newcastle and the London season. The enlarged opportunities, however, carried disadvantages. The system of 'slots', whereby the small and large theatres could operate concurrently, meant that the length of a run of a new play was tied to that of its partner production. Assessments had to be made in advance about the viability of a new play, and this could lead to overexposure. At other times, the opposite happened. A powerful production of Caryl Churchill's *Softcops* (1984), for example, had a derisory number of performances – seventeen – because of scheduling limitations. Despite promises to the contrary, the play was never revived, and this became a factor in Churchill's future absence from the RSC repertoire.

For writers the sheer size of the operation could be as off-putting as it was beneficial. Unlike in most theatres, if a writer were having a play produced by the RSC, the company's efforts were not wholly focused on that one production. It may be flattering to see one's name on a poster alongside that of Shakespeare and Chekhov, but if a director has to rush off after rehearsal to a casting meeting for the next show instead of spending time with the writer, the realities of company existence look less inviting. When the RSC agreed to stage three new plays by Edward Bond, collectively known as *The War Plays*, he was given an inexperienced staff co-director for such a project and insufficient rehearsal time uninterrupted by other company calls. Bond found himself spending too much energy in meetings trying to make the RSC system work and eventually pulled out of directing the final play.

The physical separation of the smaller theatres from the larger ones, most markedly in London during The Warehouse/Aldwych days, reinforced the idea that the small theatres were being institutionalised as ghettoes. Writers who wanted to see their plays on the RSC's big stage but could not – for example, Howard Barker – found this indeed to be the case. After the Swan opened in 1986, the lack of a London partner for its productions led to problems for new plays that originated there. They had to be squeezed into The Pit, expanded to fit the Barbican, or find a home in a third space, such as the Young Vic. Withdrawal from the Barbican in 2002 exacerbated the dilemma of how to find a further life for new plays.

Despite not being engaged with playwrights to the extent that Hall had been, Nunn pushed through the establishment of the small theatres and supported their promotion of new writing. Nunn, however, became irritated by what he saw as the narrow and, therefore, elitist approach of many new plays, and did not believe there was an audience for the likes of Barker at the Aldwych, where continued commitment to new plays was proving troublesome. In 1978, for example, Mike Leigh was asked to develop a new play through his improvisatory techniques but the project had to be abandoned when it was clear there would be no new play, and at the same time two new plays, Steve Gooch's *The Women Pirates* and David Mercer's *Cousin Vladimir*, were poorly received. Nunn's own collaboration with Edgar on *The Life and Adventures of Nicholas Nickleby* two years later underlined the continuing role of the living writer in the company's large-scale work.

After the company left The Warehouse and the 'autonomous republic' of new plays was brought back within the organisation as a whole and was no longer dominated by the taste of one director, choices were filtered through a new play committee. This comprised a playwright (David Edgar), a director drawn from the associates group who changed annually, and the literary manager. What this system lacked in focus – a weakening underpinned by the lack of profile afforded by The Pit – it gained in breadth of taste. When Adrian Noble succeeded Terry Hands, he gave responsibility for new plays to executive producer Michael Attenborough, a director with a new play track record. Contrary to Noble's expectation, however, this move was not seen by playwrights as a consolidation of the importance of new writing but as the artistic director distancing himself from it. The gradual demise of the RSC's new play profile ensued as Noble asserted the primacy of the company's classical work and new plays had to 'earn their keep' as a commodity. His 'cherry picking' approach to new plays meant only the 'best' were chosen and the rest discarded rather than inculcating a new play culture through regular production. A policy of excellence, however, can lead to the prison of good taste and a bloodless, rootless repertoire. The terms of the argument implied an accepted and universal yardstick of judgement that ignored the irregular processes whereby certain plays become seen as meaningful for different reasons at different periods in history. This approach by definition tends to downgrade or exclude the innovative or the 'other', and thereby puts at risk work that is marked by subaltern associations, whether of gender, ethnicity, class or further imaginations that deviate from the norm. If the ideal of the new play is located in Ibsen and Chekhov, the room for growth and development is limited and the company as a whole loses touch with the world it is supposed to be representing.

Under Noble's modernisation plans, bureaucratisation took over the system – writers were obliged to produce synopses – and the relationship of the company to playwrights altered. Dispensing with the old associates broke a link with many writers and, while it was healthy to bring in new names, the freelance organisation of directors meant it was harder for writers to build or sustain artistic relationships with the company. The ratio of commissioned plays that were not performed rose and there were no new big stage plays – Christmas show adaptations aside – after 1996 until the company returned to the Barbican with the 2003 dramatisation of *Midnight's Children*. The new play in 1996 was itself another adaptation, *Les enfants du paradis* and before that there had been three revivals of modern plays – *Travesties*, *The Hostage* and *A Patriot for Me* – but no new play since 1992 when Richard Nelson's *Columbus and the Discovery of Japan* had closed early. A reduction in the number of new plays at The Other Place and The Pit even led to the studio spaces having their 'right to fail' questioned. Management, for example, challenged a proposed Other Place season of Beckett short plays, a Brecht play and a Bond première on its box office potential and the plan was scrapped.

The streamlining undertaken by Noble from the mid-1990s left playwrights anxious at their future, particularly when in 2002 The Other Place was closed and the RSC withdrew from the Barbican. Any future RSC new play presence in London would require commercial backing. How problematic this would be for new plays was seen that year when the company had at its disposal three strong Stratford productions – David Edgar's *The Prisoner's Dilemma*, Peter Whelan's *A Russian in the Woods* and Martin McDonagh's *The Lieutenant of Inishmore* – but only managed to take one, the McDonagh, into the West End. Furthermore, whereas new writing had once helped keep the company in touch with contemporary currents, its falling away had left the company exposed. Solutions would not be easy. For instance, in trying to commission black writers, issues of tokenism and the culture of the RSC were raised as obstacles. The writers wanted to resist being labelled by their colour while recognising the historic reasons for this. Some also resisted being commissioned by the RSC because of the exclusively white director pool and the ethnic unevenness in casting. This did not mean they would necessarily write a play requiring black actors but they might, and if they did, they did not want this to be seen as exceptional or problematic. Nor did they want a special effort to be made to invite a 'black' audience, only for the company to revert to its predominantly 'white' mailing list for the rest of the season.

## Public role

The RSC's tradition of support for new writing at the core of its non-Shakespearean repertoire had been critical in securing its role as a court of public opinion. On occasion this role has taken on a dramatic profile; for example, the interruptions from small sections of the audience during *Destiny*, which warns of the rise of the far right, or the defacing of posters and the company notice board during *The Representative*, which criticises the wartime Pope's failure to challenge the Holocaust, and, following threats, the subsequent posting of a policeman at the stage door.[23]

Mostly, however, the public debate remained fierce but less menacing and, despite the failures – and the failures of nerve – the RSC sustained its record for committed as well as imaginative work. As a consequence, the company has made an important and distinctive contribution to the stock of the nation's plays.[24] A powerful symbol of this commitment came during the visit in 1990 of Václav Havel, the playwright turned President of Czechoslovakia, whose play *Temptation* had been given its English-language première in 1987 at The Other Place. On the opening night the cast and production team spoke by telephone to Havel, who was at the time restricted in his movements by the authorities. On his visit to London as President, he returned the compliment and instead of seeing a Shakespeare production he insisted on seeing a new play.

# SEVEN

# SHOTS IN THE DARK

At the time the RSC was founded, the tradition of theatrical training in Britain was practical, not theoretical or reflective, and could be traced back to the influence of the early Church through the medieval guild plays and *commedia dell'arte* troupes to the apprenticeships of Shakespeare's day and the beginnings of professional indoor theatre. Acting skills were passed from one actor to the next. The voice and the body's movements were developed in keeping with the size of the theatres and the visibility within them, in other words what the audience could hear and see. Following the conservatoire model of music schools in mainland Europe, formal theatre training found its place in the nineteenth century, and the notion of a general standard gained ground through the spread of the academy.

When Charles Flower published the prospectus for the new theatre in Stratford in 1875, he proposed establishing along with it a 'Dramatic Training School and College', thereby beginning Stratford's lengthy association with the idea of training and professional development. Ideas for an Academy of Acting or School of Dramatic Art at Stratford were discussed several times in the 1870s and 1880s but came to nothing, lack of funds apparently being the prime cause. In 1900, Stratford rejected the opportunity to create a training link with the Actors' Association, a forerunner of the actors' union Equity, though it was hoped something similar could happen in the future. Instead, the AA joined with Herbert Beerbohm Tree when he founded the Academy of Dramatic Art, which

subsequently became RADA. Stratford, however, did enjoy an association – albeit tangential – with a drama school; Frank Benson, director at
Stratford for more than thirty years who ran an apprentice system in his
company, employed the voice teacher Elsie Fogerty to coach his actors, and
from that collaboration she founded in 1906 the Central School of Speech
Training and Dramatic Art, later the Central School of Speech and Drama.
In 1914, Stratford hosted the first voice conference, which Fogerty helped
organise. Stratford's commitment to 'teaching, training and other educational activities, including the establishment and maintenance of a school
of acting' was reiterated in the Royal Charter of 1925. Anthony Quayle in
the early 1950s asked the Stratford governors to take over the Old Vic
School when it collapsed but they declined; although Fordham Flower was
in favour, neither his governing body nor that of the Old Vic wished for
closer links between the two rivals. Quayle also considered incorporating
RADA but made no progress and instead turned to George Devine to
run a school at Stratford, who left to take charge of the Royal Court.

The norm at Stratford in the 1950s was for leading actors to meet with
a specialist, usually in voice, on their own initiative. Directors did bring in
experts – mostly in voice and choreography – for particular productions.
As part of Hall's effort to build a company and a company spirit, he wanted
to give these disparate activities more coherence but also to make the RSC
a teaching and research institution in order to create the new type of actor,
comfortable in both classical and contemporary drama, he believed his
project required. It was a tall order. The raw material of the acting profession, he thought, fell broadly into three kinds: the old-fashioned, who lost
meaning in slow and sentimental delivery; the Noël Coward imitators,
who threw away meaning in the understatement of their charm and ease;
and the new wave with regional accents, who confused meaning with self-
expression. Drama schools were stuck teaching either technique without
inspiration or inspiration without technique; therefore in-house training
was required to make actors more versatile and more creative. Just as there
was suspicion of ensemble, there was also a widespread notion among
actors that once they had left drama school, further training was anathema. Musicians, ballet dancers and opera singers never ceased to improve
themselves, said Hall; why should actors be different?

## Verse

Hall did not wish to establish a formal theatre school but to organise
training and professional development as an organic part of the company's life, shaped by the needs of the work on stage. At first, therefore,

he would concentrate on verse (a shorthand to cover the speaking of Shakespeare's text). Until proper facilities could be introduced, this work had to be carried out in rehearsal alongside a programme of classes run by John Barton, who frequently used the sonnets for instruction. The aim of the classes was to bring consistency to the verse speaking, to make it light, swift and witty, and to use the form of the verse – its alliteration and antitheses, for example – to elucidate meaning through the imaginative creativity of each individual actor working in concert with the others. In his approach, Hall drew on the teachings of his Cambridge mentors Leavis and Rylands. Hall combined Leavis's spotlight on the meaning of the word with Rylands' spotlight on form, shape and rhythm. Rylands, who was influenced by the Renaissance revivalist William Poel, had shown Hall how he believed Shakespeare's verse should be spoken – in breathing, phrasing, line structure – and even how he believed it would have sounded in Shakespeare's day.[1] Hall later asked Edith Evans, whom Poel had directed as Cressida, to teach him everything Poel had taught her; it was an inheritance, she said, handed down from the great seventeenth-century actor Betterton through Garrick, Kean and Macready.

Hall also learned much from Barton, the parody of an absent-minded professor who, paradoxically, expounded on the pragmatic. Barton would point out that it was actors who created blank verse as a practical necessity because it worked; it was easier to get the breathing right with blank verse, it was easier to make it colloquial and irregular, and it was easier to learn than other forms available at the time. Those actors were given only their own parts and had no idea of the whole play; they rehearsed very quickly and performed the plays just a few times before moving on to the next one. Unsurprisingly, therefore, given the conditions of performance, Shakespeare's texts provide signals as when to go fast, when to go slow, when to pause or when to stress. But while Shakespeare gives the actor the shape, he does not give the reason – and that, according to Hall and Barton, is what the actor has to discover and deliver.

With a degree of youthful arrogance that overlooked the many fine speakers of Shakespeare who were working in the theatre, Hall felt that British actors did not understand the blank verse line. Either they believed the verse would take care of itself and the actor could concentrate on sense, or they ignored the sense and concentrated only on the verse. Hall insisted that *where* the actor breathed was the most important decision to take in speaking Shakespeare's verse, though in rehearsal he was less resolute. He clashed over this with Olivier, who believed an actor had to be able to say at least four lines in one breath. Hall, however, directed RSC actors to breathe in order to support meaning. They were not to take a breath in places where it was convenient for their own idiosyncratic sense of themselves but only at the end of a line or caesura. Hall recognised this was a danger in his approach, especially as in de-mystifying blank verse for the actor it was apparent that formally its requirements could be learnt very quickly.

So important was this aspect of the company's work that it came to stand for the ideology of the company. In choosing directors for his first season, for example, Hall excluded a strong candidate, Tony Richardson from the Royal Court, who had directed *Pericles* at Stratford in 1958 and *Othello* in 1959, because he told actors not to bother with the verse. Indeed, Hall considers his main achievement at the RSC not so much the creation of a company but the creation of a coherent verse-speaking style. It carried over into the RSC's modern work, most strikingly in the way in which Hall's productions of Harold Pinter's plays caught the music of his seemingly naturalistic texts. This reclamation of stage speaking was central to the 'relevance' of the company and its propulsion into the public arena, making theatre that allowed social values to be debated.

When Peter Brook returned to the company in 1970, he noticed the shortcomings of the new orthodoxy. He found the actors reluctant to experiment and sought security by their immersion in verse. Metrical exactitude had replaced dramatic meaning and the individuality of each character had become lost in a generalised rhythm that passed impersonally from one actor to the next. His emphasis was different. He found that stressing the words closed them. Instead he wanted the actor to be a medium for the word, to let the word colour the actor. He asked his cast to find the thought within the word and to expand the word from the inside. The impulse not the act was important. He challenged the separation of verse work and voice work. Both had technical aspects – for instance the former had meter, the latter, breathing and posture – but both were concerned with releasing meaning. That had always been the intention but not always the practice, and the two jostled to achieve harmony thereafter through the maze of the company's practical problems and the differences of approach of individual directors.

Hall knew his legacy would need overhauling. He recognised that the emotional temperature of stage speaking changes. Successive generations seemingly act more 'realistically' than their predecessors yet themselves become outdated within a decade or so. He was not surprised that the cool, rational style he had instigated gave way to a more romantic sweep under Trevor Nunn and Terry Hands, although they too had different emphases: Nunn focused on the individual actor and character detail, Hands on the tempo of the whole, letting the individual find his or her place within the overarching dynamic. Barton stayed true to the earlier aim but became more relaxed in its implementation while Hall – describing himself later as an iambic fundamentalist – became more punctilious, beating rhythm at rehearsals like a conductor. The RSC's verse work reached a wider public through practical workshops and a series of television programmes made by Barton in the 1980s.[2]

As the society moved from being a society of the word to being a society of the image, the consequent crisis in public language amid the proliferation of many private idioms posed acute problems for classical theatre. The psychological approach of film and television intensified the difficulties for the classical stage actor. In the 1980s the RSC responded by directing more energy into the paraphernalia of the visual than in refreshing its use of language. The actors, as a result, expended their energies on claiming their place in competition with the scenic effects. They had little strength left for listening to each other or for discovering and sharing in a contemporary way the various languages to be found within the plays, the prerequisite for the continuous need to rescue Shakespeare from his hijacking by high art into an exclusive club.

Noble's emphasis in the 1990s on the RSC being a classical company was partly a reaction to the company's lack of focus, partly a personal preference and partly a response to changes in the acting profession. Monetarist policies had undermined the system of public grants for drama schools, which at the same time had come to concentrate their efforts on the areas of expanding and dominant actor employment, namely television and film. Noble considered that actors coming from drama schools were less well equipped to handle Shakespeare's verse than before, and that this decline was a mirror of wider social change.[3] He felt there had been a loss in society of the love of language and therefore a loss of power, as command of language was command of ideas; ideas gave access to value and without value there was no democracy. He made verse speaking a priority. All RSC actors had to be acquainted with what he called the 'plumbing' of verse, the full characteristics of a line and how to read the text. He acknowledged that in the end it was the actors' choice but he did not want that choice to be made from ignorance. However, the sources on which he drew to find meaning in the verse and revitalise its delivery became so narrow and fixed that he moved the company in the opposite direction to his original intention. For example, a renewed public interest in verse as exemplified by the popularity of rap was not properly exploited. The company found it was not speaking to and with society but like a parent with a recalcitrant child, at and for society. Like the child, society was not listening.

## The Studio

When Hall first ran Stratford he could only find space for ad hoc verse classes but was always aiming to place training on a broader and more consistent base. Inspired by the example of the Moscow Art Theatre, which opened its Studio in 1912, Hall invited Michel Saint-Denis to take charge of training at the RSC as a member of the ruling triumvirate. His position in the history of British theatre training was already secure from his leadership of the pre-war London Theatre Studio and the post-war Old Vic School. With the creation of the Studio under Saint-Denis in 1962, Hall extended the scope of company-wide professional inquiry and stole a march on the incipient NT, the director of which, Laurence Olivier, was famously an enthusiast of Saint-Denis. The move was typical of Hall's buccaneering spirit.

'An actor [sic] should be a craftsman,' Hall wrote, 'but his pride in his craft should not block a quest for new expression. This quest is the basic purpose of our Studio.'[4] It would be a workshop where artists in the company could improve their craft, a place where they could get to know each other's working habits without the pressure of public performance and a means to mould the company into a more closely knit ensemble. For Saint-Denis, the Studio was a continuation of his lifetime's work, which he saw as 'an experiment directed towards the discovery of all the means by which reality can be given to fiction on the stage'.[5] He believed in the company's mission to make contact with a new generation of artists and audiences, to reconnect Shakespeare to the contemporary world.

> You can't force a contemporary meaning. But your approach must be rooted in your daily life . . . it is impossible to separate oneself from one's period without danger of death. So from your contemporary attitude you look objectively at the play's meaning, and respect its style. Then, if there is anything there that means something for your own period, it will appear naturally, unforced, in your production.[6]

For Stratford and Shakespeare to make greater impact on the young, production and acting had increasingly to possess the qualities of 'truthfulness, simplicity, directness and vigour which are demanded by the young'.[7] He called for a compromise between the demands of the present and the values of the past, which in Britain had become divorced in the name of reason and through suspicion of the lyrical. Truth had to be stripped to the bone, and revealed not concealed.

Hall shared his analysis of the problems of contemporary British acting, arrived at from the perspective of his long career. Too many actors lacked presence and acted only down to the shoulders yet, ironically, were motivated by non-intellectual forms of expression. They were not interested in physical movement, and they separated speech from movement. He blamed an excessive concentration on one particular interpretation of Stanislavsky's Method, which he thought would have appalled Stanislavsky, wherein actors were encouraged to create and perform a sub-text instead of recreating the whole part. To counter this, Saint-Denis intended to put actors into a state of improvisation, by training their voice, movement, dancing and verse acting. In terms similar to those Brook used later, Saint-Denis said an actor must be like a glove, open and flexible, but flat. By degrees the text penetrates the actor and brings the actor to life – the text, in other words, animates the glove, which is the actor's blood, nerves, breathing system and voice.

In a manifesto for the Studio, which he wrote in 1962, Saint-Denis put cross-fertilisation at the centre of his work. The highest form of traditional expression in the modern theatre was Shakespeare, recognised globally as having the greatest contemporary value from the point of view of meaning as well as form. Of the other great styles – Greek, Far Eastern, Spanish, Italian, French – Shakespeare was the only one to survive as a commercial attraction, with a popular character and of international importance. However, he had to be understood in relation to his time. He was not alone; unfortunately, the English had neglected most of their Elizabethan heritage except Shakespeare and, with him, only occasionally escaped 'pitfalls of routine, operatic artificiality or intellectual whimsicality'.[8] To renew Shakespearean production with much more daring in a way that was true for both actors and audience required 'study, understanding and appreciation of style, considered as a reality in itself'. The main purpose of the Studio was, therefore, 'to evolve the ways and means to find out the kind of work and to conduct the experiments through which a contemporary way of producing Shakespeare and the Elizabethans – and perhaps other styles, as a consequence – can be prepared'.

He also outlined the material requirements of the Studio and the type of experimental and training work he would undertake there, all of which proved to be over-ambitious. He was asking for an amphitheatre-shaped space, lighting and sound, storage, workshops for costumes, props, masks, and painting, studios for voice, movement and rehearsal work, dressing rooms and an auditorium for 200 people.

Work was to be based on freedom and collaboration, confidence and interest in progress and experiment, organisation and discipline. It would be divided into the technical (movement, dance, acrobatics, wrestling, fights; voice, diction, singing; playing of simple stage instruments) and the exploration of acting (improvisation with and without masks, theoretical and practical work on varied styles, discussion of Elizabethan and all modern theatre currents). Understudy work would also be organised through the Studio. The Studio would produce scenes from Shakespeare and the Elizabethans; poetry, singing, dancing; and selected pieces from Far Eastern theatre, Brecht, and modern dramatists. It would experiment with space and the actor–audience relationship, a strand of inquiry close to Hall's heart because both RSC stages were unsuitable for Shakespeare and weakened the impact of the company's work. This added a further responsibility to the actor's load and made training all the more important.

The Studio was to be open to all company actors on a voluntary basis, though all were expected to attend some sessions, which were 'called' like rehearsals. The plan was also to select a group of actors who had just completed drama school, and this occurred three years later. Tutors were drawn from specialist instructors and RSC personnel, including senior actors. Saint-Denis and his wife Suria Magito taught mask work, Clifford Williams acrobatics and acting verse, Gillian Alford voice, Denne Gilkes singing (in her own studio in the High Street), Molly Kenny movement, John Barton fencing, sword fighting, prosody and poetics, and Maurice Jones also taught fencing. Senior actors such as Tony Church, Hugh Sullivan, Ian Holm and Clifford Rose took tutorials on topics like make-up and verse. RSC staff gave talks on their role within the company. Visiting directors contributed too (for example, John Blatchley, who had worked with Saint-Denis and went on to co-found the Drama Centre). Saint-Denis had Williams as his assistant, mainly because he spoke fluent French, was a trained mime and was not central to Hall's directorial plans, and Abd'elkader Farrah as the Studio designer. Farrah had worked with Saint-Denis as head of the theatrical design course at Centre National Dramatique de l'Est (National Theatre School), Strasbourg, since 1955, and came with him to London to design his productions of Stravinsky's *Oedipus Rex* at Sadler's Wells and *The Cherry Orchard* for the RSC. In 1963, Saint-Denis hired as his administrator a Canadian stage manager Sandy Black, who had taught on the technical course at Strasbourg. Kaye Flanagan, who had served as secretary to artistic directors since Barry Jackson in 1946, carried out his secretarial work. The Studio was made possible by a grant given over three years from the Calouste Gulbenkian

Foundation, which took a particular interest in training and also gave money to the Royal Court for its workshops.

The Studio was meticulously planned, though the reality did not always live up to the proposals because of the demands, known and unforeseen, of the company's working life. A timetable of tutorials was devised and adjustments made to the curriculum during the preparations. Actors were divided into two groups for timetable purposes and for the rehearsals of two Studio projects, Brecht's *The Exception and the Rule* to be directed by Saint-Denis, and an excerpt from Marlowe's *Dr Faustus*, to be directed by Williams. A course of individual and group tuition ran while rehearsals were still taking place, but the real work of the Studio began after the last play of the season had opened, culminating in a 'flare-up' when the project work was shown to other members of the company.

In 1962, the final productions happened to be *King Lear* and *The Comedy of Errors* – two iconic shows. There was a terrific spirit in the company when the Studio began its four weeks of work that November in the Conference Hall (converted for hiring in 1933 from the shell of the original theatre after the fire). Space problems in the Hall became immediately apparent; Farrah and Williams needed accommodation and had to move into the stage management room as the *King Lear* production occupied all the other available space. A room in the theatre and the circle bar were also used.

A committee representing the actors was set up and met after the first week's activities. The younger actors were irritated. They had a feeling that their understudy work had not been properly noted and that they had been passed over in selection for the projects. Older actors agreed with their younger colleagues and were also worried by the burdens of extra work at the end of the season when they felt fatigue more keenly and were preoccupied with domestic and personal arrangements for leaving Stratford at the season's close. The senior actors also wondered if they were going to put more into the Studio – their presence was used to obtain financial support – than they would get out. As a result, the *Faustus* project was opened to everyone who was not participating in the Brecht project and the timetable was eased. Other adjustments to the timetable as well as suggestions for more input from the actors were proposed and accepted. It was agreed to experiment with actors choosing their own times for tutorials, subject to tutors' availability. The main plea was for thirty minutes' movement and voice work before rehearsals began but Alford was unable to meet the demand and access to the stage for voice sessions was always problematic.

When the company moved to London to rehearse the 1963 season, Studio sessions continued at the Donmar, Covent Garden, with a particular emphasis on training for new members, though much to Saint-Denis's disquiet, rehearsals frequently interrupted the work. Extra premises were sought – including the YMCA and YWCA – but such an expansion could not be sustained financially and some tutorials had to be held in dressing rooms at the Aldwych.

Premises were also an issue in Stratford in the wake of the experience of the Conference Hall. It was agreed that four rooms would be used in property the company owned not far from the theatre at Avonside to the south of Holy Trinity Church. A hired tent for classes and tutorials requiring larger space would be erected on the Avonside lawn from April to August. The tent would also be available for rehearsals but as a second priority to the Studio. The RSC governors agreed that a permanent studio space that would also be used for understudy work should be built in the Paddock in Southern Lane along with new scenic workshops and upgraded premises for the wardrobe department. A backup location was also identified, should the Paddock scheme fail. Since 1954 the Paddock had been the home of the hire wardrobe department in a small wooden hut built by the theatre's workshop staff. The RSC was denied planning permission and an alternative scheme – to build a temporary studio alongside the costume store in the Paddock – was approved in early 1965. A large corrugated aluminium shed was erected and, as happens with temporary structures, remained until 1989, becoming The Other Place in 1974.[9]

The first Studio programme in 1962 saw the involvement of approximately four-fifths of the season's total acting company. The 1963 programme saw participation rise to five-sixths and the 'flare-up' expand too, ranging from Chekhov, Brecht, Sophocles and Genet to a dance-drama improvisation, a Lorca project and songs from a choral group. In 1964 the company became larger, directors' availability for Studio work became scarcer, and the 'flare-up' consequently consisted of more and shorter excerpts, sometimes using company actors as directors. The more than thirty showings covered an enormous theatrical range, from ancient Greek and Roman drama to texts by Arnold Wesker and Harold Pinter as well as non-dramatic material, such as a John Donne sermon, to explore greater appreciation of the use of language. Under John Barton, who assumed leadership of the Studio because of Saint-Denis's ill health, the 1965 'flare-up' focused on Greek experience – science, religion, dialogues, cosmology, philosophy – and earned the tin hut where it took place the sobriquet 'The Greek Faculty' as distinct from the Conference Hall, which was known as 'The Verse Faculty'. Barton's Greek investigations subsequently led, among other things, to his twin grand projects, *The Greeks* and *Tantalus*.

As the Studio's activities grew, they placed greater strains on limited resources. Despite Saint-Denis's lucid aims, the lack of a company-wide agreed purpose for the Studio, a clear place within the organisation, and direct impact on productions made the Studio vulnerable.[10] Saint-Denis's poor health prompted the company to cancel plans to build a permanent Studio theatre, for which the RSC was preparing to raise money. The following year, 1966, when he had ceased to be active, the company's response to its first major financial crisis since securing public subsidy included closing the Studio.

The Studio in its original form may have run its course but some of the ideas that lay behind it survived. Its legacy can be seen in Theatregoround, which made its headquarters in the tin hut in the year of the Studio's demise; in The Other Place, which, in its second, updated, version acknowledged this debt when a rehearsal room was named after Saint-Denis; in the RSC's workshop programme; in the Academy under Declan Donnellan; in the RSC's education work; and in the RSC's various and diverse 'extra-curricular' activities, including the RSC Youth and Fringe festivals and the *Not the RSC* seasons run by the actors.

Generally, the Studio seems to have been welcomed as an important element of Stratford campus life. There was a tension between its role in professional training and as an experimental laboratory, and it was not always successful in serving the company's different needs. Senior actors did participate but several put in only token appearances so as not to cause offence. Young and less occupied actors liked the Studio because it gave them much appreciated extra work and acted as a showcase, despite intentions to the contrary. Others found it a distraction from the main business of the company, which was already overstretched. There were even those who resisted it as a 'foreign' idea that did not fit with the English way of doing things, though they seem to have been in a minority.

For Saint-Denis, the Studio had been his reason for joining the RSC, more so even than his advisory artistic role or his directorial work. He turned down the directorship of New York's Lincoln Center to set up the Studio but his high expectations were soon dashed. He became increasingly frustrated at the inability of the company to provide the promised support for the Studio. The practical problems of integrating the Studio into the company's working life had become more not less acute and, despite the rhetoric, it enjoyed only a low priority within the burgeoning

RSC empire. He could understand budgetary limitations and difficulties over premises but not the disruption to his carefully considered programme caused by production-specific problems and the effects of crisis management. Mostly it was actors who were taken away but in 1963 Farrah was laid off when Hall cleared the decks for *The Wars of the Roses* and Saint-Denis's production of *Squire Puntilla and His Servant Matti* was postponed. These strains were felt within the triumvirate. Hall and Brook pursued their own projects and did not find the time to make real their avowed commitment to the Studio. Saint-Denis retained tenuous links with the company as a consultant director until his death in 1971. During this period he worked on a book on training, which was edited by Suria Saint-Denis and published posthumously in 1981 as *Training for the Theatre*.

## Peter Brook

The contrast with Brook's internal experimental work was a further problem for the company's acceptance of Saint-Denis and the Studio, although it is a mark of the vitality of the early RSC that it was able to embrace both. Members of the triumvirate led both strands, and both shared a similar desire to confront the complacency of British acting by searching for a style of expression rooted in the totality of the actor's craft. One, however, was allied to the general philosophy of the company and designed to engender company spirit, the other was particular to that director's need and through productions challenged the direction the company was taking. One was open to all, the other closed to all except the group hand-picked by the director. One was hampered by financial constraint and the demands of the company it served, the other was free to explore as it wished. One was led by a man who had completed his own journey, whereas the other was led by a man who was still constantly questioning. Unlike Saint-Denis, Brook did not compromise, got what he wanted, and made a splash. He used private explorations to make public impact through renowned RSC productions that were indispensable to the definition of the company while simultaneously offering a critique of the theatrical practice underlying the company's work.

As befits the child of a scientific background, Brook's entire career had been a restless experiment. Since his first Stratford production, of *Love's Labour's Lost* in 1946, when he realised that reducing rehearsal to achieving pre-planned ideas led to deadly theatre, he had been placing greater importance on discovery in rehearsal. Yet during the rehearsal for his first RSC production, *King Lear*, he witnessed the reluctance among the actors to improvise – or to view improvisation as anything more than a game. His frustration with his own work and that of the actors grew during the following year, his busiest yet. He felt that, unlike in Shakespeare's day, there was no collective endeavour that could produce a new and common theatrical language. His response was to propose to Hall that he stage the British première of Genet's *The Screens*, written in response to the Algerian war and almost certain to be banned in Britain as deeply offensive to France, one of its closest allies. Brook, however, did not believe that British actors, whose training prepared them for character development, would be able to meet the stylistic demands Genet made. Brook resolved to form a laboratory group that would be capable of presenting *The Screens* in private to the censor and, hopefully, pave the way for a production at the Aldwych.

Despite pressure from within the governing body to resist Brook's blandishments, Hall insisted that the RSC, now Arts Council funded, should provide the conditions for Brook to continue. With Fordham Flower's backing, the company supported three months' work by ten actors, who received roughly two-fifths of a full company member's rate. The research project was mostly paid for by a Gulbenkian grant. The RSC regarded the venture as integral to its overall programme and central to its next London season, which would celebrate Shakespeare's 400th anniversary by offering a contemporary counterpoint.

With Charles Marowitz, who had been his assistant on *King Lear*, Brook was able to form what was known as the Royal Shakespeare Company Experimental Group. Marowitz had come to England from America to study, had run actor training programmes, directed and was a contributor to and co-editor of the important theatre magazine *Encore*. In assembling the group, Brook and Marowitz used audition techniques new to the RSC and to British theatre – a group of actors working together for at least an hour using improvisation and role switching. All but one was aged under thirty, and the average age was twenty-four. Sally Jacobs was the group's designer; she had come from the Royal Court to design two shows in the RSC's Arts Theatre season.

Hall courageously had agreed that the work, which had no model in Britain, could be undertaken without the pressure of a public outcome. Brook always hoped his practical research would to lead to a public airing, even if the nature of that outcome was not known at the outset, otherwise for him the project would have been incomplete. In fact, after two months of private discovery, the group presented for five weeks as work in progress a public showing in the new theatre at the London Academy of Music and Drama (LAMDA) in west London under the title *Theatre of Cruelty*.

In his approach Brook was influenced by the experimental work he had seen on tour with *King Lear* in the Soviet Union and Poland, by the non-scripted work and happenings he had seen in the US, and by the writings of Antonin Artaud, from which the much misunderstood title of the project derived. For Artaud, *Theatre of Cruelty* meant an unflinching confrontation of what it is to be human in order to restore theatre to its deepest human need. The emphasis for Brook was placed on what happened when words were taken away, because the concept of communication had become synonymous with the word, especially in a text-based company like the RSC. The programme, which varied from performance to performance, included short plays, among them Artaud's *Spurt of Blood*, sketches, a collage *Hamlet*, mimes, demonstration pieces, improvisations and debates with the audience.

Brook's desire to find a committed theatre that transcended polemics and didacticism was best expressed in *The Public Bath*, a sketch he devised with Glenda Jackson. Brook saw a correspondence between the worlds of the modern heroine – the recently bereaved Jackie Kennedy – and the modern villainess, the vilified prostitute Christine Keeler, whose liaison with War Minister John Profumo had accelerated the decline of the Conservative government. The sketch was based on *The Times* report of Keeler's trial and used the same words in relation to both women. Jackson entered to nightclub music from above the audience, dressed in the archetypal uniform of Keeler's trade – body-clinging black dress, black stockings and high heels. A judge recited over her and men begged for sex as she was led down to the floor of the theatre where she was placed in a metal bath. Without seductiveness she stripped naked. When she stepped out she was re-clothed in shapeless prison garments, thick stockings and clumsy shoes. She knelt by the bath, which became a coffin, and was now Jackie Kennedy. The music had changed to a funeral march. The men offered condolences as the coffin was carried away. The sketch, which by the standards of the time was considered shocking, became emblematic of the decade and has been celebrated as an event in its own right.

For Brook, these 'shots in the dark', as he called the season, were studies in technique, the necessary precursor to a new, expressive theatre but not that theatre itself.[11] He was challenging the traditional notion of authorship that was dominant in the 'art' theatre but also the fashion for self-expression, and was wary of replacing the actor's shallowness in using the word by a banality in using anti-naturalistic devices. Brook was asking actors to do the opposite of what they would usually be asked in the RSC: not to add character but to strip it away. By exertion of his implacable will, he believed that he was freeing actors from directorial imposition; he was training them to become untrained. This paradox led to tensions within the group. Glenda Jackson, for instance, led the others to demand that both directors join in the exercises but they declined. She also spoke out against Saint-Denis being invited to work on masks with the group because the purpose was to discover what could be expressed without extraneous props. He was asked to leave, which was ironic as this was the aspect of his work about which Brook was most interested to learn.

The experiment divided opinion within the RSC; enthusiasm was matched by scepticism and antipathy from those who smelled a whiff of pious superiority. Brook was aware that some of the work remained trivial and even conventional and much remained locked far away from the popular impulse invoked in the search for comparison with the first Elizabethans. Marowitz's radical *Hamlet* collage, for instance, meant little if the audience were not already familiar with the non-deconstructed version, and this was seen as a reinforcement of Shakespeare's capture by the elite not his liberation. Others welcomed the exercise as a valuable corrective.

If justification were needed for the RSC publicly backing theatre research, it came shortly afterwards. As intended, Brook expanded the group in order to rehearse the first dozen scenes of *The Screens* in readiness for a presentation to the censor, who, as anticipated, had deemed the play unsuitable for licence. Two performances were given at the Donmar rehearsal space. There was no stage but at one end of the room a set consisting of three mobile white screens, which the actors coloured with paint during the action. The Lord Chamberlain remained adamant that *The Screens* would not receive a licence. Instead of proceeding with a club performance as the RSC had done previously at the Arts Theatre – an experiment Brook considered safe – he abandoned the Genet production and chose to direct *Marat/Sade*. It was a theatrical *tour de force* that borrowed from both the political theatre and the Theatre of the Absurd, losing the commitment of the former in return for an aesthetic engagement of deep and wild potency that gloried in its own achievement. The production, which could not have been achieved without the preliminary research of the *Theatre of Cruelty*, ran for 144 performances on its transfer to New York where audiences saw in it the trauma of the Vietnam War. This reception convinced Brook in his inclination to research a play about how to respond to that conflict.

Despite the preparation of the *Theatre of Cruelty* season, and the participation in *Marat/Sade* of actors from that season, Brook had found the rehearsal time inadequate for the task. For the devised Vietnam project, Hall agreed to allow him what in Britain was the unheard of luxury of postponing a decision on the outcome until two-thirds of the way through rehearsal, which itself was more than double the time the RSC allotted a regular Shakespeare production. Having directed *Le Vicaire* (*The Representative*) and *The Investigation*, two plays that touch on the Holocaust, he was sharply aware of the problems of presenting horrific events. He knew he had to continue training his actors as well as himself if they were to measure up to the enormity of Vietnam. There was input from a number of quarters into what became known as *US* ('us' and America). A third of his new group were 'veterans' of *Theatre of Cruelty* and/or *Marat/Sade*: seven actors, the designer Sally Jacobs, the poet playwright Adrian Mitchell and the American composer Richard Peaslee. Albert Hunt and Geoffrey Reeves became associate directors, the writers Charles Wood and Dennis Cannan were involved at different stages, and Mike Stott and Michael Kustow joined as documentary advisers. There was also present at one moment or another a raft of experts and sympathisers, from war correspondents and historians to a Chinese theatre specialist, a Vietnamese Buddhist monk, the writer Susan Sontag and director Joe Chaikin.

Rehearsals initially were indistinguishable from research, and the quest was more important than the failures of the results. The first phase took place – bizarrely, given the content of the work – in the ballroom of the department store Bourne and Hollingsworth. The work was broad-ranging and loosely structured, and started Brook on his transcultural journey that was to take him to *The Mahabharata* years later. The actors were taught how a Vietnamese peasant might undertake everyday tasks, like cooking rice or sweeping the hut and, through improvisatory exercises, they found a way to present the self-immolation of protesting monks and a Quaker priest.

Brook moved to the Donmar rehearsal rooms for the second phase. The Polish director Jerzy Grotowski and one of the leading actors in his group, Ryszard Cieslak, narrowed down the focus and introduced the actors to a quasi-religious way of working they had never encountered: intense, personal and painful. Each actor was confronted in a series of exercises with a harsh self-scrutiny of what it meant to be an actor. The actors underwent tests designed to expose both their untapped personal resources and the accretions – psychological and theatrical – that were blocking access to those resources. Grotowski wore dark glasses and spoke in French, with Brook translating, both of which made Grotowski seem more remote and forbidding. The process was a genuine culture shock, even down to Grotowski's insistence on having the floor so clean that 'it could be kissed'.[12]

The problem of the ethics of what was being presented on stage had its counterpart in the ethics of the research practice. At what point, for example, did the necessary personal confrontation become unacceptably oppressive? Grotowski spent a whole day in a battle of wills with Jackson, who told Brook that if this treatment – 'a dehumanising waste of time' – went on, she would leave. Brook and Grotowski relented. Brook acknowledged the difficulties his 'retraining' would cause and constantly invited people to leave if they wished, but no one did.

A third phase allowed the group to switch back to the subject of the piece and prepare for Hall a rudimentary performance of the first half, accompanied by a reading of the second. The decision was taken to proceed, and Brook continued the questioning up to and beyond opening night: costumes were scrapped, the set changed, and lines were cut alongside those alterations that had to be agreed in order to gain a licence from the Lord Chamberlain.

Brook was moving in the direction that would take him away from Britain to his international research centre in Paris where he could control the entire theatrical process. By the time of *A Midsummer Night's Dream* in 1970, his heart lay across the Channel. His experiences in Stratford that year confirmed for him the rightness of his move. Rehearsal for the production was again a form of retraining, although he began with a text. He was not surprised to find the actors generally lacked creativity because the company did not provide the training he had hoped in the early 1960s it might. It had failed to build an ensemble and to ensure a consistent development of technical skill and imagination, both of which were essential for a thorough re-evaluation of Shakespeare.

Hall had supported Brook's magpie research work not only on merit but also because it would offer a bracing shock to the company. The work was pivotal in Brook's own development. He used his RSC experiences in writing the series of lectures that became the seminal book *The Empty Space* but, apart from helping to establish the company's reputation, he changed the company itself very little. Although future RSC directors may have aspired to his achievements, and a few, such as Buzz Goodbody and Katie Mitchell, may have been inspired by his example to alter the way they worked, his research methods did not influence RSC practice and can be more clearly seen to have affected others groups such as Theatre of Complicite. For the RSC, cost became a major factor in this neglect of research but also a belief that Brook was an exception.

Brook's research had been posing the same 'non-English' questions that Saint-Denis in the Studio had been asking: Why make theatre? How can theatre express the reality of the world of which it is a dynamic part?

Is it possible to develop a method that can deal with all kinds of play equally truthfully, Shakespeare as well as Chekhov, Molière as well as Pinter? Brook, like Saint-Denis, was exploring the stage space and the relationship between actor and audience. But Brook was also questioning the whole procedure of theatre: the way it is produced and the way it is received, beginning with the actors' training. The Stratford and Aldwych theatres remained part of the problem, yet it was the very fact that his productions took place *there* that gave them cultural weight. Similarly, he believed that culture showed audiences important images of their lives and yet protected audiences from thinking about the issues that gave rise to those images. By trying to penetrate that cultural shield, he was strengthening it. As Shakespeare is the ultimate mainstay of that shield, his paradox was a microcosm of the RSC's dilemma.

## Voice

One area of company life that Brook did heavily influence through his example was its voice work. Voice has always been central to the actor's craft. In the nineteenth century, elocution came to the fore because of the scale of the auditoria in which the actors had to perform and a class-based interest in 'good diction' consolidated a 'desirable' accent in what was coined as Received Pronunciation (RP). RP, with its passive tense, revealed the age-old link between voice and social power, and was itself modified as the balance of power and social habit altered.

When Hall founded the RSC, Clifford Turner, a formal and besuited teacher at RADA, represented the prevailing orthodoxy. He promoted RP and emphasised vocal mechanics and the creation of resonance. The principles were based on singing and were a part of the elocution tradition, which did not concern itself with meaning. Stratford had no overall voice policy, although it did have its own voice 'institution', in the form of Denne Gilkes, who was a singer and 'mother' figure to many of the actors. Her studio was situated at her home in the High Street where actors were also lodgers. Hall wanted to break with the RP tradition and invited Iris Warren from LAMDA to lead whole company voice sessions, which she did at weekends. Warren, who had taught under Saint-Denis, aimed to free the actor into the voice rather than train the voice in the actor. She stressed the importance of imagination and vocal play and used techniques associated with the movement teacher Rudolph Laban. Although Warren emphasised the importance of the actor finding his or her own voice, she was still seen as dealing with voice production while 'meaning' was taken care of under the verse-speaking rubric of Barton and Hall.

At the Studio under Saint-Denis there was still a technical approach. Gillian Alford led the main company activity – Warren died in 1963 – while Saint-Denis himself did speech work. He believed voice to be the most difficult aspect of actor training and thought that, because the voice changes over the years as one's body changes, an actor should never stop training her or his voice. Although he was criticised for separating the voice work from acting, he did in fact take a holistic view and stressed the inter-relationship of all the disciplines, a position that was unfashionable for most of his life. He sought to develop a correlation between the senses, and especially between speech and movement, before examining the use of words. He was very keen to explore the physical aspects of speech and wanted voice work to be fun. He disliked exercises for their own sake devoid of theatrical justification, and to encourage playfulness used non-dramatic material, such as Bible passages, newspapers extracts or even recipes. His classes dealt with diction, modulation, rhythm and vocal imagination, which he considered the most important. He was particularly concerned to encourage spontaneity in order to overcome mechanical qualities, which he found common among actors working on Shakespeare who were too conscious of technique.

In 1969 Trevor Nunn hired Cicely Berry on a part-time basis, primarily to cope with the problem actors were having in filling the space of the Stratford theatre. In the profession large-scale classical work was in decline. Actors were increasingly losing their stage voices in the dominant and naturalistic world of film and television. At the same time improvements in technology, especially in the music industry but also in the world of film and television, changed audiences' expectations. Unlike at the time when the Royal Shakespeare Theatre was built in the 1930s, audiences now expected to be able to hear everything with the same clarity wherever they sat in the auditorium. This demand pushed the RSC's voice work toward volume control, and this in turn tended to produce an RSC 'voice'. Actors – and directors – wanted to avoid this but the popular 'reality' voice suitable for the small or large screen was equally of little use. While Berry fulfilled the technical role implied in her invitation, she was also becoming aware through her work with Brook that the company was facing not a technical problem but an artistic one. From Brook she learned that to speak words should alter the actor, and she began her journey towards integrating voice and meaning.

When Nunn made her head of voice in 1970, based in Dressing Room 11, the RSC became the first company to have a permanent, full-time voice department. There had been, and continued to be, much discussion on the merits of having a head of artistic departments. There was a head of music and a literary manager and briefly a head of design, a post that did not work out. (Designers often had multiple concurrent contracts and proved difficult to co-ordinate.) Movement had also proved troublesome. Norman Ayrton and John Broome had taken company movement classes and other choreographers had worked on individual productions. Broome was briefly head of movement but had no dedicated space, which implied to him that the company was more interested in the word than the body. The associate directors, who held conflicting approaches to movement, could not agree on a single choreographer or movement teacher whom everyone could accept on a long-term basis. In voice it was different, and personality played its part here too. Berry had an openness combined with a sharp determination that allowed her to work with all kinds of directors and actors. Her dedication to the work, her intellectual liveliness, her sense of mischief and her abiding concern for the interests of actors made her an enormously popular figure in the company.

Berry, who teaches internationally and whose philosophy is contained in several practical books as well as a video about her, had studied at the Central School of Speech and Drama during the war. After two years' teaching in schools she returned there as a teacher and later opened her own studio in Drury Lane. She had always been keen on poetry but had not worked on Shakespeare until she came to the RSC, where she made voice work catch up with contemporary acting and texts. She learned a great deal working not only with Brook but with Nunn, Hands and Barton and at The Other Place with Goodbody and the young directors, producing the plays of challenging writers like Bond and Rudkin. She became a central figure in the development, education and extra-mural work of the company and in 1988 also directed *King Lear*, a production that directly transferred her voice work to the stage and was accompanied by open sessions on language with the audience, cast members and play-wright in residence Liz Lochhead.

Fashions of speech change and actors have constantly to adjust the balance between naturalism and rhetoric, between the ordinary and the extravagant, 'entering,' as Berry puts it, 'the fullness of the image yet not sounding false or melodramatic'.[13] The RSC saw its work as having a public air, and, without obscuring or avoiding meaning, the music within the language was integral to that. This did not mean the actors were being superficial or the audience passive. It was what the audience came to hear, she believed, and they would have felt cheated if it were not there. Voice work was not a matter of obtaining fuller volume and better diction but of engaging with the language itself. Berry developed simple exercises to connect the actor to words in a spontaneous way, to feel the substance of words and not just the literal meaning. She linked finding the emotional truth of the character in the language to the technical difficulties of theatre: size of auditorium, volume and clarity. She also had to be sensitive to the demands of the different directors. She had to help actors respond to the method of a particular director while keeping true to the actor's own way into the play. There was always a tension between the artistic and technical requirements because meaning was seen as the director's province. Actors look to the voice department to repair vocal damage but also to unblock them. Directors look to the department to service their production and some baulk at allowing the voice department to play a greater role than 'warming up' the actors and solving vocal problems when they arise. The size of the company in the late 1980s and the greater turnover of directors in the 1990s under Noble made it difficult to maintain the right conditions for voice work. It became harder for the voice people to get to know the actors, continuity was dissipated and the pressure to become volume controllers returned.

## The Other Place

The RSC voice department, an important conduit for leading figures in the voice world, hosted 'Theatre Voice '92', the first international conference for theatre voice teachers. It was held at the new Other Place, one of five major projects organised there that year alongside a directors' course, an exploration of language with the Asian company Tara Arts, a workshop on Derek Walcott's *The Odyssey* and a residency from the Polish group Gardzienice. This ambitious programme was a result of Noble's change in policy to formalise and enhance The Other Place's non-production activities. He put the former education head Tony Hill in charge with a brief 'to develop the skills of our artists and to establish The Other Place as a focus for regional and international training in theatre arts'.[14] To accommodate this emphasis, the number of productions presented was to be reduced, and this altered the context for both sets of activities. With the benefit of a good research and development budget, The Other Place provided an attractive range of high-quality activities, which offered opportunities to develop expertise and brought the RSC into contact with different theatre practices from Britain and abroad. The workshops, whether led by the British director Mike Alfreds, the Russian director Mikhail Mokeev or Graeae, Britain's first professional theatre group for disability, ran alongside the company's sonnet classes and The Other Place's familiar mix of complementary and extra-curricular activity.

The company used its workshop programme to question its own practices. The invitation to Tara Arts recognised the RSC's isolation from the currents of cultural diversity in Britain and to Gardzienice the continuing weakness of physical training for British actors both in general and specifically at Stratford. For Gardzienice, which takes its name from a small and remote Polish village where it is based, ensemble theatre is a way of life. The physical environment the members inhabit is a decisive inspiration, and they can spend from two to five years creating a piece of work. In an attempt to fuse two contrasting ways of working and to develop an organic relationship out of the three visits that the group eventually made to Stratford, the RSC paired Gardzienice and playwright Howard Brenton with a view to producing a piece for the RSC. The different approaches, however, turned out to be incompatible and the association between the two companies ended.

Incompatibility also featured in the invitation to Edward Bond to run a workshop with Cicely Berry in 1992. The RSC had been performing Bond's plays since Howard Davies directed *Bingo* at The Other Place in 1976. In 1988 he acknowledged that he would 'disappear' in England without the RSC's productions, though the debt was mutual: his work formed a crucial part of the RSC's mid-1970s regeneration.[15] The relationship, however, was strained. The RSC rejected *The Worlds* and he prevented the company from producing *The Human Cannon* on more than one occasion. The stress became public during the staging of *The War Plays* trilogy, which he co-directed, when he withdrew after the first two plays had opened. After the RSC production of *Restoration*, in which he described the acting as superficial, he called the company a 'vulgar mess'.[16] In this it was not alone. Bond was equally scathing about the National and the Royal Court, the other two theatres that had been the cradle of his work. Bond believed there had been a radical change in the functioning of human consciousness since Brecht's time and that consequently the purpose and character of performance and of text had also changed radically. The establishment theatre had not adjusted to this change. Through his own productions and workshops he was attempting to develop new ways of acting that met the new demands on actors that his plays made. Although he was given only three weeks instead of the four he had asked for, he proceeded with the RSC workshop as part of that attempt.[17]

Like Brook, Bond was concerned to untrain actors, in this case in relation to Shakespeare and his own plays. He believed the RSC had become 'anti-Shakespeare', making tragic tensions benign and inconsequential, and he sought to rectify this through his concept of Theatre

Eventing. This respects the structure of a play but re-organises the experience of it in order to produce alternative meanings derived from a re-examination of the play's story. Bond took excerpts from Shakespeare, his own plays and a Lorca poem to work with the actors on separating imagination from emotion. Bond explained he was not averse to emotion but believed actors must develop emotional responses that went beyond simply showing the character was being emotional. The route to this was through the actors' imagination and by being conscious not of characterisation but of themselves as individuals. He challenged the idea of making a play 'work' as a substitute for analysing its structure – a fault he laid at the door of the RSC. The nine actors seemed to have found the workshop stimulating, if perplexing. Bond, despite his pointed views of the company, was keen to run more workshops but only if the company's artistic director expressed some sympathy for the ideas he was exploring. The world was too interesting, he wrote to Noble, 'to waste time being shown round it by a medieval estate agent'.[18] There were no more Bond workshops.

Another chance for RSC actors to confront the foundation of their craft and their practice of it at the RSC came through the visit in 1997 of Augusto Boal, one of the most influential directors of the latter part of the twentieth century but working in a field far removed from that of the RSC.[19] He also was invited by Berry, who had worked with him in Brazil. His international reputation had been built first as the creator of the 'theatre of the oppressed', which aimed to turn passive spectators into protagonists, and subsequently as the exponent of the 'rainbow of desire', theatre techniques that countered subjective oppressions. Much of his work is with non-professionals, but he uses the same arsenal of techniques with professionals, only the goals are different. Although he had directed classics in conventional settings using these techniques, he had not directed Shakespeare. In this workshop there would be nothing except the process – a new experience for him as well as for the RSC actors; both would be learning.

He introduced the actors to his techniques and gradually applied them to *Hamlet*, the focus of the fortnight. The play was in the current RSC repertoire and included in its cast four members of the twenty-five-strong workshop. Boal improvised, moving from exercises he knew well to new ones, orchestrating events like a conductor, opening up speeches, moments and themes from the play to explore different ways of looking at them. Each day included discussions, in which he was frequently challenged. Berry probed him on a central issue. The techniques are introspective, about the subject, and can be used to build and develop character, but where and how does language fit into the process? He admitted that he emphasised sound rather than language and voice, and said this was an area he had not developed, possibly because he worked globally in different languages and often with semi-literate people.

Among the actors there were different opinions about the value of the workshop.[20] Some questioned the role of subjectivity in Boal's work and its relationship to changing as opposed to surviving oppressive systems, while those who felt liberated by his techniques said they were able to bring new insights to the roles they were playing in the season. There was a general welcome for the opportunity to work with a director of Boal's calibre and to explore the relationship between theatre and life. However, there was also frustration at the unavoidable limitations, which served to highlight for many the unhappiness they felt at the state of the company. One actor, Orlando Seale, later went to Brazil as a result of the workshop and became involved in a project to produce *The Tempest* in a remote rural community. Boal's proposal to build on the workshop by directing *Hamlet* at The Other Place was turned down, however, underlining the point that Stratford had never seen itself as an international centre of radical Shakespeare study through practical research and experiment alongside the more conventional work.

The reactions to the Boal workshop highlighted the general problems of the company's workshops. The projects captured the spirit of the Studio but inevitably were more eclectic, lacked overall coherence and continuity, and involved a smaller percentage of the company. As at the Studio, actor availability set the limits of participation, and workshops that could be open to everyone could only fall at the end of the season once all the productions had opened. There was also the same predicament of how the projects could benefit the company as a whole. In certain, albeit few, cases there were clear connections. Gardzienice influenced Katie Mitchell's anthropological approach, and workshops with writers, such as Derek Walcott, led to or helped shape productions. With playwrights, the danger was to prevent workshops becoming an audition for a production or a substitute for performing new plays. With actors as the main participants of the programmes, the benefits were clear at the individual level but less plain for the company as a whole. The work was important in its own right and when the company was in its infancy, the sense of active company building and mass involvement mitigated this dilemma. But when the RSC was losing its sense of company at the ground level during the 1990s' modernisation and becoming an archipelago of disparate and often differently motivated units, the quandary became more acute.

A season of well-financed projects planned well in advance for a company of actors that did not then exist necessarily replaced spontaneity with accountability. As well as producing a tendency for the value of projects to be judged by the size of their budget, the institutionalisation of projects created another layer of management, which was not always able to respond flexibly to ideas that arose outside of the planned schedule and which occasionally willed projects into being in order to fulfil the plan rather than to fulfil a need that artists had identified. A tension arose between the questioning nature of the projects and the all too manifest fact of their being officially sanctioned, especially when workshops would validate practices that found no place in the RSC rehearsal rooms. This combination of celebration at the periphery and absence at the core further undermined the reality of company for many actors.

When Noble closed The Other Place in his overhaul of the RSC, the workshop programme closed too, although verse classes continued. The Academy, which was based at the dark theatre, produced one production in the Swan in 2002, which toured and had a cast drawn from actors who had just graduated from drama school. Noble's successor, Michael Boyd, was left with the task of deciding how, or whether, to resuscitate the company's training, research and development work, which costs money and time and rarely has any direct outcome. This means it sits ill with the verities of the measurement obsessed, market-driven age, yet it keeps the company refreshed, alive and connected to the new and the imaginative.

# EIGHT

# PUBLIC ACCOUNT

The RSC set out to become a national institution in a way that the Stratford festival theatre, however prestigious and exciting, could never have been. Only the quality and appeal of the work could justify and sustain a national designation but a raft of other attributes was required to buttress public credibility. For example, gaining public subsidy, without which the young company would not have survived for more than a few years, was a necessary affirmation of public legitimacy, and one that reached beyond the merely economic. The association with Shakespeare and the broadening of the repertoire gave the company impeccable national theatre credentials; yet Hall also recognised that a base in London, which was essential for company reasons, was strategically imperative because of the unduly important role the capital played in the political as well as the cultural life of Britain. Furthermore, alongside audience building projects, disseminating the company's work as widely as possible through touring, transfers to the West End and abroad, and exploitation in television, film and recordings was crucial in the creation of national standing.[1]

Hall was deft at weaving all these strands into the fabric of his new image in order to turn Stratford into the hub of the national institution it had always aspired to be. The name he gave the company captured a suitably potent and multivalent ambiguity. As William Gaskill quipped when the Royal Shakespeare Company's title was first unveiled, it has 'everything in it except God'.[2]

The terms on which Hall achieved public authenticity for the RSC proved to be very different from those of previous Stratford ambitions. Stratford had always seen itself as emblematic of England, which, in the 1950s, was the hegemonic force in Britain. The lack of broad-based national support for Stratford's theatre did not diminish its own self-esteem. Stratford had ambitions to be seen on an equal footing with the Royal Opera House (ROH), which had received government patronage since 1930 and after the war remained the most cosseted of Britain's arts institutions. But although thoroughly Tory, Stratford did not enjoy the top-level connections sported by the ROH nor, being 'in the sticks', did it enjoy the ROH's position in the establishment's social calendar. Hall wanted the ROH status but a very different social placement. The RSC's success in repositioning itself was vital to the company's endurance as anything other than an archaic theatre.

In a formal sense, the Stratford theatre had enjoyed national status since being granted a Royal Charter in 1925. Hall exploited this connection when he secured the required royal assent to the change of title from Shakespeare Memorial Theatre. After the name change, company press releases and theatre programmes carried the rubric: 'Incorporated under Royal Charter, with the Queen as Patron, it [the RSC] virtually belongs to the nation'. Although Hall was to abandon in 1963 the most public tribute theatres then paid to Her Majesty, the habit of playing the national anthem at all performances, the royal link remained: the Queen continued serving as the company's patron and the Prince of Wales became its president in 1989. By this time, the degree to which the monarchy could be said to represent the nation was itself coming under general scrutiny, and both institutions needed to examine how they could better reflect the nation's changing multicultural profile.

## Radical image

As with the Shakespeare connection, the royal tag brought with it expectations that Hall had to challenge in order to realise the RSC's artistic vision, and he was highly skilled at negotiating the ensuing conflicts. The very 'relevance' that gave the RSC its artistic edge and, for the middle classes, its radical profile caused it problems as a national institution. The company's battles with the censor and public campaign for public subsidy won it friends among the intelligentsia but ruffled establishment feathers; Hall, none the less, was awarded a CBE in 1962.

The company's sporadic diplomatic tangles underlined the contradictory nature of its urge to be a free spirit as well as a national body. In 1963 the Aldwych Theatre was picketed because the RSC was playing host to the discredited King and Queen of Greece, whose regime had suppressed the indigenous peace movement. There were no tickets on sale to the public for the gala performance of *A Midsummer Night's Dream* because the Foreign Office had taken them all. The Royal Box was filled with security men in evening dress while police kept the protestors at a distance in the street outside and made nine arrests. Roles were reversed the following year when the Foreign Office blocked an RSC invitation to the Berliner Ensemble to come to the World Theatre Season, which meant the RSC could not take *King Lear* to East Berlin.

Establishment concern occasionally took on a mildly threatening air. When Hall and Brook signed a half-page advertisement in the *New York Times* calling for a halt to the bombing in Vietnam and for the US to recognise Vietnam's National Liberation Front, they were reinforcing a widely held view of the company as a radical force. They moved Arnold Goodman, chair of the Arts Council, to question whether the state should subsidise those who were working to overthrow it! In the turbulent years of the early 1970s the Tory arts minister Lord Eccles approached Hugh Willatt, secretary-general of the Arts Council, to ask Trevor Nunn if he could 'do something' about three or four far-left activists in the RSC. Ironically, this request came at a time when the company itself had been criticised for its left-leaning repertoire and attacked for misuse of public money by presenting a dramatisation of *The Oz Trial*. Nunn himself had recently described the company as 'basically a left-wing organisation'.[3] He and associate director David Jones had written this in a letter to *The Times* concerning the dispute the company was having with two playwrights, John Arden and Margaretta D'Arcy, who were picketing the Aldwych Theatre. The then Stratford Tory MP Angus Maude resigned from the RSC governing body over the letter. Hall defended this use of the term 'left-wing' by his successor as an aesthetic rather than a party political label. The RSC, however, was by now being criticised from the left along with the National Theatre (NT) as an irredeemably bourgeois institution, and the Arden/D'Arcy clash fuelled this criticism. The following year when Hall was about to become the NT's artistic director, he was grilled, as he saw it, by the Arts Council drama panel, and spoke for both national companies as he reflected that here was 'a perfect metaphor of how the radical dreams of yesterday become the institutions of today, to be fought and despised'.[4]

The RSC's radical reputation had dissolved by the time it moved to the Barbican in the harsh political climate of the early 1980s and thereafter the RSC did little to offend. Individual company members sustained its

earlier image, nevertheless, through support for various social and political causes and challenging unacceptable sponsorship deals. The annual
Shakespeare birthday celebrations, at which Stratford entertained representatives of all countries that had diplomatic relations with Britain, were
frequently the focus of protest. RSC members would voice their opposition to the presence of dignitaries from regimes such as the Greek and
Chilean military juntas or apartheid South Africa. In 1987 the birthday
production, *The Merchant of Venice*, only went ahead despite the attendance of the South African ambassador after management negotiations
prevented an actors' boycott. Management vetoed a proposed speech
from the stage, and the actors had to be content with airing their protests
at the celebratory procession through the town. Antony Sher, who was
cast as Shylock and is himself South African, was not content to let the
matter rest there. During the trial scene, he grabbed the Coloured actor,
Akim Mogaji, who was playing an attendant, pointed at the ambassador
in the audience, and then delivered directly to the reviled emissary the
speech that includes the lines 'You have among you many a purchas'd
slave,/Which like your asses and your dogs and mules,/You use in abject
and in slavish parts,/Because you bought them'.[5]

## The audience

The search for 'relevance' that lay at the root of the company's early profile
was also critical in the central strand of its striving for public legitimacy –
its contact with and relationship to the RSC's various audiences.

Hall and the RSC had emerged from the post-war British 'art' theatre
movement, which carried on the tradition of the pioneer repertory companies in challenging the values and organisation of the dominant
commercial theatre. The movement believed it had to educate existing
and new audiences to accept the kind of repertoire it wanted to present.
Within this process the banner of the 'right to fail' was hoisted as its standard. Paradoxically, the separation of value from the usual commercial
benchmark of box office income, which made great sense in the struggle
to create a challenging theatre of national debate, downgraded the role of
the audience. Yet Hall, who had worked in the commercial sector, regularly checked the RSC box office figures, which mostly were – and
remained – the envy of any theatre management. Hall's 'art' theatre proclivity, however, was part of his public service ethos, in which the
audience was important, though not supreme. He wanted a popular RSC,
not an avant-garde or elite one, yet he encouraged and defended the
avant-garde within his company. Indeed, *A Midsummer Night's Dream*

directed by Peter Brook, the most popular RSC Shakespeare production in terms of celebrity and audience figures, was the work of an avowed avant-gardist who once wrote an article pleading for empty seats.

Public patronage never removed the disciplines of the box office for the RSC because the level and certainty of subsidy were never sufficient to allow this, a factor that always overshadowed the RSC's relationship to its audiences. Crucially, subsidy never let the RSC keep enough of its prices sufficiently low to help attract new audiences on a consistent basis. Management manoeuvring on ticket prices became highly intricate and often led to pricing schemes that were confusing rather than encouraging to potential purchasers.

Hall's key concept of 'relevance' was drawn from the welfare state notion of social usefulness overlaid with the cultural tradition of Matthew Arnold that art was a civilising influence. There was a complex tension between the sociological and aesthetic impulses of the company in this respect, especially as 'relevance' became drained of any residual political definitions. To what extent attention to the world was expressed in the style of production shifted with time and from director to director. Use of contemporary costumes for Shakespeare made an explicit connection, in which consideration and acknowledgement of the audience were vital elements. Some, like Brook, actively built such awareness into the directorial strategies of the productions themselves. In his *Theatre of Cruelty* experiment, for example, he switched round the audience–stage relationship and included items in the programme that openly confronted the audience. At the end of *Marat/Sade* the actors stared at the audience and returned their applause with slow, antagonistic clapping. In *US*, he took this distancing further and the production ended without the customary signals of finality: after appearing to burn a butterfly, the cast remained silent, refusing to release the audience into the phase of applause, and by their silence posing the question 'Where do we stand?'

In *A Midsummer Night's Dream* Brook reversed this alienation and had the actors joining the audience in the auditorium, shaking their hands. This was an unusual violation of the separation between stage and auditorium in mainstream theatres at the time and was more frequently experienced in counter-cultural performance by groups such as the Living Theater. Brook had refused to tour *US* because that would have exacerbated a problem he found in playing it at the Aldwych; 'the liveliness of the actors waned as the immediacy of the relation with their public and their theme lessened'.[6] He overcame his scruples with *A Midsummer Night's Dream* yet still believed all his strategies were inadequate. At the RSC, the system would always accommodate the radical.

Hall took a liberal, humanist view of 'relevance' which wished to connect the theatre to society in general, and this included all classes by default. He had few illusions about the power the company possessed to make serious shifts in the class composition of the audience – that would require a massive investment of public money and equally massive cultural and social change. Nevertheless, however inadequate the means at his disposal, he did believe it was socially and artistically the right moment to try. He believed that better educational opportunities since the war, the rise of quality broadcasting and paperback sales, and changes in cinema, art and popular music had begun the slow revolution against national philistinism. The audience for serious theatre was growing as part of that development. Hall wanted the theatre he worked in to appeal to people like himself: the relevance debate was linked for him to attracting a younger, university-educated, 'upwardly mobile', theatre-going clientele, with the emphasis on age and outlook rather than class. He momentarily focused on this task in wider class terms but was most pleased when a production like his own of *Hamlet* in 1965 attracted a significant student and youth audience. Whatever the sociological results of the outcome, an awareness of speaking to a new audience expressed through the repertoire was a conscious trigger to more imaginative work and organisational innovations that supported it.

The essential element in Hall's approach of securing a London theatre meant the company having to fill every night two theatres seating some 2,000 people between them. A daunting prospect, which affected Hall's choice of London location. For Hall, the second theatre had to be situated in the West End rather than a working-class district. In this he diverged from his inspiration, Jean Vilar of the Théâtre National Populaire in Paris, as well as, closer to home, Joan Littlewood with Theatre Workshop in London's East End and before her, Lilian Baylis at the Old Vic just south of the Thames. Hall's attitude derived from his own ambition to position the RSC within the mainstream in order to challenge it on its own terms rather than being seen as a social experiment or an external critic. A mix of the practical (there was no money to convert a theatre like the Hackney Empire) and the prudent (the West End was more attractive to the stars he wished to entice and more conducive to the kind of image he was then cultivating) underpinned his view. Britain lacked the politicised cultural traditions of continental Europe, in which mass working-class parties established or supported socially engaged drama. Hall had seen Theatre Workshop – the most prominent British attempt to create such a theatre – destroyed by the need to play in the West End to compensate for Arts Council meanness. He did not want the RSC to suffer similarly. His dream was not to remain at the Aldwych but to move into a new building. At first, before the Barbican plan, it was a scheme with Ballet Rambert in which radical design was to be accompanied by a policy of cheap seats aimed at young people. This aim was carried over into the Barbican venture but by the time the RSC moved to the City, little was being done to attract the young and ticket prices reinforced a sense of the theatre's exclusivity.

At Stratford, Hall was set to tackle the prevailing conservatism that was even inscribed in the name of the Shakespeare Memorial Theatre. The change of title to the Royal Shakespeare Theatre preserved due gravitas but jettisoned the funereal and museum connotations. The audience, in which the well-heeled predominated, comprised a curious combination of visitors from near and far. At one end of the scale there was the tourist with no pre-knowledge of Shakespeare (and sometimes little or no grasp of English) and at the other end the rarefied *cognoscente*, who could compare the text being used and the interpretation being offered against previous incarnations. The RSC, Hall believed, had to educate the whole gamut to a more catholic and contemporary taste.

Unlike most reps, however, Stratford did not have an audience drawn from the local community with whom the theatre could build a relationship. Although civically Stratford maintained certain rituals connected with the theatre, such as the mayor's annual welcome to the new company, there was a degree of mutual suspicion that is commonly found in university towns. Like many universities, the RSC was, and remains, a significant landowner, local employer and nucleus for business in the region. As Stratford changed from a market crafts town when the RSC was launched to a major tourist attraction by the end of the century, the economic role of the company had become more significant yet the 'town/clown' split persisted. Local authority parsimony illustrates the divide. At the start of Hall's time, for example, a company plea for the implementation of a 50 per cent discretionary rate relief was turned down flat, and it was not until 1985 that the RSC received a grant from the district council, which agreed to support two productions, *Mary After the Queen*, the dramatisation of a Stratford story, and *The Quest*, a children's play.

Local people had acted as extras to make up the numbers in some Stratford productions but before Buzz Goodbody opened The Other Place the RSC had done little directly to involve the local community on its own terms. The Other Place remained the centre of RSC efforts to sustain this link, particularly with its workshops and shows for children. In 1983, Ron Hutchinson's *The Dillen* – the prequel to *Mary After the*

*Queen* – became a landmark production of local legitimacy and involved local people appearing in a mixed cast alongside RSC professionals. Set before the First World War, it formed the first part of the Hewins family story, which was continued in the later play. The production began and ended in The Other Place; in between, scenes were played out in nearby locations. The audience followed the peripatetic cast as George Hewins searched for work, a grim echo down the years of the callous injunction issued to the unemployed by Thatcher's minister Norman Tebbit 'to get on their bikes'. The production countered the pretty postcard view of Stratford and robustly celebrated community at a time when government was disparaging the very idea.[7]

Although the company's education department undertook a great deal of local work, the community aspect of the RSC repertoire faded until Katie Mitchell's brief attempt in the 1990s to make The Other Place a local theatre, if only as a place to rest and have a cup of tea. April de Angelis's *A Warwickshire Testimony*, another play inspired by local history and seen at The Other Place in 1999, seemed more of a last gasp than a new beginning. The closure of The Other Place two years later and the loss of many jobs due to the company's restructuring did little to assuage local antagonism.

For the RSC the issue of 'audience' could not be reduced to box office statistics. It had to be seen in a more complex as well as unstable context, shaped by many factors. Theatre, because of its closeness to and need for the audience, is continually forced to reassess its methods. If it does not, it dies. A 'nation's vocabulary', wrote Hall, 'its accents, its whole culture, are always shifting and modern mass communications make the tempo of change distressingly fast.'[8] He knew public legitimacy had to be earned, and would have to be earned repeatedly. This involved conscious intervention at many levels, not only in theatre-making but also in theatre-going – from the buildings, their ease of access, layout, location and decoration to ticket prices, marketing, publicity, dress conventions, behaviour codes, style of catering and methods of looking after the audience.

As part of his new deal with the audience, Hall – and subsequent artistic directors – not only offered a new style of production but changed the arrangement and look of the auditoria in the search for a better actor–audience relationship. Hall also wanted to alter the front-of-house arrangements but could not afford to, although he did institute changes to the programmes and publicity material. The spirit of greater equality and company openness was channelled through the creation of the RSC Club and its offshoot Theatregoround (TGR). In the mid-1970s, the establishment of The Other Place and The Warehouse played a similar role, reflecting new artistic thinking as well as a response to new social diversity.

At this juncture the company also decided to refocus its disparate educational work by appointing in 1976 its first development officer, Maurice Daniels. Daniels, who until then had assumed the role of the company's planning controller, had acted in the early 1950s with the remarkable Century Theatre, which toured in lorries carrying its own stage. He was committed to the public service, missionary ethos of his new job and extended the work of the Club and TGR in opening up the RSC further to its existing and potential audiences. Daniels used his experience of scheduling problems to match the advanced planning needs of educational institutions against the practicalities of the company, especially in terms of actor availability. The RSC visited the expected range of venues – schools, training colleges, universities, polytechnics and youth, adult and community centres – as well as some unexpected ones, such as Long Lartin Prison, which housed prisoners serving life sentences. These activities were supplemented by backstage tours, question-and-answer sessions, readings, extra-mural performances and working rehearsals in Stratford. Alongside the annual summer school, which had begun in 1948, and work with Birmingham University's Shakespeare Institute, which is based in Stratford, further educational activity was undertaken by the RSC Gallery, a department embodying the contradiction of preserving the company's past while emancipating the company from it.

Nunn, in particular, believed the RSC had a duty to influence the way Shakespeare is taught, and in this the company exercised considerable sway. Actors, directors and other RSC members used workshops, seminars, demonstrations and lectures to span the gulf between those who present Shakespeare in the professional theatre and those who engage with the plays in an educational context, be they teachers or students. Especially popular were weekend workshops for teachers led by Cicely Berry, which arose out of Saturday sessions at The Other Place. Contacts with local education authorities, individual schools and universities expanded rapidly at the end of the 1970s. In the wake of this momentum, and following the initial RSC/W.H. Smith Youth Festival in 1982, the RSC appointed its first head of education, Tony Hill. The department grew in both Stratford and London to keep in step with the expanding role of education across the arts world. In 1993, the Prince of Wales, the company's president, sponsored an annual RSC Shakespeare school for English and drama teachers working in the secondary sector. The company undertook vocational work too – for example, classes at the Guildhall School of Music and Drama in voice, text, acting and stage management.[9]

Apart from isolated examples such as the Antigones Project in 1991/92, in which young people around Britain created new plays in collaboration with RSC-nominated playwrights, the company's educational work focused on Shakespeare. It rarely exploited the RSC's contemporary repertoire. External pressure pushed the RSC and other arts organisations to compensate in their educational work for the cutbacks in school arts provision and for the failures of wider social policy. Despite some excellent initiatives, in trying to meet the increasing demand the RSC education department became overstretched and suffered as an adjunct to rather than an integral part of the company's work. There was insufficient contact between the upper echelons of the RSC and the education activity, which became an arm of marketing, driven by government policy and funders' requirements rather than by internal need – a familiar story of the times.

## Touring and transfers

Public legitimacy was also secured through imaginative use of touring as well as exploitation of the company's work in transfers and other media. No other arts organisation has managed an accomplishment like the twenty-five years of the Newcastle upon Tyne residency, which earned the company the freedom of the city on its twenty-first visit in 1998. Unfortunately, a similar feat could not be achieved in the south-west. The small-scale regional tour began in 1978 as a 'first eleven' venture but over the years it proved hard to sustain the idealism. On occasion it was used as the testing ground – or siding – for directors and was often under-cast, with actors playing lead roles who would not have been offered those parts on the Royal Shakespeare Theatre stage. The middle- and large-scale touring of the late 1980s and 1990s, made possible by sponsorship and association with commercial producers, filled a vacuum left by the demise of touring companies such as Prospect, Renaissance and Compass. In 1998/99 the RSC had seven shows on tour in the UK along with its two residencies in Newcastle and Plymouth; yet, as with the Stratford operation, size did not always equal quality. Christopher Hampton's *Les Liaisons Dangereuses*, for instance, had become a staple of RSC touring but productions soon lost their shine, an example of commercial imperative supplanting artistic need.

International touring was revived in 1962 after a break of three years and continued more or less annually. The RSC's enterprise in this field was recognised in 1986 by receipt of the Queen's Award for Export. Geographic expansion in the mid-1990s/early 2000s as part of the international rebranding of the company took the RSC for the first time to South America, India, Pakistan and China. There was, however, too often an uncomfortable gap between the reception of work at home and abroad and the ambassadorial function could not conceal uneasiness about core activity in Stratford and London.

From the transfer of *Becket* in 1961, RSC productions moving to the commercial sector have helped maintain the reassuring rather than the radical thread of the company brand name. The attributes of the brand, a gold standard for high-class entertainment, became more important than any individual or individual production as far as the target audience was concerned. When *Wild Oats*, written by an unknown author, succeeded in the West End in 1977, the RSC image and the associated ensemble playing was the selling point. On the other hand, when the musical *Les Misérables* transferred in 1985 for its very long West End run, it attracted a different kind of audience for whom the RSC probably meant little, if anything at all. The show swelled the RSC's funds – it was by far the company's greatest transfer earner – yet, as a barely acknowledged RSC production in the West End, it does not appear to have added greatly to the audience numbers at the RSC's own theatres.

Exploitation of RSC productions on television did bring the company's name to a wider audience, especially in the early days when it had the edge on the NT in this regard. From the first Aldwych season, *The Hollow Crown* was featured on BBC TV's *Monitor* programme and *The Cherry Orchard* was broadcast on the same network. They were quickly followed by *As You Like It*, *The Comedy of Errors* and, in what was to become a major television event, *The Wars of the Roses*. This level of incursion could not be maintained as TV broadcasting changed. Yet Nunn made the most sustained use of television with productions such as *Antony and Cleopatra*, *Macbeth* and *Nicholas Nickleby*, in each of which with his collaborators he skilfully addressed the problems of transferring theatre work to the small screen. Another of his shows, *The Thwarting of Baron Bolligrew*, was the subject of a 1965 Redifusion 'backstage' documentary, a precursor of London Weekend Television's programmes in the 1980s on John Barton and verse speaking and Channel Four's *Behind the Scenes* 1998 programme on the RSC's technical and production departments.

The RSC's move into film was less successful, despite Hall's self-deluding pronouncement in the mid-1960s that 'The future of our company is bound up with films.'[10] Cinema was the seductive fantasy for theatre directors of a certain ambition – Ingmar Bergman, as master of both media, was the model. A deal with CBS in 1966 was designed to bring the company much-needed funds and involved three Hall productions: *A Midsummer Night's Dream*, *Macbeth* (planned for 1967) and an adaptation of Henry Livings' *Eh?*, which became *Work is a Four Letter Word*. The first to be made, and Hall's first feature film, was the Livings project, but inexperience, over-work and poor judgement on the script – Hall rejected Livings' version for one by the RSC Literary Manager Jeremy Brooks – resulted in a flop. The stage failure of *Macbeth* jeopardised the deal but Hall did make *A Midsummer Night's Dream* in 1968. He was exhausted and the film was poorly received. CBS ended the contract. Brook's film versions of his RSC productions *King Lear*, *Marat/Sade* and *US* (as *Tell Me Lies*), although useful for theatre historians, did not rescue the RSC's awkward relationship to film, which continued intermittently through to the 1990s.[11] RSC directors who did enjoy a successful transition to film – Danny Boyle, David Jones, Sam Mendes and Roger Michell – made their mark independently of the company and not by filming Shakespeare. Ironically, the resurgence of Shakespeare in Hollywood in the 1990s was triggered by Kenneth Branagh's film of *Henry V* based on the RSC production by Adrian Noble. Much to Noble's annoyance, neither he nor the company received proper credit.

All these strands of exploitation of the company's work at first helped establish the RSC profile and later reinforced it. For example, the many awards won in the Hall years made the RSC seem like a thrilling and attractive company at the heart of the British theatre, whereas their relative dearth in the 1990s reflected the decline of the company's image. Creating a public profile was a conscious strategy and involved not only existing but also potential audience members and maximising the number who felt they had a stake in the RSC's existence as taxpayers and as citizens of the society the company was investigating. Hall appreciated the power of the media and realised that controversy built interest in the company. He was keen to meet and accommodate journalists and used the press to campaign on the RSC's behalf. He made first nights start at 6.30 pm to help the critics yet was not afraid to tackle them, usually considered a rash tactic to pursue. He even threatened to ban one.[12] As well as appearing in newspapers with Leslie Caron, he was featured in a TV series *The Young Tigers*, in a survey by London's *Evening Standard* on the 'New Elite', and was lampooned in the newly launched satirical magazine *Private Eye*.[13]

After Hall, the fact of the RSC's existence was understandably no longer news but neither was its eternal financial crisis. The personal profile of the artistic directors became of less importance than the RSC brand, epitomised by a mention in the radio saga *The Archers*. This change related to differences in the personalities of subsequent RSC leaders but also marked a shift in the nature and likely source of celebrity as well as a perceived decline in the national importance of theatre. The company was inevitably caught up in the media denigration of theatre people in the 1980s as politicians and pundits reached for the 'lefties', 'luvvies' and 'whingers' clichés. Nunn's earnings in the commercial sector and his absenteeism from the RSC excited press hostility, to which in one case he responded with a libel suit, and Hands's stewardship further aroused media wrath at the path the RSC was following. In the wake of Noble's streamlining plans in the next decade, 'trouble at the RSC' became the refrain. There were good productions during Noble's time just as there were bad ones during Hall's, but the context was different and in Noble's final years the RSC story became one of disintegration not growth. The company became less adept at handling the media, and Noble was criticised for losing the plot and falling prey to events rather than directing them. The more he professed that he was protecting the values of the great company, the more he was undermined. His plea to pull down the Royal Shakespeare Theatre and replace it with a Shakespeare village gave rise to accusations of the 'Disney-fication' of Stratford, often from the very people who already believed the town was in thrall to tourism. His unexpected resignation was widely covered, and his chosen heir Michael Boyd, after sensibly speaking up for himself as his appointment was announced, equally sensibly decided to lie low while he gave himself time to consider the size of the task he had taken on.

The bond between company and audience was built up over many years and in many ways. *The Wars of the Roses*, for example, was played in one day on the anniversary of the Battle of Bosworth, a new and audacious idea in 1963 that deliberately sought to forge links of sharing. Here was an echo of the Oberammergau passion, which Hall had seen during his national service, a return to the epic play-going of the Greeks, creating a theatre experience beyond the habitual. As a result of such initiatives, through its choice and delivery of the repertoire and through its various strategies for being held to public account, the RSC came to enjoy a dedicated following akin to that of a football club. People would see the shows because it was the RSC. They would follow the development of particular actors from a Shakespeare play in one space to a new play in another and from one season to the next. There was a spark that belied the institutional side of the company and tapped a seam of creativity that was linked to its popularity.

In the 1980s, the edifice of corporate hospitality allied to the inhospitality of the Barbican centre and the catalogue of cancelled performances, which the public blamed on an infatuation with technology, undermined the 'contract' between the audience and the company. The goodwill built up over the Aldwych years was dissipated. The company's erratic pattern of operation from the mid-1990s in both Stratford and London induced disorientation internally and externally. The institution lumbered on but the company, despite intermittent examples to the contrary, seemed to have lost the public dimension and could not find new strategies to reconnect to the concerns of its fractured society. While the RSC kept up to date in using sophisticated marketing techniques, its targets did not represent the wide and diverse social coalition with which a national theatre needs to engage. The RSC may have been a brand leader but what did that now stand for? The company did not seem sure how to develop its brand in a world where the struggle to assert diverse identities had become a key social dynamic.

# NINE

# COMPANY OR CORPORATION?

After just over four decades of existence, the central issue facing the RSC was, as ever, artistic but, as ever, it had an organisational dimension. Peter Hall had created a company for artistic reasons; Trevor Nunn had refined it for artistic reasons; and for artistic reasons Adrian Noble had fractured what was left of it. His departure raised many questions beyond the immediate one of survival and at their core was the issue of company: could – or should – the RSC still enjoy the word 'company' in its title and is this significant? Does the relationship between size and identity ineluctably disbar the RSC from any meaningful use of the word? And if so, at what point does such a disjuncture occur? Most importantly, what does 'company' mean at the beginning of the twenty-first century when the economic basis required to support the RSC has turned it into a corporation?

'Company' had been the unique early characteristic, and subsequently provided the abiding cohesion, of the RSC. It lay at the root of what made it distinctive. All Hall's initial innovations – offering long-term contracts, taking the Aldwych, establishing the Studio, and introducing modern work and experiment – stemmed from his desire to develop a company. Thirty years later, the Arts Council's appraisal of the institution, coming in 1990 at the end of turbulent times as Noble was about to take charge, described the concept of company as 'crucial' for the RSC. In 2002, Noble still talked 'company', even though he had reduced any such idea as originally envisaged to rubble. Yet, it was a group of twenty-eight

actors performing in the Swan Theatre a repertory of five plays by
Shakespeare and his contemporaries who enjoyed the warmest reception
and highest accolades of Noble's final season. This 'dedicated ensemble',
however, had been thrown together in haste, revealing symptomatically a
pragmatism that often cuts across planning in the theatre. Two directors
left in the early stages of the project and one of the leading actors was
hired after the opening plays had begun rehearsals and only a day before
his own productions were due to start their preparations. In microcosm,
this was not dissimilar to the problems Hall had to confront when putting
together his first season. The achievements of the Swan group represented the work of an ensemble only in so far as the actors displayed
admirable 'teamwork'. They were hired for the season and departed when
the productions finished their runs. While it was true that many had
appeared with the RSC before, the longevity of the company's existence
and extent of its disparate and disconnected work rendered this a negligible affirmation of ensemble credentials. Hall's vaunted companies and
their successors were also hybrids predicated on compromises. But, as
with the Swan experiment, the issue was to what degree the compromises permitted or prohibited creativity, not whether the institutional
form was perfect. Theatre is the eternal scavenger and in a constant state
of adulteration. There is no reason to expect a company to be any purer.
Hall, however, was trying to create the conditions for the company as a
whole to develop its skills over time, whereas the Swan season was an isolated and limited example of a repertoire company that highlighted its
absence at the heart of the parent RSC.

'Company' was the ideal that Hall and Nunn both returned to once
they had left the RSC. Hall oversaw a company system in the National
Theatre and later attempted the impossible trick of running his own
troupe in the West End. Nunn also established companies within the
larger embrace of the NT. 'Company' was also the motif linking many of
the most important British theatre groups of the post-war years, from
Theatre Workshop and the English Stage Company to Joint Stock and
Complicite. Being a company can resolve the inherent tension between
the freelance, itinerant existence of theatre people and the collective
nature of theatre itself. Yet company is not a prefabricated system but an
approach that gives rise to certain organisational forms. Its strength lies in
the artistic security it gives to all to experiment and be creative but, if that
is not to become a straitjacket, it has to be renewed through challenging
work, training and at some point dispersal. The initial impetus behind a
company, which often lasts for only three or four years, has to be picked
up and reanimated if further survival is to be contemplated. The RSC

endured for more than four decades by responding to such creative cycles. The radical impulses came from outside and then formed the establishment; the establishment then had to repeat the process to thrive. This became harder the longer the RSC continued, and the institution resisted the new outsiders or welcomed them in but not on their terms. Experiment was pushed to the margins, and that reinforced the prevailing sclerotic practices.

Being a company cannot guarantee creativity; there is no perfect system and adjustment is needed continually. But being a company did bring clear benefits to the RSC, like the interaction between the classical and the contemporary and the collaborative developing of work over a period of time through the repertoire system, the exchange of ideas and open, mutual criticism.[1] In the early seasons, the augmented respect for the actor made possible by company work enhanced the actor's imaginative power and the actor's force and variety of means of expression. This and the associated sharing were lost later in the relentless tread of routine and the increased volume of output. It did not mean the actors beforehand had necessarily been better actors but that they often acted more coherently together because, as part of a company, they brought more to rehearsal as well as more to performance.

The company system as it developed at the RSC had its own intrinsic problems, however. Despite shared views, there had never been a consensus on what acting was, let alone what constituted an ensemble, and those with power in the company jostled for their own honourable aims within a common goal that took its definition from the strength of leadership on offer. It was in the nature of the system that different directors had to use the same actors and accept those with whom they were not comfortable in order to achieve a season. This affected the whole repertoire, from classical work to the new plays, which raised their own particular casting quandaries. The RSC system often resulted in directors' pressing actors into a uniform approach to meet the deadlines of the complex schedule because that was the expedient way to cope in the allotted time with the different styles of acting and levels of experience they faced. Another attempt to deliver the schedule at the expense of creative inquiry arose from external criticism of verse speaking, which was usually misdirected disapproval of poor acting or poor directing, and sometimes encouraged directorial insistence on consensus where there was none. The demands of the schedule also led to a 'hit and run' culture where directors did not give sufficient time to a production once it had opened but moved on to the next project.

None of these problems was confined to any one period in the company's life, although the accumulation of other and related troubles made this progressively seem the case. By the time Noble resigned he was being blamed for all the RSC's ills. The crisis under him inevitably fed nostalgia about the old days, burying memories of the bad productions, poor planning and withering rows that were as much the features of the 'golden' period as the accomplishments that are rightly remembered and celebrated. Hall believed there would be something wrong with the company if it were all sweetness and light. He set the tone by creating a machismo atmosphere; a thick skin was necessary for survival. Actors were summarily dispensed with at the end of the season if deemed surplus to requirements and Hall showed through his sacking of John Barton from *The Taming of the Shrew* that friendship was no obstacle to being professionally pitiless.[2]

The RSC in its first seasons was not a visionary band defending its purity against the depredations of an antagonistic social order or the unmuddied source of incessant successes. There is no doubt, nevertheless, that creating the RSC was an exciting new venture and acted as a magnet for the profession. It offered exceptional opportunities; for younger actors it was like a further phase in their training; for established actors it was a rare chance to regenerate and develop skills. It did have its own charisma, especially in the British context where ensembles were still seen as something foreign. But, as an entity that was always only an approximation of an idea and was continually being remade in pursuit of that idea, it is important to remember the limitations.

Michael Murray offered his own perspective on being an actor with the company from 1961–63 playing minor roles, including in *The Wars of the Roses*. He wrote openly of his time there in 'Diary of a Small-Part Actor' published in the theatre magazine *Encore*.[3] Since there had been a social revolution, he asked in the article, was not a theatrical one overdue but, if so, could the RSC be the agent of such a transformation? His answer was pessimistic and cast doubt on whether communal art could be developed in Britain at all. Indeed, he wondered, was it even desirable? In weighing the arguments about ensembles (stars versus small parts), he asked if anyone wanted to see Peggy Ashcroft playing Hedda Gabler one night and Marina in *Measure for Measure* the next. Hall had set this type of juxtaposition as the aim of the company – as he put it, an actor playing Hamlet on Monday and the butler on Tuesday – but knew himself he had only just begun the journey.[4]

Murray concurred. He reported that getting noticed was still the order of the day, and despite all the talk of company, RSC life was replete with the usual petty jealousies and actors trying to best each other. He also reflected on contrasting styles of rehearsal and their relationship to company. Murray believed that the 'European' approach of a director like

Michel Saint-Denis, in which he created a world of clarity and precision derived from intricate pre-rehearsal thinking, offered greater scope than the pragmatism of Hall, who had already abandoned the Saint-Denis type of work process. Hall favoured a freewheeling approach based on the actor's spontaneity. This impressionistic but exciting method left little time for detailed orchestration and tended to reproduce the pre-given strengths, weaknesses and status of the cast rather than transform them. It became the dominant method at the RSC.

Ian Holm, who had appeared as a spear-carrier at Stratford in 1954 and had stayed since his return in 1957, playing among other parts Puck, Ariel, Troilus and Richard III in *The Wars of the Roses*, replied in the same edition of *Encore* that the RSC was making an important challenge to the prevailing commercial system. As a result, actors were paying far more attention to the needs of the play.[5]

Ironically, Peter Brook, the director who radicalised the RSC, was not a company man, though he created his own companies. Brook was very demanding of his casts and of the company as an institution, and Hall gave him what he wanted. Brook thought RSC actors had an undemanding understanding of ensemble, as if knowing each other were adequate. He emphasised an active interpretation of ensemble, which had to be more than just public school team spirit. The role of individual commitment and effort was central. His own companies within the larger company posed a dilemma that recurred later in the RSC: to what extent could an individual be given his or her head whilst staying true to a company ideal? If the company reins in the distinctive individual, how does it avoid conformity? If it does not, how does it avoid fragmentation? Brook was opposed to the expansion of the RSC and preferred another model, a smaller nucleus of actors led by a charismatic figure such as himself. In Brook's case, his singular vision, which was criticised by some within the RSC as a combination of pretentiousness, ruthlessness and arrogance, was tolerated and encouraged because of the results.

After Hall's departure, Nunn took the company idea to its furthest RSC limit. In his experiment with an egalitarian model based on a reduced number of actors, Murray's scenario came true – leading actors played small as well as major roles – but the experiment was short-lived. It could not provide the basis for future growth and other avenues returning to the larger companies were explored. As was always going to be the case, some actors believed the experiment to be valid and welcome while others viewed it as a mechanical interpretation of the ensemble idea. Richard Pasco said: 'I don't believe that you can have an ensemble company in the truest sense when you have young actors straight out of drama school working alongside people who have spent twenty-five years in the theatre.'[6] He cited his own experience in 1971 of being asked to 'walk on' and to understudy a small part, which was exactly what he had been doing for Tyrone Guthrie almost twenty years before. He believed in a middle way between the star system and the genuine ensemble, and that is the path the RSC trod.[7]

Although certain acting companies achieved a special identity, such as those in Terry Hands's history productions and Adrian Noble's *Plantagenets,* and a few, thanks to circumstance, acquired an unusually distinct focus as happened with *Nicholas Nickleby,* there were no more variations to the standard RSC model until Noble's streamlining in the late 1990s when the idea of company as a guiding force collapsed under the weight of institutional change.

## Actors

The RSC was never a single or fixed entity, although it had dominant values even when it included and encouraged oppositional views. Its size meant that at any given moment it actually comprised several companies under one overarching company umbrella; each component within it – for example, a Stratford company, the Other Place or a tour – needed its own identity within the greater RSC identity, and this was feasible until the company passed its optimum size and the artistic leadership was no longer able to bind the constituent parts together.

Actors were the life-blood of the various companies, although the gap between actors and administration reinforced the feeling that ownership of 'the' company resided with the long-serving members of the senior management. In structural terms there was little power given to actors. Peggy Ashcroft (and briefly Paul Scofield) was a member of the largely nominal RSC direction, though her relationship to Hall and Nunn was important to both directors. The planning committee had places for leading actors, such as Alan Howard and Ian McKellen, but they found that their own schedules made attendance difficult and key decisions were as likely to be taken elsewhere. McKellen led the first small-scale tour and Sheila Hancock, as a director, led the one in 1983 when it returned after a break and the company needed her profile to relaunch it. Sinead Cusack was elected to the new board of governors in 1999. Within the company, actors exercised their collective strength both through the normal union channels and also informally in the pursuit of extra-mural activities, such as the *Not the RSC* festivals organised independently, though with the help, of the parent company. Actors' artistic input was mainly confined to

traditional practices, although on one occasion the cast vetoed a proposed production of Arnold Wesker's *The Journalists* and in individual
cases actors have refused to appear in certain plays, such as Barrie Keeffe's
*Frozen Assets* because of its attack on upper-class attitudes and behaviour.[8]

Principally, however, actor power resided where it does in commercial
theatre, in the standing of the actor, in the actor's ability to negotiate a
deal, which for a few means being able to choose the director but for most
the need to ride the RSC casting process as best they can, in their contribution to rehearsal and in their performance on stage. While, generally
speaking, directors instigated the basic concept of a production, it could
not work in detail without the agreement of the actors, and was sometimes changed because of actor involvement. The RSC never became a
directors' theatre in the continental sense and acknowledged that actors
controlled how an idea was to be realised and delivered. The company
enjoyed a strong sense of identification with a large number of actors, and
not only those on the honorary and associate artist lists.[9] Terry Hands
once described an NT production directed by an ex-RSC associate that
included several ex-RSC actors as an RSC production in exile. Inevitably,
as more and more people passed through the company's ranks, the RSC
'diaspora' grew to a point where the sheer numbers and turnover weakened this sense of association.

Actors have been an important source of observation on the company
as well as on their roles through interviews and their own self-generated
comment in memoirs and autobiographies. Judi Dench in a biography
pays tribute to the RSC as a co-operative endeavour, while Ian McKellen
in his biography believed the RSC to be a monolith until he worked there
in the 1970s.[10] He found it to be a series of small, intimate groups, not a
company in the traditional sense but hierarchical and more like a limited
company producing a product. There have been notable attacks, however;
some have appeared in the press, from the likes of Helen Mirren and Ian
McDiarmid, while others have recorded their critical thoughts in their
books, such as Brian Cox, who found the RSC of the 1980s 'dry in
manner, precious in execution, lacking virility, a bit posh – undergradu-
ate made good'.[11] Antony Sher has offered a day-by-day account of the
serpentine intricacies of the RSC's internal life as seen from the actor's
point of view, while Nigel Hawthorne complained at the lack of care the
company takes of its actors.[12] Robert Stephens complains of the poor
pay and argues the RSC should slash the price of accommodation in
Stratford to compensate. With less Shakespeare being produced, he writes,
'actors are forced into the trap of working for peanuts in Stratford'.[13]
Sheila Hancock recounts the frustrations of trying to plan and run the

small-scale tour, the difficulty of meeting the joint artistic directors, but having succeeded, of being 'trevved' and 'handled' by them in turn, and of the reluctance of the RSC to discuss money.[14] Kenneth Branagh tells of dramatising his feelings in an RSC fringe play *Tell Me Honestly*, which he believed resulted in a bitter pay dispute with the company and his feeling unwanted, like an ungrateful child.[15]

## Family

References to the RSC as a family abound. In the early years of company building, there was a palpable sense of belonging to an enclosed order like the Masons, which was reinforced by the relative seclusion of Stratford. The advance of car ownership and the extension of the M40 through Warwickshire in 1991 undermined this remoteness, by which time the company had already outgrown its sequestered phase through expansion. The corollary was the ideology of the family, which persisted and bridged the gap between actors and administration, between past and present and between 'a' and 'the' company, even when the RSC was manifestly too large to be considered in familial terms but had become more of a dispersed clan. Official documents would refer to the RSC as a family, while an extensive and esoteric apparatus – ranging from honorary and associate artists, the RSC Advisory Direction and honorary posts such as emeritus director (Hands and Nunn) to honorary governors and even honorary emeritus governors – supported the notion.

The use of the family metaphor, however, contrasted jarringly with the splintered family lives of the RSC's directors and their string of broken marriages. The RSC family was all-consuming, and this fed the pride that tipped over into smugness at the family's considerable achievements. The family was protective, and would not criticise its own in public while being capable of savagery in private. At senior management level there was concern for people yet ruthlessness once an individual had been deemed to have forfeited the family's support.

Formal relations with actors and production staff were subject to union agreements, and, unlike the other national performing arts institutions, the RSC has not suffered from major strikes. The handling of the changes in the 1990s belied this tradition of care. Among the administration, which was not unionised, the problem of low wages was compounded for many years by an annual pay review that was arcane, tardy, entirely at the discretion of the general manager and not subject to proper external scrutiny. The warning to the company in the 1983 Priestley Report not to take the staff for granted nor to regard them as infinitely elastic was not heeded, and nor was his advice to take great care in the making of pay settlements. In this paternalistic set-up, individual bargaining was possible but difficult. An obvious remedy – to join a union – was available in theory but to achieve collective bargaining rights, more than 50 per cent of a whole category would have to be persuaded to vote for membership. In the absence of any formal mechanism for the procedure, few people knew who was in which category, and anyone willing to campaign faced the obstacle of being identified as a troublemaker.

The 'family' was also primarily patriarchal, heterosexual and white. Although it was a male culture that derided 'camp' as much as changing-room atavism, men dominated the rehearsal room as well as the company, which was serviced mainly by women. Even in the 1980s women directors were still exceptional enough to raise comment, and the shadow of Buzz Goodbody's suicide still hung over the company. The associate system generated a cut-throat, hothouse atmosphere of intense competitiveness that affected the whole planning, casting and production process in which the obstacles were much higher for women than for men. Given the sexual nature of much casting, however unacknowledged, there were huge disadvantages facing female directors in the planning of a season. The strain on female casting directors (with one exception the norm at the RSC) in having to second-guess the tastes of the mostly heterosexual male directors was another burden to add to their massive workload. Efforts were made, nevertheless, to counter the gender imbalance in Shakespeare's plays through other areas of the repertoire, especially new plays, and in commissioning women playwrights. Women in the company also fought back, both in rehearsal and collectively within the company. There were sporadic female discussion groups in the 1970s and 1980s, a decade that saw a concerted resistance to male stereotyping of Shakespeare's female roles. Internal pressure from women in the company led to the Women's Project, which spawned a production in 1986 of Deborah Levy's *Heresies*, appropriately a play exploring female creativity. This moment of institutional recognition, however, became no more than a token response when it was not followed through after its begetters left the company.

The RSC, like most other major theatre companies, also suffered from the institutional racism that was eventually recognised at the end of the twentieth century as scarring Britain. The company was, in Peter Brook's words, 'perhaps the freest and most enlightened national theatre organisation in the world', yet no British black or Asian director has been given an RSC production and the administration has remained astonishingly and embarrassingly white.[16] The company made noticeable, though inconsistent, attempts at 'integrated' casting, which, in the context of the profession, were significant, but it did not achieve a situation where 'non-white' actors were nurtured and equal opportunity was the custom. For many actors, skin colour remained an important element in their identity and 'colour blind' casting was not the ideal they sought. It tended to reinforce prevailing prejudices, which meant a 'white' benchmark, and could be seen as coercive, encouraging assimilation instead of acknowledging or celebrating difference. The RSC had viewed its national remit in terms of offering a range of different spaces and spreading its geographical reach but it had failed adequately to represent on or off stage the multicultural diversity of the society it was serving.

## The future

Michael Boyd, who became artistic director in 2003, inherited a huge financial crisis, like Nunn, Hands and Noble before him, but he was also bequeathed an institution shaken to its core.

The unravelling of the company in Noble's final years reflected the uncertainty of the times and the degree to which social cohesion and the possibility of a collective response among the audience had significantly diminished. Answers to such questions as 'What is a national theatre like the RSC for?' and 'What spaces and forms of organisation are appropriate to it?' became harder to find. Having set the standard against which modern Shakespeare production was judged, the kind of theatre the RSC presented suffered a decline in prestige in an ever more transient and image-driven world. The wellspring of creativity in the company was running dry. The various RSC activities seemed increasingly unrelated and held together not by the existence of a company but by its transformation into a corporation. This was a response to the wider historical trend of 'commodification', in which the audience ceased to be partners or participants and became instead consumers or customers. In this bargain, with its relentless focus on audience figures as the benchmark of success, the 'goods' on offer – the productions – were distinguished by packaging not content, novelty took centre stage, and experiment was consigned to the margins.

When the RSC's 'house style' had become so broad that its heterodoxy had become self-defeating, the balance between evolution and change and between continuity and innovation had been damagingly disturbed. Having escaped the prison of 1950s decorative theatre, the company did not want to find itself trapped by another constraint of political significance, yet in the 1980s and 1990s the sources of its inspiration and renewal had become less able to provide coherence or a sufficient basis for sustained work of contemporary relevance. Art has many purposes other than the artistic and it may operate autonomously, but that does not mean it operates in a social vacuum or that its codes are not susceptible to social interpretation. This is not to suggest the theatrical aesthetic should be directly determined by the social, which often leads to over-simplified and patronising productions, merely to recognise the dynamic of the relationship, a dynamic that is particularly potent in a performance art like theatre.

The RSC's relevance, however broadly defined, depended on the company keeping itself open to as full a range as possible of society's influences. The obvious absence or under-representation of whole sections of the population, defined especially by class and ethnicity, could only be addressed by inter-related strategies permeating all the company's activity that linked audience development to changes both in the way the repertoire was presented and what the repertoire was 'saying'.

For Michael Boyd there were urgent questions: revitalising the Shakespeare work, the balance within the repertoire between Shakespeare and other, particularly new, work and the RSC's relationship to living playwrights; whether or not to re-establish a permanent presence in London; the future of the Royal Shakespeare Theatre and the nature of any new spaces created in Stratford; whether or in what combination The Other Place would remain as a school, expand as an education centre or be restored to its earlier function as a theatre; and the rebuilding of the RSC's internal culture through greater care of the actor, restoring rehearsals as the prime site for discovery allied to a new training, research and development programme. And there was the most pressing issue: would the direction the RSC takes be towards company or corporation? The RSC will be pulled in both directions; how the art and the management co-exist will be critical and time will tell to what extent company aspirations and corporate reality are compatible with each other and where the breaking point between the burden of the past and reform for the future might come.

Once again the RSC would have to examine the sources of its public legitimacy and, while attempting to swell its private coffers, justify again the sums of public money expended on supporting the company, a registered charity, in post-welfare state Britain. Large sums were found to bail the RSC out of its troubles during the Noble modernisation process, but to what extent would the Arts Council support the new RSC and on what conditions? Some commentators believed that without the national glue of Shakespeare to hold the RSC together, it would not have continued to receive state funding in the last years of the twentieth century. If in the twenty-first it were simply to be a very large theatrical organisation, however prestigious an international player in the global entertainment market, on what basis could it lay claim to this subsidy? Other national arts bodies, like the English National Opera, were also in difficulties and competition for the subsidy cake was fierce. How would the RSC fare? Unless it returned to its public service roots as a company, would it be any different to other national organisations operating in areas of economic activity for which state help is controversial and vulnerable, such as shipbuilding, aviation, agriculture and energy?

There are signs that Michael Boyd is tackling his daunting task head on. Plans for his inaugural season in 2004 show a return to first principles: he is seeking a new London home and to recreate a dedicated core ensemble of actors at the heart of the RSC. There will be increased time for preparation, a revived interest in text and voice work, a new emphasis on movement, and a more organic relationship between Shakespeare production and new writing. He has also seen the resignation of managing director Chris Foy, who, like one of his predecessors Derek Hornby, was also appointed from the business world and departed a short while into the tenure of a new artistic director. Foy's close association with the RSC's corporate stance and the re-organisation shambles that led to Noble's resignation suggests that Boyd has asserted the primacy of his own ideas. Indeed, he will need to provide strong and resolute leadership in order to set and maintain clarity of purpose, lift morale and navigate a clear course in the reinvention of the RSC artistically and organisationally.

The RSC story has been one of many achievements and much struggle, both internal and external. In the battles as well as in the triumphs, the issue of company has been central, and it will remain so in the future. The value of company can be seen in the scope, scale and quality of the RSC's work, particularly in the renaissance of large-stage, publicly committed Shakespeare for which it was responsible. The company added durability to recognition as a mark of its legitimacy as an institution of national and international standing and kept itself alive through an inner, creative discontent, a feeling that no problem had been solved definitively. This search to find integrity and passion in presenting plays – in the speaking of the words, the movement, the sets, the costumes, the sounds, the supporting apparatus – can never be finished because theatre is ephemeral, a series of partial successes and failures that do not endure. But how to find the institutional forms that serve that creative impulse, retain knowledge and develop expertise? What happens when the inner discontent subsides or is overwhelmed by the needs of the institution?

The bursts of renewal that revivified the RSC defied expectation but the pattern was jeopardised by the company's very size and success. At the beginning of the twenty-first century the tension between company and corporation caused the institution to spiral out of control. In the breach between the RSC's original desire, which was still invoked, and the actual practice, it had become clear that the company's heartbeat was growing fainter and the body was in danger of becoming a corpse. The legacy of the RSC as one of the great international theatre organisations with a rich history of remarkable attainment made the task of rebirth in the new conditions of a new century all the more onerous. It is an issue that concerns the theatrical profession but it is also an issue that society should care about and become engaged in, not only because the health of the nation can be read in the health of its cultural institutions – however indirectly – but because of the crisis in national institutions generally.

Whether or not the RSC can regenerate again as an innovative company at the centre of theatrical creativity or becomes an institution enslaved to corporate demands is a question as critical for an increasingly uncertain Britain as it is for the company itself.

# APPENDIX

# PRODUCTIONS 1960–2002/3

The list runs from the first season under Peter Hall to the last under Adrian Noble. It is arranged chronologically by year for ease of reference but it should be noted that seasons in Stratford and London varied in length and did not coincide exactly with calendar years. Tours and transfers also often ran or occurred beyond the calendar year in which they appear here. Titles are given for the year in which productions opened and are not repeated for subsequent years if the run is continuous. The list omits Theatregoround shows (save those that formed part of an RSC season), residencies, fringe productions and festival productions.

The name of the play is followed by its author – with the exception of titles by Shakespeare – and by the director. For example, *The Homecoming* (Harold Pinter; Peter Hall). 'T' indicates a transfer. 'R' indicates a revival (or occasionally a return of a production that has only recently left the repertoire).

## 1960

### Shakespeare Memorial Theatre

*The Two Gentlemen of Verona* (Peter Hall) [first performance by new company, 5 April]
*The Merchant of Venice* (Michael Langham)
*Twelfth Night* (Peter Hall)
*The Taming of the Shrew* (John Barton)
*Troilus and Cressida* (Peter Hall and John Barton; UK tour)
*The Winter's Tale* (Peter Wood)

### Aldwych Theatre

*The Duchess of Malfi* (John Webster; Donald McWhinnie) [first performance by new company, 15 December]
*Twelfth Night* (Peter Hall; T)

## 1961

### Royal Shakespeare Theatre

*Much Ado About Nothing* (Michael Langham)
*Hamlet* (Peter Wood)
*Richard III* (William Gaskill)
*As You Like It* (Michael Elliott)
*Romeo and Juliet* (Peter Hall)
*Othello* (Franco Zeffirelli)

## Aldwych Theatre

[season began December 1960 with *The Duchess of Malfi* and *Twelfth Night*]
*Ondine* (Jean Giraudoux; Peter Hall)
*The Devils* (John Whiting; Peter Wood; UK tour)
*The Hollow Crown* (adapt. and directed John Barton; T from UK tour; toured UK and
   abroad)
*Becket* (Jean Anouilh, trans. Lucienne Hill; Peter Hall; transfers to West End)
*The Taming of the Shrew* (Maurice Daniels; T)
*The Cherry Orchard* (Anton Chekhov, adapt. John Gielgud; Michel Saint-Denis)

## 1962

## Royal Shakespeare Theatre

*Measure for Measure* (John Blatchley)
*A Midsummer Night's Dream* (Peter Hall; R of 1959 production; UK tour)
*The Taming of the Shrew* (Maurice Daniels; R)
*Macbeth* (Donald McWhinnie)
*Cymbeline* (William Gaskill)
*The Comedy of Errors* (Clifford Williams)
*King Lear* (Peter Brook)

## Aldwych Theatre

*As You Like It* (Michael Elliott; T)
*The Art of Seduction* (Choderlos de Laclos, adapt. and directed John Barton)
*The Caucasian Chalk Circle* (Bertolt Brecht, trans. John Holmstrom; William Gaskill)
*Playing with Fire* (August Strindberg, trans. Michael Meyer; John Blatchley) and
*The Collection* (Harold Pinter; Peter Hall and Harold Pinter)
*A Penny for a Song* (John Whiting; Colin Graham)
*Curtmantle* (Christopher Fry; Stuart Burge; from UK tour)
*Troilus and Cressida* (Peter Hall; R)
*The Devils* (Peter Wood; R)
*King Lear* (Peter Brook; T; toured abroad)
*The Comedy of Errors* (Clifford Williams; T; toured abroad)

## Arts Theatre

*Everything in the Garden* (Giles Cooper; Donald McWhinnie; transfers to West End)
*Nil Carborundum* (Henry Livings; Anthony Page)
*The Lower Depths* (Maxim Gorky, adapt. Derek Marlowe; Toby Robertson)
*Afore Night Come* (David Rudkin; Clifford Williams)
*Women Beware Women* (Thomas Middleton; Anthony Page)
*The Empire Builders* (Boris Vian, trans. Simon Watson Taylor; David Jones)
*Infanticide in the House of Fred Ginger* (Fred Watson; William Gaskill)

## 1963

## Royal Shakespeare Theatre

*The Tempest* (Clifford Williams in collaboration with Peter Brook)
*Julius Caesar* (John Blatchley)
*The Comedy of Errors* (Clifford Williams; R)
*The Wars of the Roses:*

*Henry VI* (Peter Hall, with John Barton and Frank Evans)
*Edward IV* ((Peter Hall, with John Barton and Frank Evans)
*Richard III* ((Peter Hall, with John Barton and Frank Evans)

## Aldwych Theatre

*The Physicists* (Friedrich Dürrenmatt, trans. James Kirkup; Peter Brook; UK tour)
*A Midsummer Night's Dream* (Peter Hall; T; UK tour)
*The Beggar's Opera* (John Gay; Peter Wood)
*The Representative* (Rolf Hochhuth, trans. Robert David MacDonald; Clifford Williams)
*The Hollow Crown* (John Barton; R)
*The Comedy of Errors* (Clifford Williams; T)

# 1964

## Royal Shakespeare Theatre

*Richard II* (Peter Hall, John Barton and Clifford Williams)
*Henry IV Part 1* (Peter Hall, John Barton and Clifford Williams)
*Henry IV Part 2* (Peter Hall, John Barton and Clifford Williams)
*Henry V* (Peter Hall and John Barton)
*The Wars of the Roses:*
*Henry VI* (Peter Hall and John Barton; R)
*Edward IV* ((Peter Hall and John Barton; R)
*Richard III* ((Peter Hall and John Barton; R)

## Aldwych Theatre

*The Wars of the Roses:*
*Henry VI* (Peter Hall, with John Barton and Frank Evans; T)
*Edward IV* ((Peter Hall, with John Barton and Frank Evans; T)
*Richard III* ((Peter Hall, with John Barton and Frank Evans; T)
*King Lear* (Peter Brook; R; toured abroad)
*The Comedy of Errors* (Clifford Williams; R; toured abroad)
*The Rebel* (devised and directed Patrick Garland)
[World Theatre Season]
*The Birthday Party* (Harold Pinter; Harold Pinter)
*Afore Night Come* (David Rudkin; Clifford Williams; R)
*Expeditions One* (James Saunders, Jean Tardieu, Samuel Beckett, Fernando Arrabal, John
    Whiting; Robin Midgley, Garry O'Connor, Elsa Bolam, John Schlesinger)
*Endgame* (Samuel Beckett; Donald McWhinnie)
*Victor* (Roger Vitrac, trans. Lucienne Hill; Robin Midgley)
*Marat/Sade* (Peter Weiss, trans. Geoffrey Skelton; Peter Brook)
*The Jew of Malta* (Christopher Marlowe; Clifford Williams)
*Eh?* (Henry Livings; Peter Hall)
*The Merry Wives of Windsor* (John Blatchley)

*Theatre of Cruelty* season under Peter Brook and Charles Marowitz at LAMDA (varied
    programme) and Donmar Rehearsal Rooms (scenes from *The Screens*, Jean Genet,
    trans. Bernard Frechtman)

# 1965

## Royal Shakespeare Theatre

*Love's Labour's Lost* (John Barton)
*The Jew of Malta* (Christopher Marlowe; Clifford Williams; T)
*The Merchant of Venice* (Clifford Williams)
*The Comedy of Errors* (Clifford Williams; R)
*Timon of Athens* (John Schlesinger)
*Hamlet* (Peter Hall)

## Aldwych Theatre

*Expeditions Two* (Charles Wood, Johnny Speight, Irene Coates, David Mercer; David
    Jones with Trevor Nunn)
*The Comedy of Errors* (Clifford Williams; R; UK tour)
[World Theatre Season]
*Henry V* (John Barton and Trevor Nunn)
*The Homecoming* (Harold Pinter; Peter Hall; UK tour and transfer to US)
*Squire Puntilla and His Servant Matti* (Bertolt Brecht, adapt. Jeremy Brooks; Michel
    Saint-Denis)
*The Hollow Crown* (John Barton; R)
*The Investigation* (Peter Weiss, trans. Alexander Gross; Peter Brook and David Jones)
*Marat/Sade* (Peter Brook; R; transfer to US)
*The Thwarting of Baron Bolligrew* (Robert Bolt; Trevor Nunn)
*Hamlet* (Peter Hall; T)


[Theatregoround launched]

# 1966

## Royal Shakespeare Theatre

*Henry IV Part 1* (John Barton, Clifford Williams and Trevor Nunn; R)
*Henry IV Part 2* (John Barton, Clifford Williams and Trevor Nunn; R)
*Twelfth Night* (Clifford Williams)
*Henry V* (John Barton and Trevor Nunn; R)
*Hamlet* (Peter Hall; R)
*The Revenger's Tragedy* (Cyril Tourneur; Trevor Nunn)

## Aldwych Theatre

*The Government Inspector* (Nikolai Gogol, adapt. Jeremy Brooks; Peter Hall)
*The Investigation* (Peter Brook and David Jones; R)
[World Theatre Season]
*Tango* (Sławomir Mrożek, adapt. Tom Stoppard; Trevor Nunn)
*Days in the Trees* (Marguerite Duras, trans. Sonia Orwell; John Schlesinger)
*The Meteor* (Friedrich Dürrenmatt, trans. James Kirkup; Clifford Williams)
*US* (collectively created; Peter Brook)
*Staircase* (Charles Dyer; Peter Hall; played Brighton)
*Belcher's Luck* (David Mercer; David Jones)
*The Homecoming* (Peter Hall; R)
*The Thwarting of Baron Bolligrew* (Trevor Nunn; R)

# 1967

## Royal Shakespeare Theatre

*The Taming of the Shrew* (Trevor Nunn; toured UK and abroad)
*Coriolanus* (John Barton)
*The Revenger's Tragedy* (Trevor Nunn; R)
*All's Well That Ends Well* (John Barton; toured abroad)
*As You Like It* (David Jones; toured UK and abroad)
*Macbeth* (Peter Hall; toured abroad)
*Romeo and Juliet* (Karolos Koun)

## Aldwych Theatre

[World Theatre Season]
*Ghosts* (Henrik Ibsen, adapt. Denis Cannan; Alan Bridges; UK tour)
*Little Murders* (Jules Feiffer; Christopher Morahan)
*As You Like It* (David Jones; T)
*The Taming of the Shrew* (Trevor Nunn; T)
*The Relapse* (John Vanbrugh; Trevor Nunn; UK tour)
*The Criminals* (José Triana; Terry Hands)
*The Hollow Crown* (John Barton; R)

# 1968

## Royal Shakespeare Theatre

*Julius Caesar* (John Barton; UK tour)
*King Lear* (Trevor Nunn)
*The Merry Wives of Windsor* (Terry Hands; UK tour)
*As You Like It* (David Jones; R)
*Dr Faustus* (Christopher Marlowe; Clifford Williams; toured abroad)
*Troilus and Cressida* (John Barton)
*Much Ado About Nothing* (Trevor Nunn; toured abroad)

## Aldwych Theatre

*Macbeth* (Peter Hall; T)
*All's Well That Ends Well* (John Barton; T)
*Under Milk Wood* (Dylan Thomas; Terry Hands; Theatregoround)
[World Theatre Season]
*Indians* (Arthur Kopit; Terry Hands)
*The Merry Wives of Windsor* (Terry Hands; T)
*The Relapse* (Trevor Nunn; R)
*The Latent Heterosexual* (Paddy Chayevsky; Terry Hands)
*God Bless* (Jules Feiffer; Geoffrey Reeves)
*Julius Caesar* (John Barton; T)

# 1969

## Royal Shakespeare Theatre

*Pericles* (Terry Hands)
*The Merry Wives of Windsor* (Terry Hands; R; toured abroad)
*The Winter's Tale* (Trevor Nunn)

*When Thou Art King* (adapt. and directed John Barton; Theatregoround)
*Women Beware Women* (Thomas Middleton; Terry Hands)
*Twelfth Night* (John Barton)
*Henry VIII* (Trevor Nunn)

### Aldwych Theatre

*A Delicate Balance* (Edward Albee; Peter Hall)
*A Dutch Uncle* (Simon Gray; Peter Hall)
[World Theatre Season]
*Troilus and Cressida* (John Barton; T; toured abroad)
*Landscape* and *Silence* (Harold Pinter; Peter Hall)
*Much Ado About Nothing* (Trevor Nunn; T)
*The Silver Tassie* (Sean O'Casey; David Jones)
*Bartholomew Fair* (Ben Jonson; Terry Hands)
*The Revenger's Tragedy* (Trevor Nunn; R)

## 1970

### Royal Shakespeare Theatre

*Measure for Measure* (John Barton)
*Richard III* (Terry Hands)
*Dr Faustus* (Christopher Marlowe; Gareth Morgan; Theatregoround)
*Hamlet* (Trevor Nunn)
*King John* (Buzz Goodbody; Theatregoround)
*The Two Gentlemen of Verona* (Robin Phillips)
*A Midsummer Night's Dream* (Peter Brook)
*The Tempest* (John Barton)

### Aldwych Theatre

*Tiny Alice* (Edward Albee; Robin Phillips)
*After Haggerty* (David Mercer; David Jones; transferred to West End)
[World Theatre Season]
*London Assurance* (Dion Boucicault; Ronald Eyre; transfer to West End and US)
*The Winter's Tale* (Trevor Nunn; T; toured abroad)
*The Plebeians Rehearse the Uprising* (Günter Grass, trans. Ralph Mannheim; David Jones)
*Twelfth Night* (John Barton; T; toured abroad)
*When Thou Art King* (John Barton; R)
*Major Barbara* (George Bernard Shaw; Clifford Williams)
*Henry VIII* (Trevor Nunn; T)
*The Two Gentlemen of Verona* (Robin Phillips; T)

### Round House

Theatregoround Festival:
*When Thou Art King* (John Barton; T)
*Arden of Faversham* (anon; Buzz Goodbody)
*King John* (Buzz Goodbody; T)
*Dr Faustus* (Gareth Morgan; T)
*A Midsummer Night's Dream* (Peter Brook; T) ⎫
*Richard III* (Terry Hands; T)                 ⎬ studio performances
*Hamlet* (Trevor Nunn; T)                      ⎭

## 1971

### Royal Shakespeare Theatre

*The Merchant of Venice* (Terry Hands)
*Twelfth Night* (John Barton; R)
*Richard II* (John Barton; Theatregoround)
*Henry V* (John Barton; Theatregoround)
*Much Ado About Nothing* (Ronald Eyre)
*The Duchess of Malfi* (John Webster; Clifford Williams)
*Othello* (John Barton)

### Aldwych Theatre

*Old Times* (Harold Pinter; Peter Hall; UK tour, transfer to US)
[World Theatre Season]
*A Midsummer Night's Dream* (Peter Brook; T; toured abroad)
*Enemies* (Maxim Gorky; trans. Kitty Hunter Blair and Jeremy Brooks; David Jones)
*The Man of Mode* (George Etherege; Terry Hands)
*Exiles* (James Joyce; Harold Pinter)
*The Balcony* (Jean Genet, trans. Barbara Wright and Terry Hands; Terry Hands)
*Much Ado About Nothing* (Ronald Eyre; T)

### The Place

*Occupations* (Trevor Griffiths; Buzz Goodbody)
*Subject to Fits* (Robert Montgomery; A.J. Antoon)
*Miss Julie* (August Strindberg, trans. Michael Meyer; Robin Phillips)

[Theatregoround closed]

## 1972

### Royal Shakespeare Theatre

*Toad of Toad Hall* (A.A. Milne; Euan Smith)
*The Romans:*
*Coriolanus* (Trevor Nunn, with Buzz Goodbody)
*Julius Caesar* (Trevor Nunn, with Buzz Goodbody and Euan Smith)
*The Comedy of Errors* (Clifford Williams; R)
*Antony and Cleopatra* (Trevor Nunn, with Buzz Goodbody and Euan Smith)
*Titus Andronicus* (Trevor Nunn, with John Barton, Buzz Goodbody and Euan Smith)

### Aldwych Theatre

*All Over* (Edward Albee; Peter Hall)
*The Oz Trial* (adapted by David Illingworth and Geoffrey Robertson; Buzz Goodbody)
[World Theatre Season]
*The Merchant of Venice* (Terry Hands; T)
*The Lower Depths* (Maxim Gorky, trans. Kitty Hunter Blair and Jeremy Brooks; David Jones)
*Othello* (John Barton; T)
*A Midsummer Night's Dream* (Peter Brook; R)
*Murder in the Cathedral* (T.S. Eliot; Terry Hands)
*The Island of the Mighty* (John Arden and Margaretta D'Arcy; David Jones)

# 1973

## Royal Shakespeare Theatre

*A Midsummer Night's Dream* (Peter Brook; R)
*Romeo and Juliet* (Terry Hands)
*Richard II* (John Barton)
*As You Like It* (Buzz Goodbody)
*Love's Labour's Lost* (David Jones)
*The Taming of the Shrew* (Clifford Williams)
*Toad of Toad Hall* (Euan Smith; R)

## The Studio

*Three Women* (Sylvia Plath; Barry Kyle; later, with material added by Kyle, *Sylvia Plath*)
*Christopher Columbus* and *Escurial* (Michel de Ghelderode; Patrick Tucker)

## Aldwych Theatre

*Suzanna Andler* (Marguerite Duras, trans. Barbara Bray; Howard Sackler)
[World Theatre Season]
*Antony and Cleopatra* (Trevor Nunn, assisted by Euan Smith; T)
*Julius Caesar* (Trevor Nunn, with Buzz Goodbody and Euan Smith; T)
*Titus Andronicus* (Trevor Nunn, with Buzz Goodbody and Euan Smith; T)
*Landscape* (Harold Pinter; Peter Hall; R) and
*A Slight Ache* (Harold Pinter; Peter James)
*Coriolanus* (Trevor Nunn, with Buzz Goodbody and Euan Smith; T)
*Midwinter Spring* (Nicol Williamson; Nicol Williamson)

## The Place

*Cries from Casement as His Bones Are Brought to Dublin* (David Rudkin; Terry Hands)
*Section Nine* (Philip Magdalany; Charles Marowitz)
*Hello and Goodbye* (Athol Fugard; Peter Stevenson)
*Sylvia Plath* (devised and directed Barry Kyle)
*A Lesson in Blood and Roses* (John Wiles; Clifford Williams)

# 1974

## Royal Shakespeare Theatre

*King John* (John Barton with Barry Kyle)
*Richard II* (John Barton; R; toured)
*Cymbeline* (John Barton with Barry Kyle and Clifford Williams)
*Twelfth Night* (Peter Gill)
*Measure for Measure* (Keith Hack)
*Macbeth* (Trevor Nunn)

## The Other Place

*King Lear* (Buzz Goodbody; toured) [first performance, 10 April]
*I Was Shakespeare's Double* (John Downie with Penny Gold; Howard Davies)
*Babies Grow Old* (devised and directed Mike Leigh; toured)
*The Tempest* (Keith Hack)
*Afore Night Come* (David Rudkin; Ron Daniels)
*Uncle Vanya* (Anton Chekhov, trans. Mike Nichols and Albert Todd; Nicol Williamson)

## Aldwych Theatre

*Sherlock Holmes* (adapt. William Gillette; Frank Dunlop; toured, transfer to US)
*Section Nine* (Charles Marowitz; R)
*Duck Song* (David Mercer; David Jones)
*The Bewitched* (Peter Barnes; Terry Hands)
*Travesties* (Tom Stoppard; Peter Wood; transfer to US)
*Summerfolk* (Maxim Gorky, trans. Kitty Hunter Blair and Jeremy Brooks; David Jones; toured)
*Dr Faustus* (Christopher Marlowe; John Barton; toured)
*Richard II* (John Barton; T)
*The Marquis of Keith* (Frank Wedekind, adapt. Ronald Eyre and Alan Best; Ronald Eyre)
*Cymbeline* (John Barton with Barry Kyle and Clifford Williams; T)

## The Place

*Comrades* (August Strindberg, adapt. Jeremy Brooks; Barry Kyle)
*The Can Opener* (Victor Lanoux, adapt. Charles Wood; Walter Donohue)
*King Lear* (Buzz Goodbody; T)
*The Beast* (Snoo Wilson; Howard Davies)

# 1975

## Royal Shakespeare Theatre

*Midwinter Spring* (Nicol Williamson; R)
[new season]
*Henry V* (Terry Hands)
*Henry IV Part 1* (Terry Hands)
*Henry IV Part 2* (Terry Hands)
*The Merry Wives of Windsor* (Terry Hands; R)

## The Other Place

*Hamlet* (Buzz Goodbody)
*The Mouth Organ* (devised and directed Ralph Koltai and Clifford Williams)
*Perkin Warbeck* (John Ford; Barry Kyle and John Barton)
*Man is Man* (Bertolt Brecht, trans. Steve Gooch; Howard Davies)
*Richard III* (Barry Kyle)

## Aldwych Theatre

*King John* (John Barton with Barry Kyle; T)
*Twelfth Night* (Peter Gill; T)
*Macbeth* (Trevor Nunn; T)
*Midwinter Spring* (Nicol Williamson; R)
*Love's Labour's Lost* (David Jones; R; toured)
*Travesties* (Peter Wood; R; transfer to US)
*Hedda Gabler* (Henrik Ibsen, adapt. Trevor Nunn; Trevor Nunn; toured abroad)
*Jingo* (Charles Wood; Ronald Eyre)
*The Marrying of Anne Leete* (Harley Granville Barker; David Jones)
*Too True to Be Good* (George Bernard Shaw; Clifford Williams; transfer to West End)
*The Return of A.J. Raffles* (Graham Greene; David Jones)

# 1976

## Royal Shakespeare Theatre

*The Return of A.J. Raffles* (David Jones; T)
[new season]
*Romeo and Juliet* (Trevor Nunn and Barry Kyle)
*Much Ado About Nothing* (John Barton)
*The Winter's Tale* (John Barton and Trevor Nunn)
*Troilus and Cressida* (John Barton and Barry Kyle)
*The Comedy of Errors* (Trevor Nunn)
*King Lear* (Trevor Nunn, John Barton and Barry Kyle)

## The Other Place

*Schweyk in the Second World War* (Bertolt Brecht, trans. Sue Davies; Howard Davies)
*Dingo* (Charles Wood; Barry Kyle)
*Macbeth* (Trevor Nunn)
*Destiny* (David Edgar; Ron Daniels)
*Bingo* (Edward Bond; Howard Davies)

## Aldwych Theatre

*Henry V* (Terry Hands; T; toured)
*Henry IV Part 1* (Terry Hands; T)
*Henry IV Part 2* (Terry Hands; T)
*The Merry Wives of Windsor* (Terry Hands; T)
*The Zykovs* (Maxim Gorky, trans. Kitty Hunter Blair and Jeremy Brooks; David Jones)
*The Iceman Cometh* (Eugene O'Neill; Howard Davies)
*The Devil's Disciple* (George Bernard Shaw; Jack Gold)
*Ivanov* (Anton Chekhov, trans. Jeremy Brooks and Kitty Hunter Blair; David Jones)
*Old World* (Alexei Arbuzov, trans. Ariadne Nicolaeff; Terry Hands)
*Wild Oats* (John O'Keeffe; Clifford Williams)

## Round House

*Hamlet* (Buzz Goodbody; T)
*Man is Man* (Howard Davies; T)

# 1977

## Royal Shakespeare Theatre

*Wild Oats* (John O'Keeffe; Clifford Williams; T; transfer to West End)
[new season]
*Macbeth* (Trevor Nunn; T)
*A Midsummer Night's Dream* (John Barton and Gillian Lynne)
*The Comedy of Errors* (Trevor Nunn; R)
*Henry VI Part 1* (Terry Hands)
*Henry VI Part 2* (Terry Hands)
*Henry VI Part 3* (Terry Hands)
*Henry V* (Terry Hands; R)
*As You Like It* (Trevor Nunn)
*Coriolanus* (Terry Hands)

## The Other Place

*The Alchemist* (Ben Jonson; Trevor Nunn)
*'Tis Pity She's a Whore* (John Ford; Ron Daniels)
*The Lorenzaccio Story* (Paul Thompson after Alfred de Musset; Ron Daniels)
*Queen Christina* (Pam Gems; Penny Cherns)
*The Sons of Light* (David Rudkin; Ron Daniels)

## Aldwych Theatre

*Privates on Parade* (Peter Nichols; Michael Blakemore; transfer to West End)
*King Lear* (Trevor Nunn, John Barton and Barry Kyle; T)
*Destiny* (Ron Daniels; T)
*The Comedy of Errors* (Trevor Nunn; T)
*A Midsummer Night's Dream* (John Barton and Gillian Lynne; T)
*Much Ado About Nothing* (John Barton; T)
*Romeo and Juliet* (Trevor Nunn and Barry Kyle; T)
*Pillars of the Community* (Henrik Ibsen, adapt. Inga-Stina Ewbank; John Barton)
*Troilus and Cressida* (John Barton and Barry Kyle; T)
*The Days of the Commune* (Bertolt Brecht, trans. Clive Barker and Arno Reinfrank; Howard Davies)
*The Alchemist* (Trevor Nunn; T)

## The Warehouse

*Schweyk in the Second World War* (Howard Davies; T) [first performance 18 July]
*Macbeth* (Trevor Nunn; T)
*That Good Between Us* (Howard Barker; Barry Kyle)
*Bandits* (C.P. Taylor; Howard Davies)
*Bingo* (Howard Davies; T)
*Factory Birds* (James Robson; Bill Alexander)
*Frozen Assets* (Barrie Keeffe; Barry Kyle)
*The Bundle* (Edward Bond; Howard Davies)
*Dingo* (Charles Wood; Barry Kyle; T [1978])
[West End: *Man and Superman* (George Bernard Shaw; Clifford Williams)
First annual Newcastle-upon-Tyne residency]

# 1978

## The Royal Shakespeare Theatre

*The Taming of the Shrew* (Michael Bogdanov)
*The Tempest* (Clifford Williams)
*Measure for Measure* (Barry Kyle)
*Love's Labour's Lost* (John Barton)
*Antony and Cleopatra* (Peter Brook)

## The Other Place

*The Merchant of Venice* (John Barton)
*Captain Swing* (Peter Whelan; Bill Alexander)
*The Churchill Play* (Howard Brenton; Barry Kyle)
*Piaf* (Pam Gems; Howard Davies)
*Hippolytus* (Euripides, adapt. David Rudkin; Ron Daniels)
*The Shepherd's Play* (adapt. John Barton; David Tucker)

## Aldwych Theatre

*The Way of the World* (William Congreve; John Barton)
*Henry V* (Terry Hands; T)
*Henry VI Part 1* (Terry Hands; T)
*Henry VI Part 2* (Terry Hands; T)
*Henry VI Part 3* (Terry Hands; T)
*Coriolanus* (Terry Hands; T; toured abroad)
*A Miserable and Lonely Death* (dramatisation of Steve Biko inquest by Norman Fenton
  and Jon Blair; Walter Donohue; T)
*The Dance of Death* (August Strindberg, trans. Michael Meyer; John Caird; T)
*The Women Pirates* (Steve Gooch; Ron Daniels)
*As You Like It* (Trevor Nunn; T)
*Cousin Vladimir* (David Mercer; Jane Howell)
*The Changeling* (Thomas Middleton and William Rowley; Terry Hands)
*Saratoga* (Bronson Howard; Ronald Eyre)

## The Warehouse

*Dingo* (Charles Wood; Barry Kyle; T)
[new season]
*The Lorenzaccio Story* (Paul Thompson after Alfred de Musset; Ron Daniels; T)
*The Dance of Death* (August Strindberg, trans. Michael Meyer; John Caird)
*'Tis Pity She's a Whore* (John Ford; Ron Daniels; T)
*The Sons of Light* (David Rudkin; Ron Daniels; T)
*The Jail Diary of Albie Sachs* (adapt. David Edgar; Howard Davies)
*Savage Amusement* (Peter Flannery; John Caird)
*A & R* (Pete Atkin; Walter Donohue)
*Shout Across the River* (Stephen Poliakoff; Bill Alexander)
*Look Out . . . Here Comes Trouble* (Mary O'Malley; John Caird)
*The Hang of the Gaol* (Howard Barker; Barry Kyle)
*The Adventures of Awful Knawful* (Peter Flannery and Mick Ford; John Caird and
  Howard Davies)

## Young Vic

*Macbeth* (Trevor Nunn; T)

## Small-scale Tour

*Twelfth Night* (Jon Amiel)
*Three Sisters* (Anton Chekhov, trans. Richard Cottrell; Trevor Nunn)
*And Is There Honey Still For Tea?* (devised and directed Roger Rees)

# 1979

## Royal Shakespeare Theatre

*The Merry Wives of Windsor* (Trevor Nunn)
*Cymbeline* (David Jones)
*Twelfth Night* (Terry Hands)
*Othello* (Ronald Eyre)
*Julius Caesar* (Barry Kyle)

## The Other Place

*Pericles* (Ron Daniels)
*The Jail Diary of Albie Sachs* (Howard Davies; T)
*The Suicide* (Nikolai Erdman, trans. Peter Tegel; Ron Daniels)
*Baal* (Bertolt Brecht, trans. Peter Tegel; David Jones)
*Anna Christie* (Eugene O'Neill; Jonathan Lynn)
*Three Sisters* (Trevor Nunn; T)

## Aldwych Theatre

*Love's Labour's Lost* (John Barton; T)
*The Taming of the Shrew* (Michael Bogdanov; T)
*The White Guard* (Mikhail Bulgakov, trans. Michael Glenny; Barry Kyle)
*Antony and Cleopatra* (Peter Brook; T)
*Wild Oats* (John O'Keeffe; Clifford Williams; R)
*Once in a Lifetime* (Moss Hart and George S. Kaufman; Trevor Nunn; transfer to West
    End)
*Children of the Sun* (Maxim Gorky, trans. Jeremy Brooks and Kitty Hunter Blair; Terry
    Hands)
*Measure for Measure* (Barry Kyle; T)
*Piaf* (Howard Davies; T; transfer to West End)
*The Greeks: The War, The Murders, The Gods* (John Barton and Kenneth Cavander; John
    Barton [1980])

## The Warehouse

*The Churchill Play* (Barry Kyle; T)
*The Merchant of Venice* (John Barton; T)
*The Innocent* (Tom McGrath; Howard Davies)
*Piaf* (Howard Davies; T)
*Hippolytus* (Ron Daniels; T)
*Captain Swing* (Bill Alexander; T)
*Much Ado About Nothing* (Howard Davies; T)
*Bastard Angel* (Barrie Keeffe; Bill Alexander [1980])
*The Caucasian Chalk Circle* (John Caird; T [1980])
*The Loud Boy's Life* (Howard Barker; Howard Davies [1980])

## Small-scale Tour

*Much Ado About Nothing* (Howard Davies)
*The Caucasian Chalk Circle* (Bertolt Brecht, trans. James and Tania Stern with W.H.
    Auden; John Caird)

# 1980

## Royal Shakespeare Theatre

*As You Like It* (Terry Hands)
*Romeo and Juliet* (Ron Daniels)
*Hamlet* (John Barton)
*Richard II* (Terry Hands)
*Richard III* (Terry Hands)
*The Swan Down Gloves* (Billie Brown and Nigel Hess; Ian Judge [1981])

## The Other Place

*The Shadow of the Gunman* (Sean O'Casey; Michael Bogdanov)
*The Maid's Tragedy* (Francis Beaumont and John Fletcher; Barry Kyle)
*The Fool* (Edward Bond; Howard Davies)
*Timon of Athens* (Ron Daniels)
*Hansel and Gretel* (David Rudkin; Ron Daniels)

## Aldwych Theatre

*The Greeks: The War, The Murders, The Gods* (John Barton and Kenneth Cavander; John
    Barton)
[new season]
*Twelfth Night* (Terry Hands; T)
*The Merry Wives of Windsor* (Trevor Nunn; T)
*The Life and Adventures of Nicholas Nickleby, Parts One and Two* (Charles Dickens, adapt.
    David Edgar; Trevor Nunn and John Caird)
*Othello* (Ronald Eyre; T)
*Juno and the Paycock* (Sean O'Casey; Trevor Nunn)

## The Warehouse

*Bastard Angel* (Barrie Keeffe; Bill Alexander)
*The Caucasian Chalk Circle* (John Caird; T)
*The Loud Boy's Life* (Howard Barker; Howard Davies)
[new season]
*Three Sisters* (Trevor Nunn; T)
*Pericles* (Ron Daniels; T)
*Anna Christie* (Jonathan Lynn; T)
*Educating Rita* (Willy Russell; Mike Ockrent; transfer to West End)
*The Suicide* (Ron Daniels; T)
*Baal* (David Jones; T)
*No Limits to Love* (David Mercer; Howard Davies)
*The Irish Play* (Ron Hutchinson; Barry Kyle)
*Television Times* (Peter Prince; Stephen Frears)
*Naked Robots* (Jonathan Gems; John Caird [1981])

## Regional Tour

*Henry IV, Parts 1* and *2* (Bill Alexander)

# 1981

## Royal Shakespeare Theatre

*The Merchant of Venice* (John Barton)
*A Winter's Tale* (Ronald Eyre)
*A Midsummer Night's Dream* (Ron Daniels)
*Titus Andronicus/The Two Gentlemen of Verona* (John Barton)
*All's Well That Ends Well* (Trevor Nunn; revived in New York)

## The Other Place

*The Forest* (Alexander Ostrovsky, trans. Jeremy Brooks and Kitty Hunter Blair; Adrian
    Noble)
*The Twin Rivals* (George Farquhar; John Caird)
*A Doll's House* (Henrik Ibsen, trans. Michael Meyer; Adrian Noble)

*The Witch of Edmonton* (Thomas Dekker, John Ford and William Rowley; Barry Kyle)
*Money* (Edward Bulwer-Lytton; Bill Alexander)

## Aldwych Theatre

*Passion Play* (Peter Nichols; Mike Ockrent)
*The Suicide* (Ron Daniels; T)
*Juno and the Paycock* (Trevor Nunn; R)
[new season]
*The Knight of the Burning Pestle* (Francis Beaumont; Michael Bogdanov)
*The Life and Adventures of Nicholas Nickleby, Parts One and Two* (Trevor Nunn and John
    Caird; R; transfer to New York)
*Troilus and Cressida* (Terry Hands)
*The Merchant of Venice* (John Barton; T)
*As You Like It* (Terry Hands; T)
*The Love Girl and the Innocent* (Alexander Solzhenitsyn, trans. Jeremy Brooks and Kitty
    Hunter-Blair; Clifford Williams)
*Hamlet* (John Barton; T)
*Romeo and Juliet* (Ron Daniels; T)
*Richard II* (Terry Hands; T)
*Richard III* (Terry Hands; T)
*The Swan Down Gloves* (Terry Hands; R)
*La Ronde* (Arthur Schnitzler, adapted John Barton and Sue Davies; John Barton [1982])
*The Forest* (Adrian Noble; T [1982])

## The Warehouse

*Naked Robots* (Jonathan Gems; John Caird)
[new season]
*The Accrington Pals* (Peter Whelan; Bill Alexander)
*Outskirts* (Hanif Kureishi; Howard Davies)
*Thirteenth Night* (Howard Brenton; Barry Kyle)
*The Forest* (Adrian Noble; T)
*The Shadow of the Gunman* (Michael Bogdanov; T)
*Good* (C.P. Taylor; Howard Davies)
*The Fool* (Howard Davies; T)
*The Maid's Tragedy* (Barry Kyle; T)
*Timon of Athens* (Ron Daniels; T)
*Hansel and Gretel* (Ron Daniels; T)

## Fortune Season

*The Hollow Crown* (John Barton; R)
*Pleasure and Repentance* (devised and directed Terry Hands)

# 1982

## Royal Shakespeare Theatre

*Macbeth* (Howard Davies)
*Much Ado About Nothing* (Terry Hands)
*King Lear* (Adrian Noble)
*The Tempest* (Ron Daniels)
*The Taming of the Shrew* (Barry Kyle)
*The Roaring Girl* (Thomas Middleton and Thomas Dekker; Barry Kyle [1983])

## The Other Place

*Our Friends in the North* (Peter Flannery; John Caird)
[new season]
*Arden of Faversham* (anon; Terry Hands)
*Peer Gynt* (Henrik Ibsen, adapt. David Rudkin; Ron Daniels)
*Lear* (Edward Bond; Barry Kyle)
*Molière* (Mikhail Bulgakov, adapt. Dusty Hughes; Bill Alexander)
*Antony and Cleopatra* (Adrian Noble)

## Aldwych Theatre

*La Ronde* (Arthur Schnitzler, adapted John Barton and Sue Davies; John Barton)
*The Forest* (Adrian Noble; T)
[*Richard II* (Terry Hands; T) is the final RSC performance, 13 March]

## Barbican Theatre

*The Swan Down Gloves* (Terry Hands; R) [plays before the Queen on official opening, 3 March]
*Henry IV, Parts 1* and *2* (Trevor Nunn) [open first RSC season, 9 June]
*A Midsummer Night's Dream* (Ron Daniels; T)
*All's Well That Ends Well* (Trevor Nunn; T; revived in New York)
*The Winter's Tale* (Ronald Eyre; T)
*Poppy* (Peter Nichols and Monty Norman; Terry Hands; transfer to West End)
*Peter Pan* (J.M. Barrie; John Caird and Trevor Nunn)

## The Warehouse

[last RSC performance *Timon of Athens* (Ron Daniels; T), 13 March]

## The Pit

*Our Friends in the North* (John Caird; T) [opens RSC season, 10 June]
*A Doll's House* (Adrian Noble; T)
*Money* (Bill Alexander; T)
*The Twin Rivals* (John Caird; T)
*The Witch of Edmonton* (Barry Kyle; T)
*Clay* (Peter Whelan; Bill Alexander)

# 1983

## Royal Shakespeare Theatre

*The Roaring Girl* (Thomas Middleton and Thomas Dekker; Barry Kyle)
[new season]
*Julius Caesar* (Ron Daniels)
*Twelfth Night* (John Caird)
*Henry VIII* (Howard Davies)
*The Comedy of Errors* (Adrian Noble)
*Measure for Measure* (Adrian Noble)

## The Other Place

*The Time of Your Life* (William Saroyan; Howard Davies)
*A New Way to Pay Old Debts* (Philip Massinger; Adrian Noble)
*The Dillen* (Angela Hewins, adapt. Ron Hutchinson; Barry Kyle)
*Volpone* (Ben Jonson; Bill Alexander)

*Life's a Dream* (Pedro Calderon de la Barca, adapt. John Barton and Adrian Mitchell; John Barton)

## Barbican Theatre

*The Roaring Girl* (Barry Kyle; T)
*The Taming of the Shrew* (Barry Kyle; T)
*Much Ado About Nothing* (Terry Hands; T; continental tour)
*King Lear* (Adrian Noble; T)
*Cyrano de Bergerac* (Edmond Rostand, trans. Anthony Burgess; Terry Hands; continental tour)
*Macbeth* (Howard Davies; T)
*The Tempest* (Ron Daniels; T)
*Maydays* (David Edgar; Ron Daniels)
*Peter Pan* (John Caird; R)

## The Pit

*Antony and Cleopatra* (Adrian Noble; T)
*The Body* (Nick Darke; Nick Hamm)
*Lear* (Barry Kyle; T; continental tour)
*Peer Gynt* (Ron Daniels; T)
*Tartuffe* (Molière, trans. Christopher Hampton; Bill Alexander)
*Arden of Faversham* (Terry Hands; T)
*Molière* (Bill Alexander; T)
*The Custom of the Country* (Nicholas Wright, from Francis Beaumont and John Fletcher; David Jones)
*Softcops* (Caryl Churchill; Howard Davies [1984])

## Regional Tour

*A Midsummer Night's Dream* (Sheila Hancock)
*Romeo and Juliet* (John Caird)

# 1984

## Royal Shakespeare Theatre

*Henry V* (Adrian Noble)
*The Merchant of Venice* (John Caird)
*Richard III* (Bill Alexander)
*Hamlet* (Ron Daniels)
*Love's Labour's Lost* (Barry Kyle)

## The Other Place

*A Midsummer Night's Dream* (Sheila Hancock; T)
*Camille* (Alexander Dumas fils, adapt. Pam Gems; Ron Daniels; transfer to West End)
*Romeo and Juliet* (John Caird; T)
*Golden Girls* (Louise Page; Barry Kyle)
*The Party* (Trevor Griffiths; Howard Davies with David Edgar)
*Today* (Robert Holman; Bill Alexander)
*The Desert Air* (Nicholas Wright; Adrian Noble)

## Barbican Theatre

*Measure for Measure* (Adrian Noble; T)
*The Comedy of Errors* (Adrian Noble; T)
*Julius Caesar* (Ron Daniels; T)
*The Happiest Days of Your Life* (John Dighton; Clifford Williams)
*Twelfth Night* (John Caird; T)
*Henry VIII* (Howard Davies; T)
*Mother Courage* (Bertolt Brecht, adapt. Hanif Kureishi; Howard Davies)
*Peter Pan* (John Caird; R)

## The Pit

*Volpone* (Bill Alexander; T)
*Life's a Dream* (John Barton; T)
*The Time of Your Life* (Howard Davies; T)
*Red Star* (Charles Wood; John Caird)
*The Devils* (John Whiting; John Barton)
*A New Way to Pay Old Debts* (Adrian Noble; T)
*Breaking the Silence* (Stephen Poliakoff; Ron Daniels; transfer to Mermaid Theatre)

## Regional Tour

*The Winter's Tale* (Adrian Noble)
*The Crucible* (Arthur Miller; Barry Kyle)

# 1985

## Royal Shakespeare Theatre

*The Merry Wives of Windsor* (Bill Alexander)
*As You Like It* (Adrian Noble)
*Troilus and Cressida* (Howard Davies)
*Othello* (Terry Hands)
*Nicholas Nickleby, Parts 1* and *2*, (Trevor Nunn, John Caird; R; UK, continental tour)

## The Other Place

*Philistines* (Maxim Gorky, adapt. Dusty Hughes; John Caird)
*The Dillen* (Barry Kyle; R)
*Les Liaisons Dangereuses* (Choderlos de Laclos, adapt. Christopher Hampton; Howard Davies)

## The Warehouse [temporary Stratford venue]

*Mary After the Queen* (Angela Hewins; Barry Kyle)
*The Taming of the Shrew* (Di Trevis; T)
*Happy End* (Di Trevis; T)

## Barbican Theatre

*Hamlet* (Ron Daniels; T)
*Richard III* (Bill Alexander; T)
*Henry V* (Adrian Noble; T)
*Red Noses* (Peter Barnes; Terry Hands)
*Love's Labour's Lost* (Barry Kyle; T)
*Les Misérables* (Alain Boublil, Claude-Michel Schönberg, after Victor Hugo; Trevor Nunn and John Caird; transfer to West End)

## The Pit

*Waste* (Harley Granville Barker; John Barton; transfer to West End)
*The Party* (Howard Davies with David Edgar; T)
*Golden Girls* (Barry Kyle; T)
*Today* (Bill Alexander; T)
*The War Plays:*
*Parts One and Two: Red Black and Ignorant* and *The Tin Can People* (Edward Bond; Edward Bond and Nick Hamm)
*Part Three: Great Peace* (Edward Bond; Nick Hamm)
*Dreamplay* (August Strindberg, adapt. John Barton; John Barton)
*The Desert Air* (Adrian Noble; T)
*Howard Barker Season:*
*Crimes in Hot Countries* (Bill Alexander)
*The Castle* (Nick Hamm)
*Downchild* (Bill Alexander and Nick Hamm)
*Melons* (Bernard Pomerance; Alison Sutcliffe)

## Regional Tour

*The Taming of the Shrew* (Di Trevis)
*Happy End* (Dorothy Lane, Kurt Weill, Bertolt Brecht, trans. Michael Feingold; Di Trevis)

# 1986

## Royal Shakespeare Theatre

*Romeo and Juliet* (Michael Bogdanov)
*The Winter's Tale* (Terry Hands)
*A Midsummer Night's Dream* (Bill Alexander)
*Richard II* (Barry Kyle)
*Macbeth* (Adrian Noble)

## Swan Theatre

*The Two Noble Kinsmen* (William Shakespeare and John Fletcher; Barry Kyle) [first performance, 28 April]
*Every Man in His Humour* (Ben Jonson; John Caird)
*The Rover* (Aphra Behn; John Barton)
*The Fair Maid of the West* (Thomas Heywood; Trevor Nunn [played at official opening before the Queen, 13 November])

## The Other Place

*Flight* (David Lan; Howard Davies)
*The Art of Success* (Nick Dear; Adrian Noble)
*Worlds Apart* (José Triana, adapt. Peter Whelan; Nick Hamm)
*Country Dancing* (Nigel Williams; Bill Alexander)

## Barbican Theatre

*As You Like It* (Adrian Noble; T)
*Othello* (Terry Hands; T)
*The Merry Wives of Windsor* (Bill Alexander; T)
*Mephisto* (Ariane Mnouchkine after Klaus Mann, trans. Timberlake Wertenbaker; Adrian Noble)
*Troilus and Cressida* (Howard Davies; T)

*The Danton Affair* (Stanisława Przybyszewska, adapt. Pam Gems; Ron Daniels)
*Misalliance* (George Bernard Shaw; John Caird)
*Scenes from a Marriage* (Georges Feydeau, adapt. Peter Barnes; Terry Hands)
*A Penny for a Song* (John Whiting; Howard Davies)

### The Pit

*Les Liaisons Dangereuses* (Howard Davies; T; transfer to West End and New York)
*Philistines* (John Caird; T)
*Il Candelaio* (Giordano Bruno, adapt. Frank Dotterell; Clifford Williams and Paul Marcus)
*Real Dreams* (Trevor Griffiths; Ron Daniels)
*The Dead Monkey* (Nick Darke; Roger Michell)
*Principia Scriptoriae* (Richard Nelson; David Jones)
*The Archbishop's Ceiling* (Arthur Miller; Nick Hamm)
*Heresies* (Deborah Levy; Susan Todd)

### Regional Tour

*Much Ado About Nothing* (Ron Daniels)
*The Merchant of Venice* (Roger Michell)

## 1987

### Royal Shakespeare Theatre

*Kiss Me Kate* (Cole Porter, Sam and Bella Spewack; Adrian Noble; UK tour and transfer to Old Vic)
[new season]
*Julius Caesar* (Terry Hands)
*The Merchant of Venice* (Bill Alexander)
*Twelfth Night* (Bill Alexander)
*The Taming of the Shrew* (Jonathan Miller)
*Measure for Measure* (Nicholas Hytner)

### Swan Theatre

*Hyde Park* (James Shirley; Barry Kyle)
*Titus Andronicus* (Deborah Warner)
*The Jew of Malta* (Christopher Marlowe; Barry Kyle)
*The Revenger's Tragedy* (Cyril Tourneur; Di Trevis)
*The New Inn* (Ben Jonson; John Caird)

### The Other Place

*Fashion* (Doug Lucie; Nick Hamm)
*Temptation* (Václav Havel, trans. George Theiner; Roger Michell)
*Indigo* (Heidi Thomas; Sarah Pia Anderson)
*A Question of Geography* (John Berger and Nella Bielski; John Caird)
*Cymbeline* (Bill Alexander)

### Barbican Theatre

*The Merry Wives of Windsor* (Bill Alexander; R)
[new season]
*Macbeth* (Adrian Noble; T)
*Romeo and Juliet* (Michael Bogdanov; T)

*Richard II* (Barry Kyle; T)
*The Balcony* (Jean Genet, trans. Terry Hands and Barbara Wright; Terry Hands)
*A Midsummer Night's Dream* (Bill Alexander; T)
*The Winter's Tale* (Terry Hands)
*The Wizard of Oz* (L. Frank Baum, adapt. John Kane; Ian Judge)

## The Pit

*Country Dancing* (Bill Alexander; T)
*Sarcophagus* (Vladimir Gubaryev, trans. Michael Glenny; Jude Kelly)
*Worlds Apart* (Nick Hamm)
*The Storm* (Alexander Ostrovsky, adapt. Stephen Lowe; Nick Hamm)
*Flight* (David Lan; Howard Davies)
*The Art of Success* (Nick Dear; Adrian Noble)
*Deathwatch* and *The Maids* (Jean Genet, adapt. David Rudkin; Gerard Murphy and
    Ultz)
*Old Year's Eve* (Peter Speyer; Sarah Pia Anderson)
*Speculators* (Tony Marchant; Barry Kyle)

## Mermaid Theatre

*The Fair Maid of the West* (Trevor Nunn; T)
*Every Man in His Humour* (John Caird; T)
*The Two Noble Kinsmen* (Barry Kyle)
*They Shoot Horses Don't They?* (Horace McCoy, adapt. Ray Herman; Ron Daniels)
*The Great White Hope* (Howard Sackler; Nicholas Kent)
*Sarcophagus* (Jude Kelly; T)
*The Rover* (John Barton; T)

## Regional Tour

*Hamlet* (Roger Michell)
*The Comedy of Errors* (Nick Hamm)

# 1988

## Royal Shakespeare Theatre

*Carrie* (Michael Gore, Dean Pitchford, Lawrence D. Chen, after Stephen King; Terry
    Hands)
[new season]
*Much Ado About Nothing* (Di Trevis)
*Macbeth* (Adrian Noble; R)
*The Tempest* (Nicholas Hytner)
*The Plantagenets*:
*Henry VI* (Adrian Noble)
*The Rise of Edward IV* (Adrian Noble)
*Richard III, His Death* (Adrian Noble)

## Swan Theatre

*The Constant Couple* (George Farquhar; Roger Michell)
*The Plain Dealer* (William Wycherley; Ron Daniels)
*The Man of Mode* (George Etherege; Garry Hynes)
*Restoration* (Edward Bond; Roger Michell)

## The Other Place

*Across Oka* (Robert Holman; Sarah Pia Anderson)
*King John* (Deborah Warner)
*The Love of the Nightingale* (Timberlake Wertenbaker; Garry Hynes)
*King Lear* (Cicely Berry)

## Barbican Theatre

*The Jew of Malta* (Barry Kyle; T)
*Twelfth Night* (Bill Alexander; T)
*The Merchant of Venice* (Bill Alexander; T)
*Julius Caesar* (Terry Hands; T)
*Three Sisters* (Anton Chekhov, adapt. John Barton from a literal trans. by Helen Rappaport; John Barton)
*The Taming of the Shrew* (Jonathan Miller; T)
*Measure for Measure* (Nicholas Hytner)
*The Churchill Play* (Howard Brenton; Barry Kyle)
*The Wizard of Oz* (Ian Judge; R)

## The Pit

*Cymbeline* (Bill Alexander; T)
*Fashion* (Nick Hamm; T)
*Temptation* (Roger Michell; T)
*The Revenger's Tragedy* (Di Trevis; T)
*Titus Andronicus* (Deborah Warner; T; continental tour)
*Hyde Park* (Barry Kyle; T)
*The Bite of the Night* (Howard Barker; Danny Boyle)
*Divine Gossip* (Stephen Lowe; Barry Kyle)
*A Question of Geography* (John Caird; T)
*Electra* (Sophocles, trans. Kenneth McLeish; Deborah Warner)

## Almeida Theatre

*Hello and Goodbye* (Athol Fugard; Janice Honeyman)
*Keeping Tom Nice* (Lucy Gannon; Bill Buffery)
*Oedipus* (Seneca, adapt. Ted Hughes; Donald Sumpter)

## UK Tour

*Hamlet* (Ron Daniels)

## Regional Tour

*The Beaux' Stratagem* (George Farquhar; Clifford Williams)
*A Midsummer Night's Dream* (Bill Buffery)

# 1989

## Royal Shakespeare Theatre

*The Wizard of Oz* (Ian Judge; T)
[new season]
*A Midsummer Night's Dream* (John Caird)
*Hamlet* (Ron Daniels; T)
*Cymbeline* (Bill Alexander)
*As You Like It* (Barry Kyle)

*All's Well That Ends Well* (Barry Kyle)
*Coriolanus* (Terry Hands with John Barton)

## Swan Theatre

*Romeo and Juliet* (Terry Hands)
*Dr Faustus* (Christopher Marlowe; Barry Kyle)
*The Silent Woman or Epicoene* (Ben Jonson; Danny Boyle)
*Pericles* (David Thacker)
*Singer* (Peter Flannery; Terry Hands)
*The Duchess of Malfi* (John Webster; Bill Alexander)

## The Other Place

*Othello* (Trevor Nunn; transfer to Young Vic) [final performance, 16 September. Theatre demolished; replaced with new theatre in 1991]

## Barbican Theatre

*The Plantagenets*:
*Henry VI* (Adrian Noble; T)
*The Rise of Edward IV* (Adrian Noble; T)
*Richard III, His Death* (Adrian Noble; T)
*Macbeth* (Adrian Noble; T)
*The Tempest* (Nicholas Hytner; T)
*The Man Who Came to Dinner* (Moss Hart and George S. Kaufman; Gene Saks)
*The Master Builder* (Henrik Ibsen, trans. Michael Meyer; Adrian Noble)
*Hamlet* (Ron Daniels; T)
*A Midsummer Night's Dream* (John Caird; T; UK tour)
*A Clockwork Orange* (Anthony Burgess; Ron Daniels [1990])

## The Pit

*Restoration* (Roger Michell; T)
*The Man of Mode* (Garry Hynes; T)
*King John* (Deborah Warner; T)
*The Plain Dealer* (Ron Daniels; T)
*Some Americans Abroad* (Richard Nelson; Roger Michell)
*Across Oka* (Sarah Pia Anderson; T)
*The Love of the Nightingale* (Garry Hynes; T)
*Mary and Lizzie* (Frank McGuinness; Sarah Pia Anderson)
*Playing with Trains* (Stephen Poliakoff; Ron Daniels)
*Dr Faustus* (Barry Kyle; T)
*Romeo and Juliet* (Terry Hands; T; regional tour)
*Have* (Julius Hay, trans. Peter Hay; Janice Honeyman [1990])

## Almeida Theatre

*King Lear* (Cicely Berry; T)
*Kissing the Pope* (Nick Darke; Roger Michell)
*H.I.D. (Hess is Dead)* (Howard Brenton; Danny Boyle)

## UK Tour

*A Midsummer Night's Dream* (John Caird)

## Regional Tour

*Romeo and Juliet* (Terry Hands)

## 1990

### Royal Shakespeare Theatre

*Show Boat* (Jerome Kern, Oscar Hammerstein II, after Edna Ferber; Ian Judge; co-production with Opera North; T from Leeds; transfer to West End)
[new season]
*Much Ado About Nothing* (Bill Alexander)
*The Comedy of Errors* (Ian Judge)
*King Lear* (Nicholas Hytner)
*Love's Labour's Lost* (Terry Hands)
*Richard II* (Ron Daniels)

### Swan Theatre

*The Last Days of Don Juan* (Tirso de Molina, adapt. Nick Dear; Danny Boyle)
*Troilus and Cressida* (Sam Mendes)
*Edward II* (Christopher Marlowe; Gerard Murphy)
*Two Shakespearean Actors* (Richard Nelson; Roger Michell)
*The Seagull* (Anton Chekhov, trans. Michael Frayn; Terry Hands)

### Barbican Theatre

*A Clockwork Orange* (Anthony Burgess; Ron Daniels; transfer to West End)
[new season]
*All's Well That Ends Well* (Barry Kyle; T)
*As You Like It* (Barry Kyle; T)
*Coriolanus* (Terry Hands with John Barton; T)
*Singer* (Terry Hands; T)
*Barbarians* (Maxim Gorky, trans. Jeremy Brooks and Kitty Hunter-Blair; David Jones)
*Moscow Gold* (Tariq Ali and Howard Brenton; Barry Kyle)

### The Pit

*Have* (Julius Hay, trans. Peter Hay; Janice Honeyman)
[new season]
*Singer* (Terry Hands; T)
*Pericles* (David Thacker; T)
*The Duchess of Malfi* (Bill Alexander; T)
*Earwig* (Paula Milne; Ron Daniels)
*A Dream of People* (Michael Hastings; Janet Suzman)

[Barbican Theatre and The Pit closed 3 November; reopened 21 March 1991]

### UK Tour

*Show Boat* (Ian Judge; T)

### UK and Continental Tour

*Les Liaisons Dangereuses* (West End production taken over by David Leveaux)

### Regional Tour

*The Taming of the Shrew* (Bill Alexander; tour abroad)

## 1991

### Royal Shakespeare Theatre

*Henry IV Part 1* (Adrian Noble)
*Twelfth Night* (Griff Rhys Jones)
*Henry IV Part 2* (Adrian Noble)
*Romeo and Juliet* (David Leveaux)
*Julius Caesar* (Steven Pimlott)

### Swan Theatre

*The Virtuoso* (Thomas Shadwell; Phyllida Lloyd)
*The Two Gentlemen of Verona* (David Thacker)
*'Tis Pity She's a Whore* (John Ford; David Leveaux)
*The Alchemist* (Ben Jonson; Sam Mendes)
*The Thebans* (Sophocles' three Oedipus plays, trans. Timberlake Wertenbaker; Adrian Noble)

### The Other Place

*The Blue Angel* (Pam Gems, after Heinrich Mann; Trevor Nunn) [first performance at new theatre 7 August 1991]
*Measure for Measure* (Trevor Nunn)
*A Woman Killed with Kindness* (Thomas Heywood; Katie Mitchell)

### Barbican Theatre

*Love's Labour's Lost* (Terry Hands; T)
*Much Ado About Nothing* (Bill Alexander; T)
*King Lear* (Nicholas Hytner; T)
*The Comedy of Errors* (Ian Judge; T)
*The Seagull* (Terry Hands; T)
*Richard II* (Ron Daniels; T)
*A Woman of No Importance* (Oscar Wilde; Philip Prowse)
*The Strange Case of Dr Jekyll and Mr Hyde* (Robert Louis Stevenson, adapt. David Edgar; Peter Wood)

### The Pit

*Two Shakespearean Actors* (Roger Michell; T)
*The Last Days of Don Juan* (Danny Boyle; T)
*Edward II* (Gerard Murphy; T)
*Troilus and Cressida* (Sam Mendes; T)
*Curse of the Starving Class* (Sam Shepard; Robin Lefevre)
*The Pretenders* (Henrik Ibsen, adapt. Chris Hannan; Danny Boyle)
*The Bright and Bold Design* (Peter Whelan; Bill Alexander)

### UK Tour

*Les Liaisons Dangereuses* (David Leveaux; T)

### Regional Tour

*The Blue Angel* (Trevor Nunn; T; transfer to West End)
*Measure for Measure* (Trevor Nunn; T; transfer to Young Vic)

# 1992

## Royal Shakespeare Theatre

*The Taming of the Shrew* (Bill Alexander)
*As You Like It* (David Thacker)
*The Winter's Tale* (Adrian Noble)
*The Merry Wives of Windsor* (David Thacker)
*Antony and Cleopatra* (John Caird)

## Swan Theatre

*The Beggar's Opera* (John Gay; John Caird)
*A Jovial Crew* (Richard Brome, adapt. Stephen Jeffreys; Max Stafford-Clark)
*All's Well That Ends Well* (Peter Hall)
*Tamburlaine the Great* (Christopher Marlowe; Terry Hands)
*The Changeling* (Thomas Middleton and William Rowley; Michael Attenborough)

## The Other Place

*The Odyssey* (Derek Walcott; Gregory Doran)
*Richard III* (Sam Mendes)
*The School of Night* (Peter Whelan; Bill Alexander)

## Barbican Theatre

*Henry IV Part 1* (Adrian Noble; T)
*The Alchemist* (Sam Mendes; T)
*Henry IV Part 2* (Adrian Noble; T)
*Romeo and Juliet* (David Leveaux; T)
*Columbus and the Discovery of Japan* (Richard Nelson; John Caird)
*The Two Gentlemen of Verona* (David Thacker; T)
*The Thebans* (Adrian Noble; T)
*Hamlet* (Adrian Noble)
*The Comedy of Errors* (Ian Judge; T)

## The Pit

*The Virtuoso* (Phyllida Lloyd; T)
*A Woman Killed with Kindness* (Katie Mitchell; T)
*'Tis Pity She's a Whore* (David Leveaux; T)
*The Dybbuk* (Solomon Anski, trans. Mira Rafolowicz; Katie Mitchell)
*Amphibians* (Billy Roche; Michael Attenborough)
*Artists and Admirers* (Alexander Ostrovsky, adapt. Kevin Elyot; Phyllida Lloyd)
*The Gift of the Gorgon* (Peter Shaffer; Peter Hall; transfer to West End)
*King Baby* (James Robson; Simon Usher [1993])

## UK Tour

*The Comedy of Errors* (Ian Judge; T; toured abroad)
*A Woman of No Importance* (Philip Prowse; T; transfer to West End)

## Regional Tour

*Richard III* (Sam Mendes; T; toured abroad; transfer to Donmar Warehouse)

# 1993

## Royal Shakespeare Theatre

*Hamlet* (Adrian Noble; T)
*King Lear* (Adrian Noble)
*The Merchant of Venice* (David Thacker)
*The Tempest* (Sam Mendes)
*Love's Labour's Lost* (Ian Judge)

## Swan Theatre

*Richard III* (Sam Mendes; T)
*Murder in the Cathedral* (T.S. Eliot; Steven Pimlott)
*The Venetian Twins* (Carlo Goldoni, adapt. Ranjit Bolt; Michael Bogdanov)
*The Country Wife* (William Wycherley; Max Stafford-Clark)
*Elgar's Rondo* (David Pownall; Di Trevis)

## The Other Place

*Ghosts* (Henrik Ibsen, trans. Michael Meyer; Katie Mitchell)
*Julius Caesar* (David Thacker)
*Moby Dick* (Rod Wooden, after Herman Melville; Gerry Mulgrew)

## Barbican Theatre

*The Beggar's Opera* (John Caird; T)
*As You Like It* (David Thacker; T)
*Antony and Cleopatra* (John Caird; T)
*The Winter's Tale* (Adrian Noble; T)
*The Taming of the Shrew* (Bill Alexander; T)
*Travesties* (Tom Stoppard; Adrian Noble; transfers to West End)
*The Two Gentlemen of Verona* (David Thacker; R)
*Tamburlaine the Great* (Terry Hands; T)
*Macbeth* (Adrian Noble)

## The Pit

*King Baby* (James Robson; Simon Usher [new season])
*The School of Night* (Michael Attenborough; T)
*A Jovial Crew* (Max Stafford-Clark; T)
*The Changeling* (Michael Attenborough; T)
*Wallenstein* (Friedrich Schiller, trans. Francis Lamport, adapt. Tim Albery; Tim Albery)
*All's Well That Ends Well* (Peter Hall; T)
*The Odyssey* (Gregory Doran; T)
*Misha's Party* (Richard Nelson and Alexander Gelman; David Jones)
*Wildest Dreams* (Alan Ayckbourn; Alan Ayckbourn)
*Unfinished Business* (Michael Hasting; Steven Pimlott [1994])

## UK Tour

*The Two Gentlemen of Verona* (David Thacker; T, includes West End)
*Les Liaisons Dangereuses* (Michael Attenborough; R; toured abroad)

## UK and Continental Tour

*The Winter's Tale* (Adrian Noble; T)

## Regional Tour

*Julius Caesar* (David Thacker; T; tours abroad)

# 1994

## Royal Shakespeare Theatre

*Macbeth* (Adrian Noble; T)
*Henry V* (Matthew Warchus)
*Twelfth Night or What You Will* (Ian Judge)
*A Midsummer Night's Dream* (Adrian Noble)
*Measure for Measure* (Steven Pimlott)

## Swan Theatre

*Wildest Dreams* (Alan Ayckbourn; T)
*Peer Gynt* (Henrik Ibsen, adapt. John Barton from Christopher Fry; John Barton)
*Coriolanus* (David Thacker)
*The Wives' Excuse* (Thomas Southerne; Max Stafford-Clark)
*The Broken Heart* (John Ford; Michael Boyd)

## The Other Place

*After Easter* (Anne Devlin; Michael Attenborough)
*Henry VI, The Battle for the Throne* (Katie Mitchell)
*Pentecost* (David Edgar; Michael Attenborough)

## Barbican Theatre

*The Merchant of Venice* (David Thacker; T)
*Love's Labour's Lost* (Ian Judge; T)
*King Lear* (Adrian Noble; T)
*The Tempest* (Sam Mendes; T)
*The Hostage* (Brendan Behan; Michael Bogdanov)
*The Venetian Twins* (Michael Bogdanov; T)
*A Christmas Carol* (Charles Dickens, adapt. John Mortimer; Ian Judge)

## The Pit

*Unfinished Business* (Michael Hasting; Steven Pimlott)
[new season]
*Ghosts* (Katie Mitchell; T)
*The Country Wife* (Max Stafford-Clark; T)
*Elgar's Rondo* (Di Trevis; T)
*Murder in the Cathedral* (Steven Pimlott; T)
*Moby Dick* (Gerry Mulgrew; T)
*Ion* (Euripides, adapt. David Lan; Nicholas Wright)
*The Shakespeare Revue* (devised and directed Chris Luscombe, Malcolm McKee)
*New England* (Richard Nelson; Peter Gill)
*Easter* (August Strindberg, trans. Inga-Stina Ewbank; Katie Mitchell [1995])

## UK Tour

*Macbeth* (Adrian Noble; T)
*The Two Gentlemen of Verona* (David Thacker; T)
*Love's Labour's Lost* (Ian Judge; T; visited Tokyo)

## Regional Tour

*Henry VI, The Battle for the Throne* (Katie Mitchell; T; toured abroad)

# 1995

## Royal Shakespeare Theatre

*Romeo and Juliet* (Adrian Noble)
*The Taming of the Shrew* (Gale Edwards)
*Julius Caesar* (Peter Hall)
*Richard III* (Steven Pimlott)

## Swan Theatre

*The Devil is an Ass* (Ben Jonson; Matthew Warchus)
*The Relapse or Virtue in Danger* (John Vanbrugh; Ian Judge)
*The Cherry Orchard* (Anton Chekhov, adapt. Peter Gill; Adrian Noble)
*The Tempest* (David Thacker; T)
*Bingo* (David Thacker; T)
*Faust, Parts 1* and *2* (Wolfgang von Goethe, adapt. Howard Brenton; Michael Bogdanov)

## The Other Place

*The Painter of Dishonour* (Pedro Calderon de la Barca, adapt. Laurence Boswell and David Johnston; Laurence Boswell)
*Lord of the Flies* (William Golding, adapt. Nigel Williams; Elijah Moshinsky)
*The Phoenician Women* (Euripides, trans. David Thompson; Katie Mitchell)

## Barbican Theatre

*Twelfth Night or What You Will* (Ian Judge; T)
*A Midsummer Night's Dream* (Adrian Noble; T)
*Measure for Measure* (Steven Pimlott; T)
*Coriolanus* (David Thacker; T)
*Henry V* (Matthew Warchus; T)
*A Patriot for Me* (John Osborne; Peter Gill)
*A Christmas Carol* (Ian Judge; R)
*Les enfants du paradis* (Simon Callow, after Jacques Prévert; Simon Callow [1996])

## The Pit

*Easter* (August Strindberg, trans. Inga-Stina Ewbank; Katie Mitchell)
[new season]
*After Easter* (Michael Attenborough; T)
*The Wives' Excuse* (Max Stafford-Clark; T)
*The Broken Heart* (Michael Boyd; T)
*The Shakespeare Revue* (Chris Luscombe and Malcolm McKee; R; transfer to West End)
*Spring Awakening* (Frank Wedekind, adapt. Ted Hughes; Tim Supple)
*The Park* (Botho Strauss, trans. Jeremy Sams; David Fielding)
*Son of Man* (Dennis Potter; Bill Bryden)
*Cain* (Lord Byron; John Barton)
*Slaughter City* (Naomi Wallace; Ron Daniels [1996])

## Young Vic

*Pentecost* (Michael Attenborough; T)
*The Tempest* (David Thacker)

*Bingo* (Edward Bond; David Thacker)
*Zenobia* (Nick Dear; Mike Ockrent)
*Peer Gynt* (John Barton; T)

## UK and Continental Tour

*A Midsummer Night's Dream* (Adrian Noble; T)

## Regional Tour

*The Tempest* (David Thacker; T; toured abroad)
*Bingo* (David Thacker; T; toured abroad)

# 1996

## Royal Shakespeare Theatre

*Twelfth Night* (Ian Judge; R)
[new season]
*As You Like It* (Steven Pimlott)
*Macbeth* (Tim Albery)
*Troilus and Cressida* (Ian Judge)
[new season]
*A Midsummer Night's Dream* (Adrian Noble; R)
[new season]
*Much Ado About Nothing* (Michael Boyd)
*The Merry Wives of Windsor* (Ian Judge)
*Cymbeline* (Adrian Noble [1997])
*Hamlet* (Matthew Warchus [1997])

## Swan Theatre

*The White Devil* (John Webster; Gale Edwards)
*Three Hours after Marriage* (John Gay, Alexander Pope and John Arbuthnot; Richard Cottrell)
*The General from America* (Richard Nelson; Howard Davies)
[new season]
*The Cherry Orchard* (Anton Chekhov, adapt. Peter Gill; Adrian Noble; R; transfer to West End)
[new season]
*Henry VIII* (Gregory Doran)
*Little Eyolf* (Henrik Ibsen, trans. Michael Meyer; Adrian Noble)
*Camino Real* (Tennessee Williams; Steven Pimlott [1997])
*The Spanish Tragedy* (Thomas Kyd; Michael Boyd [1997])

## The Other Place

*The Herbal Bed* (Peter Whelan; Michael Attenborough)
*The Comedy of Errors* (Tim Supple)
*The Learned Ladies* (Molière, trans. A.R. Waller; Steven Pimlott)
[new season]
*Everyman* (anon.; Kathryn Hunter and Marcello Magni)
*The Mysteries:*
*The Creation* (anon., adapt. Katie Mitchell and Ed Kemp; Katie Mitchell [1997])
*The Passion* (anon., adapt. Katie Mitchell and Ed Kemp; Katie Mitchell [1997])

## Barbican Theatre

*Les enfants du paradis* (Simon Callow, after Jacques Prévert; Simon Callow)
[new season]
*The Taming of the Shrew* (Gale Edwards; T)
*Romeo and Juliet* (Adrian Noble; T)
*Julius Caesar* (Peter Hall; T)
*Richard III* (Steven Pimlott; T)
*A Midsummer Night's Dream* (Adrian Noble; R)
[new season]
*As You Like It* (Steven Pimlott; T)
*Macbeth* (Tim Albery; T)
*Troilus and Cressida* (Ian Judge; T)

## The Pit

*Slaughter City* (Naomi Wallace; Ron Daniels)
[new season]
*The Relapse or Virtue in Danger* (Ian Judge; T)
*The Devil is an Ass* (Matthew Warchus; T)
*The Painter of Dishonour* (Laurence Boswell; T)
*The Phoenician Women* (Katie Mitchell; T)
*Faust, Parts 1* and *2* (Michael Bogdanov; T)
[new season]
*In the Company of Men* (Edward Bond; Edward Bond)
*The Herbal Bed* (Michael Attenborough; T; transfer to West End and US)
*The Learned Ladies* (Steven Pimlott; T)
*The White Devil* (Gale Edwards; T )
*Three Hours after Marriage* (Richard Cottrell; T [1997])
*The General from America* (Howard Davies; T [1997])

## UK and Continental Tour

*Twelfth Night* (Ian Judge; T)
*A Midsummer Night's Dream* (Adrian Noble; T)

## Regional Tour

*The Comedy of Errors* (Tim Supple; T; toured abroad)

# 1997

## Royal Shakespeare Theatre

*Cymbeline* (Adrian Noble)
*Hamlet* (Matthew Warchus)
[new season]
*Henry V* (Ron Daniels)
*Twelfth Night* (Adrian Noble)
*The Merchant of Venice* (Gregory Doran)
*The Tempest* (Adrian Noble [1998])
*Measure for Measure* (Michael Boyd [1998])

## Swan Theatre

*Camino Real* (Tennessee Williams; Steven Pimlott)
*The Spanish Tragedy* (Thomas Kyd; Michael Boyd)

*Kenneth's First Play* (written and directed Richard Nelson and Colin Chambers)
[new season]
*Cyrano de Bergerac* (Edmond Rostand, trans. Anthony Burgess; Gregory Doran)
*Romeo and Juliet* (Michael Attenborough; T)
*Bartholomew Fair* (Ben Jonson; Laurence Boswell)
*The Two Gentlemen of Verona* (Edward Hall [1998])
*Talk of the City* (Stephen Poliakoff; Stephen Poliakoff [1998])

## The Other Place

*The Mysteries:*
*The Creation* (anon., adapt. Katie Mitchell and Ed Kemp; Katie Mitchell)
*The Passion* (anon., adapt. Katie Mitchell and Ed Kemp; Katie Mitchell)
*Krapp's Last Tape* (Samuel Beckett; Edward Petherbridge and David Hunt)
*More Words* (devised and directed Cicely Berry and Andrew Wade)
[new season]
*Beckett Shorts* ((Samuel Beckett; Katie Mitchell; toured abroad) comprising: *Out of the Dark: Footfalls, Rockaby, Not I*
*Over the Years: Embers, A Piece of Monologue, That Time*
[new season]
*Roberto Zucco* (Bernard-Marie Koltès, adapt. Martin Crimp; James Macdonald)
*Goodnight Children Everywhere* (Richard Nelson; Ian Brown)
*Shadows* (dir. John Crowley [1998]) comprising: *Purgatory* (W.B. Yeats); *Riders from the Sea* and *In the Shadow of the Glen* (J.M. Synge)
*Bad Weather* (Robert Holman; Steven Pimlott [1998])

## Barbican Theatre

*Henry V* (Ron Daniels; T)
*Hamlet* (Matthew Warchus; T)
*The Merry Wives of Windsor* (Ian Judge; T)
*Cymbeline* (Adrian Noble; T [1998])
*Much Ado About Nothing* (Michael Boyd; T [1998])

## The Pit

*Three Hours after Marriage* (Richard Cottrell; T)
*The General from America* (Howard Davies; T)
[new season]
*Romeo and Juliet* (Michael Attenborough)
*The Spanish Tragedy* (Michael Boyd; T)
*Little Eyolf* (Adrian Noble; T)
*The Mysteries:*
*The Creation* (Katie Mitchell; T [1998])
*The Passion* (Katie Mitchell; T [1998])
*Everyman* (Kathryn Hunter and Marcello Magni; T [1998])
*The Unexpected Man* (Yasmina Reza, trans. Christopher Hampton; Matthew Warchus [1998])
*Krapp's Last Tape* (Edward Petherbridge and David Hunt; T [1998])
*More Words* (devised and directed Cicely Berry and Andrew Wade; T [1998])

## Young Vic

*The Comedy of Errors* (Tim Supple; T)
*Henry VIII* (Gregory Doran; T)
*Camino Real* (Steven Pimlott; T)

*Uncle Vanya* (Anton Chekhov, adapt. David Lan; Katie Mitchell)
*Kenneth's First Play* (Richard Nelson and Colin Chambers; T)

## UK Tour

*Henry V* (Ron Daniels; T)
*Cyrano de Bergerac* (Gregory Doran; T; transfer to West End)

## Regional Tour

*Romeo and Juliet* (Michael Attenborough; T; toured abroad)

[First Plymouth residency]

# 1998

## Royal Shakespeare Theatre

*The Tempest* (Adrian Noble)
*Measure for Measure* (Michael Boyd)
[new season]
*The School for Scandal* (Richard Brinsley Sheridan; Declan Donnellan)
*Richard III* (Elijah Moshinsky)
*The Lion, the Witch and the Wardrobe* (C.S. Lewis, adapt. Adrian Mitchell; Adrian Noble)
*The Winter's Tale* (Gregory Doran)

## Swan Theatre

*The Two Gentlemen of Verona* (Edward Hall)
*Talk of the City* (Stephen Poliakoff; Stephen Poliakoff)
[new season]
*Troilus and Cressida* (Michael Boyd; T)
*A Month in the Country* (Brian Friel after Ivan Turgenev; Michael Attenborough)

## The Other Place

*Shadows* (dir. John Crowley) comprising: *Purgatory* (W.B. Yeats); *Riders from the Sea* and
    *In the Shadow of the Glen* (J.M. Synge)
*Bad Weather* (Robert Holman; Steven Pimlott)

## Barbican Theatre

*Cymbeline* (Adrian Noble; T)
*Much Ado About Nothing* (Michael Boyd; T)
[new season]
*The School for Scandal* (Declan Donnellan; T)
*The Merchant of Venice* (Gregory Doran; T)
*The Tempest* (Adrian Noble; T)
*Measure for Measure* (Michael Boyd; T [1999])
*The Lion, the Witch and the Wardrobe* (Adrian Noble; T [1999])
*The Winter's Tale* (Gregory Doran; T [1999])

## The Pit

*The Mysteries:*
*The Creation* (Katie Mitchell; T)
*The Passion* (Katie Mitchell; T)
*Everyman* (Kathryn Hunter and Marcello Magni; T)

*The Unexpected Man* (Yasmina Reza, trans. Christopher Hampton; Matthew Warchus; transfer to West End)
*Krapp's Last Tape* (Edward Petherbridge and David Hunt; T; tour; transfer to Arts, with *Breath*)
*More Words* (devised and directed Cicely Berry and Andrew Wade; T)
[new season]
*Troilus and Cressida* (Michael Boyd)
*Shadows: Purgatory, Riders from the Sea* and *In the Shadow of the Glen* (John Crowley; T)
*The Two Gentlemen of Verona* (Edward Hall; T)
*Bad Weather* (Steven Pimlott; T [1999])
*Goodnight Children Everywhere* (Ian Brown; T [1999])
*Roberto Zucco* (James Macdonald; T [1999])
*A Month in the Country* (Michael Attenborough; T [1999])

## UK Tour

*The Herbal Bed* (Peter Whelan; Michael Attenborough; R)
*Richard III* (Elijah Moshinsky; T; transfer to West End)

## Regional Tour

*Romeo and Juliet* (Michael Attenborough; R)

[First US residency (New York, Washington DC)]

# 1999

## Royal Shakespeare Theatre

*A Midsummer Night's Dream* (Michael Boyd)
*Othello* (Michael Attenborough)
*Antony and Cleopatra* (Steven Pimlott)
*Timon of Athens* (Gregory Doran)
[new season]
*King Lear* (Yukio Ninagawa; T from Tokyo)
*The Lion, the Witch and the Wardrobe* (C.S. Lewis, adapt. Adrian Mitchell, Adrian Noble; R)

## Swan Theatre

*Volpone* (Ben Jonson; Lindsay Posner)
*Tales from Ovid* (Ted Hughes, adapt. Tim Supple and Simon Reade; Tim Supple; visit abroad)
*The Family Reunion* (T.S. Eliot; Adrian Noble)
[new season]
*Macbeth* (Gregory Doran)
*The Taming of the Shrew* (Lindsay Posner)
*The Seagull* (Anton Chekhov, adapt. Peter Gill; Adrian Noble [2000])

## The Other Place

*The Dispute* (Pierre Marivaux, trans. Neil Bartlett; Neil Bartlett; co-production with Lyric Theatre, Hammersmith)
[new season]
*Oroonoko* (Aphra Behn, adapt. Biyi Bandele; Gregory Doran)
*Don Carlos* (Friedrich Schiller, trans. Robert David MacDonald; Gale Edwards)
*A Warwickshire Testimony* (April de Angelis; Alison Sutcliffe)

[new season]
*A Servant of Two Masters* (Carlo Goldoni, adapt. Lee Hall; Tim Supple; co-production with Young Vic)

## Barbican Theatre

*Measure for Measure* (Michael Boyd; T)
*The Lion, the Witch and the Wardrobe* (Adrian Noble; T)
*The Winter's Tale* (Gregory Doran; T)
[new season]
*King Lear* (Yukio Ninagawa; T)
*A Midsummer Night's Dream* (Michael Boyd; T)
*Othello* (Michael Attenborough; T)
*Antony and Cleopatra* (Steven Pimlott; T)
*Timon of Athens* (Gregory Doran; T)
*The Seagull* (Adrian Noble; T)

## The Pit

*Bad Weather* (Steven Pimlott; T)
*Goodnight Children Everywhere* (Ian Brown; T)
*Roberto Zucco* (James Macdonald; T)
*A Month in the Country* (Michael Attenborough; T)
[new season]
*The Taming of the Shrew* (Lindsay Posner; T)
*Volpone* (Lindsay Posner; T)
*Oroonoko* (Gregory Doran; T)
*Don Carlos* (Gale Edwards; T [2000])
*The Family Reunion* (Adrian Noble; T [2000])
*Victoria* (David Greig; Ian Brown [2000])

## Young Vic

*Talk of the City* (Stephen Poliakoff; T)
*Bartholomew Fair* (Laurence Boswell; T)

## Lyric Theatre, Hammersmith

*The Dispute* (Neil Bartlett; T; toured UK and abroad)

## UK and Continental Tour

*The Seagull* (Adrian Noble; T)
*Macbeth* (Gregory Doran; T)

## Regional Tour

*Troilus and Cressida* (Michael Boyd; T; toured abroad)
*A Month in the Country* (Michael Attenborough; T; toured abroad)

## 2000

## Royal Shakespeare Theatre

*As You Like It* (Gregory Doran)
*The Comedy of Errors* (Lynne Parker)
*Romeo and Juliet* (Michael Boyd)
*Henry V* (Edward Hall)

[new season]
*The Secret Garden* (Frances Hodgson Burnett, adapt. Marsha Norman; Adrian Noble;
     transfer to West End)
*The Duchess of Malfi* (John Webster; Gale Edwards; T [2001])

## Swan Theatre

*The Seagull* (Anton Chekhov, adapt. Peter Gill; Adrian Noble)
[new season]
*The Rivals* (Richard Brinsley Sheridan; Lindsay Posner)
*Henry IV, Part 1* (Michael Attenborough)
*Henry IV, Part 2* (Michael Attenborough)
[new season]
*Henry VI, Part 1* (Michael Boyd; US visit)
*Henry VI, Part 2* (Michael Boyd; US visit)
*Henry VI, Part 3* (Michael Boyd; US visit)
*Richard III* (Michael Boyd; US visit [2001])

## The Other Place

*La Lupa* (Giovanni Verga, adapt. David Lan; Simona Gonella)
*Back to Methusaleh* (George Bernard Shaw; David Fielding)
*Richard II* (Steven Pimlott)
[new season]
*The Tempest* (James Macdonald; T)

## Barbican Theatre

*The Duchess of Malfi* (John Webster; Gale Edwards)
*The Comedy of Errors* (Lynne Parker; T)
*The Rivals* (Lindsay Posner; T)
*Romeo and Juliet* (Michael Boyd; T [2001])
*Henry IV, Part 1* (Michael Attenborough; T [2001])
*Henry IV, Part 2* (Michael Attenborough; T [2001])
*Henry V* (Edward Hall; T [2001])

## The Pit

*Don Carlos* (Gale Edwards; T)
*The Family Reunion* (Adrian Noble; T)
*Victoria* (David Greig; Ian Brown)
[new season]
*The Tempest* (James Macdonald)
*As You Like It* (Gregory Doran; T)
*Richard II* (Steven Pimlott; T)
*La Lupa* (Simona Gonella; T [2001])
*Back to Methusaleh* (David Fielding; T [2001])

## Young Vic

*A Servant of Two Masters* (Tim Supple; T)
*Macbeth* (Gregory Doran; T)
*Tales from Ovid* (Tim Supple; T)

## Sadler's Wells

*The Lion, the Witch and the Wardrobe* (C.S. Lewis, adapt. Adrian Mitchell; Adrian Noble;
     R)

### UK and Continental Tour

*A Servant of Two Masters* (Tim Supple)

### UK Tour

*The Duchess of Malfi* (Gale Edwards; T)

### Regional Tour

*The Taming of the Shrew* (Lindsay Posner; T; toured abroad)

### Denver Centre for the Performing Arts

*Tantalus* (John Barton, additional text Colin Teevan; Peter Hall and Edward Hall):
*Outbreak*
*War*
*Homecomings*


### 2001

### Royal Shakespeare Theatre

*The Duchess of Malfi* (John Webster; Gale Edwards; T [2001])
[new season]
*Hamlet* (Steven Pimlott)
*Twelfth Night* (Lindsay Posner)
*Julius Caesar* (Edward Hall)
[new season]
*Alice in Wonderland* and *Through the Looking Glass* (Rachel Kavanaugh; T)

### Swan Theatre

*Richard III* (Michael Boyd)
[new season]
*King John* (Gregory Doran)
*Love in a Wood* (William Wycherley; Tim Supple)
*Jubilee* (Peter Barnes; Gregory Doran)
[new season]
*The Merchant of Venice* (Loveday Ingram; T)

### The Other Place

*A Russian in the Woods* (Peter Whelan; Robert Delamere)
*The Lieutenant of Inishmore* (Martin McDonagh; Wilson Milam)
*The Prisoner's Dilemma* (David Edgar; Michael Attenborough) [final performance by
   RSC at theatre, 13 October]

### Barbican Theatre

*Romeo and Juliet* (Michael Boyd; T)
*Henry IV, Part 1* (Michael Attenborough; T)
*Henry IV, Part 2* (Michael Attenborough; T)
*Henry V* (Edward Hall; T)
[new season]
*Tantalus* (Peter Hall and Edward Hall; T)
[new season]
*Alice in Wonderland* and *Through the Looking Glass* (Lewis Carroll, adapt. Adrian
   Mitchell; Rachel Kavanaugh)

[new season]
*Hamlet* (Steven Pimlott; T)
*Twelfth Night* (Lindsay Posner; T)
*Julius Caesar* (Edward Hall; T [2002])

## The Pit

*La Lupa* (Simona Gonella; T)
*Back to Methusaleh* (David Fielding; T)
*This Other Eden:*
*Loveplay* (Moira Buffini; Anthony Clark )
*Luminosity* (Nick Stafford; Gemma Bodinez)
*Brixton Stories* (Biyi Bandele; Roxana Silbert)
*Epitaph for the Official Secrets Act* (Paul Greengrass and Simon Reade; Simon Reade)
[new season]
*The Merchant of Venice* (Loveday Ingram)
[new season]
*King John* (Gregory Doran; T)
*The Lieutenant of Inishmore* (Wilson Milam; T; transfer to West End)
*The Prisoner's Dilemma* (Michael Attenborough; T [2002])
*A Russian in the Woods* (Robert Delamere; T [2002])

## Young Vic

*The Thoughts of Joan of Arc on the English as She Burns at the Stake* (David Farr; David
    Farr)
*Henry VI, Part 1* (Michael Boyd; T)
*Henry VI, Part 2* (Michael Boyd; T)
*Henry VI, Part 3* (Michael Boyd; T)
*Richard III* (Michael Boyd; T)

## Tricycle Theatre, London and West Yorkshire Playhouse, Leeds

*Brixton Stories* (Roxana Silbert; T)

## Regional Tour

*The Tempest* (James Macdonald; T; toured abroad)

## 2002

## Royal Shakespeare Theatre

*A Midsummer Night's Dream* (Richard Jones)
[new season]
*Much Ado About Nothing* (Gregory Doran; transfer to West End)
*Antony and Cleopatra* (Michael Attenborough; transfer to West End)
[new season]
*The Tempest* (Michael Boyd; T)
*The Winter's Tale* (Matthew Warchus; T)
*Pericles* (Adrian Noble; T)
[new season]
*The Lion, the Witch and the Wardrobe* (C.S. Lewis, adapt. Adrian Mitchell; Adrian
    Noble; R)

## Swan Theatre

*The Prince of Homburg* (Heinrich von Kleist, adapt. Neil Bartlett with David Bryer; Neil Bartlett; co-production with Lyric Theatre, Hammersmith)
[new season]
*Edward III* (Anthony Clark)
*Eastward Ho!* (Ben Jonson, John Marston and George Chapman; Lucy Pitman-Wallace)
*The Roman Actor* (Philip Massinger; Sean Holmes)
*The Island Princess* (John Fletcher; Gregory Doran)
*The Malcontent* (John Marston; Dominic Cooke)
[the above five plays transferred as a repertoire to the West End]
[new season]
*King Lear* (Declan Donnellan; the RSC Academy Company)
[new season]
*The Merry Wives of Windsor* (Rachel Kavanaugh; transfer to Old Vic)
*Coriolanus* (David Farr; transfer to Old Vic)

## Barbican Theatre

*Julius Caesar* (Edward Hall; T)
*A Midsummer Night's Dream* (Richard Jones; T) [final performance by RSC 11 May]

## The Pit

*The Prisoner's Dilemma* (Michael Attenborough; T)
*A Russian in the Woods* (Robert Delamere; T)
[new season]
*Night of the Soul* (David Farr; David Farr) [final performance by RSC 11 May]

## Young Vic

*King Lear* (Declan Donnellan; T; toured abroad)

## Round House

*The Tempest* (Michael Boyd)
*The Winter's Tale* (Matthew Warchus)
*Pericles* (Adrian Noble)

## Lyric Theatre, Hammersmith

*The Prince of Homburg* (Neil Bartlett; T)

## UK and Continental Tour

*A Midsummer Night's Dream* (Richard Jones; T)

## Regional Tour

*The Merchant of Venice* (Loveday Ingram; T; toured abroad)

# 2003

## Barbican Theatre

[first return visit by RSC]
*Midnight's Children* (Salman Rushdie, adapt. Salman Rushdie, Simon Reade and Tim Supple; Tim Supple)

## Regional Tour

*The Merry Wives of Windsor* (Rachel Kavanaugh; T; toured abroad)
*Coriolanus* (David Farr; T; toured abroad)

Information on RSC productions can be found in the Royal Shakespeare Company's Archives 'FESTE' database at www.pads.ahds.ac.uk or at the Shakespeare Centre Library, Stratford-upon-Avon, UK (library@Shakespeare.org.uk).

# NOTES

## INTRODUCTION

1 In Britain, there is demand for the 'outcome' but little readiness to pay for the process, i.e. research and development. No other industry would be expected to survive on these terms. The National Theatre, the theatre that receives the highest level of public subsidy, has to rely on private finance to run its studio; even the Royal Opera House, the most heavily state subsidised of the live arts organisations, requires the support of a Cuban-born millionaire, Alberto Vilar, for its development work.

2 In researching the book it became clear that certain statistically based comparisons are difficult to make both between different periods within the RSC's history and between the RSC and other organisations, as different costing methods are used at different times. At the RSC, for example, the method of preparing payrolls changed from 1968/69 to 1969/70, until 1972 figures were available only for total production costs not individual production costs, and the cost of a permanent stage was not counted against individual shows although a percentage of administration/production staff costs were. Under Adrian Noble, the new working model involved a new accountancy policy because the theatrical season was no longer the same as the financial year.

3 Quoted in Sally Beauman, *The Royal Shakespeare Company: A History of Ten Decades*, Oxford, Oxford University Press, 1982, p. 244.

## ONE: ALL IN A STATE OF FINDING

1 Stratford's parliamentary constituency regularly returned a Conservative MP. From 1950–63 it was John Profumo, an RSC governor, who helped bring down the government as war minister in the Christine Keeler sex-and-spy scandal. After Profumo, Angus Maude became Stratford's MP (1963–83). He was an RSC governor until he resigned in 1972 over remarks made by Trevor Nunn, the RSC's artistic director, and David Jones, an RSC associate director, in a letter to *The Times* that the RSC was 'basically a left-wing organisation'. Maude was a deputy chairman of the Tory Party and Margaret Thatcher's first paymaster general. When Hall took over at Stratford, its president was Lord Avon, former Conservative MP for neighbouring Warwick and Leamington (1923–57) and, as Anthony Eden, Prime Minister during the Suez débâcle.

2 Anthony Quayle, reported in *The Birmingham Mail*, 17 September 1965.

3 Following a period of intense industrial unrest during his leadership of the NT, including a strike in the election year 1979 which nearly broke the theatre, Hall voted for Thatcher because he believed the unions had become corrupt. He did not vote Tory again. See Peter Hall, *Making an Exhibition of Myself*, London, Sinclair-Stevenson, 1993, pp. 294–97.

4  Quoted in Stephen Fay, *Power Play: The Life and Times of Peter Hall*, London, Hodder & Stoughton, 1996, p. 85.

5  The National Theatre was for a time called the Royal National Theatre but later reverted to its original title. To avoid confusion, it is always referred to as the National Theatre or the NT.

6  Quoted in David Addenbrooke, *The Royal Shakespeare Company: The Peter Hall Years*, London, William Kimber, 1974, p. 47.

7  Peter Hall in 'Avoiding a Method', an article taken from a talk given to the company, published in *Crucial Years*, an RSC booklet, London, Max Reinhardt, 1963, p. 18.

8  Peter Hall, Introduction to the Illustrated Programme of the World Theatre Season, Aldwych Theatre, Royal Shakespeare Company, 1964.

9  Quoted in Fay, op. cit., p. 85.

10  Hall, 'Avoiding a Method', op. cit., p. 14.

11  Quoted in Addenbrooke, op. cit., p. 46.

12  The list of those signing up to the long-term contract showed a mix of the old and the new. As well as Peggy Ashcroft, the list included: Max Adrian, Harry Andrews, Ian Bannen, Roy Dotrice, Paul Hardwick, Ian Holm, Richard Johnson, Peter O'Toole, Eric Porter, Dorothy Tutin and Patrick Wymark.

13  Peter Hall, 'Shakespeare and the Modern Director', in John Goodwin (ed.), *The Royal Shakespeare Theatre Company, 1960–63*, London, Max Reinhardt, 1964, p. 44.

14  Quoted from Associated Television 'Look Around' programme in Royal Shakespeare Company Theatre Records, vol. 56 (June 1962–October 1962).

15  Quoted in Fay, op. cit., p. 168. The Rambert plans went through several phases. The RSC was to occupy the new theatre for nine months of the year and Rambert for three months. The costs were to be met privately. Hall did not like plans drawn up by Seifert architects. Basil Spence, who had designed Coventry Cathedral, was brought in and his plans went on public display at the Royal Academy in May 1964. The theatre was due to open in four years' time but fundraising was slow and the Barbican offer diverted Hall to the City of London project, leaving the Rambert people feeling unhappy. Rambert was to be a part of the Barbican project but the ballet company went its own way and opened premises in west London, though not on the scale of the original scheme.

16  The full title is *The Persecution and Assassination of Marat as Performed by the Inmates of the Asylum of Charenton under the Direction of the Marquis de Sade*.

17  Born in Cardiff, Williams did not attend university but trained to be an economist and worked in mining. He became a ballet dancer, founded in 1950 what was then Britain's only professional mime company, directed in South Africa and had been director of productions at Canterbury and Hornchurch. He had also been an assistant stage manager and an actor and director with Theatre Workshop. Hall once considered Williams as his successor but, according to Williams, thought his work had become too casual. He was fired with six months' notice but as Hall's successor Trevor Nunn did not know this, Williams stayed.

18  *The Observer*, 16 September 1962.

19  This paragraph is based on an interview with Clifford Williams by the author.

20  Buckingham Palace agreed to the name Royal Shakespeare Theatre, and the company was known at first as the Royal Shakespeare Theatre Company. Hall felt that was 'too Stratford' (Fay, op. cit., p. 166) and chose the Royal Shakespeare Company in preference. The RSC is incorporated under Royal Charter as the Royal Shakespeare Theatre, Stratford-upon-Avon.

21  Hall, *Making an Exhibition of Myself*, p. 203.

22 Quoted in Fay, op. cit., p. 187
23 Paddy Donnell was already at the NT when Hall arrived but Hall brought with him Harold Pinter and John Bury on the artistic side and on the administrative side Gillian Diamond, Michael Kustow and John Goodwin. The NT board was sensitive to this and blocked Hall from directing in the RSC's first Barbican season in case it might blur the distinction between the two companies. Eventually, in 1997, Hall's successor at the RSC, Trevor Nunn, also came to run the NT.
24 To take one example: in 1979–80, the NT added sixteen new shows, gave 909 performances, had box office revenue of £1,611,913, and subsidy from the Arts Council (omitting funding from the Greater London Council) of £4,125,652. The RSC added twenty new productions, gave 1209 performances, had box office revenue of £2,785,655, and an Arts Council grant of £1,900,000. The NT received £8.69 subsidy per paid admission, the RSC £2.30. The disparity meant the RSC had to raise its seat prices more quickly (e.g. in 1981 the RSC top Stratford price was £10 and in London £7.50 whereas for the NT it was £6.90). In addition, the NT could pay more to staff and artists. The RSC that year also outperformed the Council's two other national clients, the Royal Opera House and English National Opera, yet remained under-funded. With annual inflation running at 15 per cent, these two and the NT received a 20 per cent rise. The RSC was given only 7.46 per cent. Later the grant was supplemented but the new total still only amounted to a rise of 13.4 per cent.

## TWO: IN THE MARKETPLACE OF NOW

1 Speaking to the 1966 Club annual meeting, quoted in the *Stratford-upon-Avon Herald*, 4 March 1966.
2 Interview by Frank Cox in *Plays and Players*, May 1964.
3 Interview with the author.
4 Interview with the author.
5 The RSC music department, under Woolfenden's leadership for most of the period covered by this book, supported live music and encouraged and/or nurtured new composers, such as Stephen Oliver, Ilona Sekacz, Nigel Hess, Shaun Davey, Gary Yershon and Jason Carr.
6 Quoted in Richard Pearson, *A Band of Arrogant and United Heroes: The Story of the Royal Shakespeare Company production of 'The Wars of the Roses'*, London, The Adelphi Press, 1990, p. 26. This book was a primary source for the section on the trilogy, supported by interviews with the author.
7 *The Daily Mail*, 21 August 1963.
8 *Independent on Sunday*, 6 January 1991.
9 Michael Billington, *Peggy Ashcroft*, London, John Murray, 1988, p. 204.
10 Foreword to Pearson, op. cit., p. ix.
11 The *Stratford-upon-Avon Herald*, op. cit.
12 David Addenbrooke, *The Royal Shakespeare Company: The Peter Hall Years*, London, William Kimber, 1974, p. 230.
13 Ken Kesey, US novelist and cult figure in the psychedelic hippy culture. He journeyed across the USA in a multicoloured bus. He was the author of *One Flew Over the Cuckoo's Nest*.
14 Littler's views were reported in *The Daily Telegraph*, 24 August 1964. Hall believed the ruckus also to be associated with the fact that he gave evidence in a court case brought by Littler against the BBC for transmitting a satirical song purporting to be sung by Littler, which included the line 'I don't like other people's dirty plays, I only like mine' (a reference to a controversial play he was presenting). Commentators

have noted that the row occurred in the summer 'silly season' when news is light and that it helped boost revenue in the West End.

15  The poem was called 'I Sing of Olaf'.

16  Quoted in Stephen Fay, *Power Play: The Life and Times of Peter Hall*, London, Hodder & Stoughton, 1996, p. 228.

17  Peter Hall, *Making an Exhibition of Myself*, London, Sinclair-Stevenson, 1993, p. 207.

18  Ibid., p. 208.

19  Some commentators believe the play to have been written by Thomas Middleton.

20  Nunn offers this account of himself in the 'Afterword' he wrote for Addenbrooke, op. cit., p. 180.

21  The project eventually surfaced in 1971 (Cockpit Theatre, London) as *What a Way to Run a Revolution* by David Benedictus, music by Guy Woolfenden.

22  The RSC Club newspaper *Flourish* had asked its readers to nominate a play for this slot. *The Revenger's Tragedy*, which Nunn had read at university, came third in the poll behind Marlowe's *Edward II* and Webster's *The White Devil*.

23  *The Observer*, 9 October 1966.

24  Press release, 29 January 1968.

25  Hall, op. cit., p. 168.

26  Ibid., p. 159.

27  Ibid., p. 169. The interview was with Peter Lewis in the magazine *Nova*, August 1967.

28  Ibid., pp. 139–40.

29  Peter Brook, 'Peter Hall by Peter Brook', *RSC Annual Report*, 1968.

## THREE: THE AGE OF EXPANSION

1  Trevor Nunn, 'Afterword' in David Addenbrooke, *The Royal Shakespeare Company: The Peter Hall Years*, London, William Kimber, 1974, p. 182.

2  Peter Brook, 'Peter Hall by Peter Brook', *RSC Annual Report*, 1968.

3  As with the three-year contract, the two-year contract was a commitment rather than a binding document. Equity, the actors' union, continued to limit negotiations to a fifty-two-week contract and the second year of the 'two-year contract' remained subject to renegotiation.

4  Quoted in Sally Beauman, *The Royal Shakespeare Company: A History of Ten Decades*, Oxford, Oxford University Press, 1982, p. 308.

5  *The Times*, 25 October 1973.

6  Peter Hall, *Peter Hall's Diaries: The Story of a Dramatic Battle*, London, Hamish Hamilton, 1983, p. 56.

7  This and the following quotation, Nunn, op. cit., p. 183.

8  In 1970 a group of actors formed around Martin Bax and Hugh Keays Byrne took the name Chaff and Bran (from a line by Pandarus in *Troilus and Cressida* referring to foot soldiers) in order to organise extra-mural activities. They converted the Rotunda in the gardens behind the Stratford theatre into a flexible space for private performances and dubbed it the Little Roundhouse. It had been part of an orangerie and later became a brass-rubbing centre. All kinds of shows were seen there and the actors hoped it would become a second auditorium open to RSC Club members and local people. This role was taken on by The Other Place.

9  Terry Hands believed the importance of The Other Place was purely aesthetic and worked there only once.

10  Internal RSC document on second Stratford auditorium, December 1973.

11  Nunn directed one new production in 1974, one in 1975 and six in 1976.

12 According to Leon Rubin (in *The Nicholas Nickleby Story: The Making of the Historic Royal Shakespeare Company Production*, London, Heinemann, 1981), of a possible fifty-two actors, forty-six accepted.

## FOUR: BARBICAN BOUND

1 Paid admissions had dropped by 14 per cent from 1979/80–81/2 but rose by 22 per cent in 1982/83. On the downside, however, the policy raised production and stage operating costs, which were higher at the Barbican than at the Aldwych.

2 Peter Hall, *Making an Exhibition of Myself*, London, Sinclair-Stevenson, 1993, p. 206.

3 Clive Priestley, 'Love Letter on White Paper? The "Special Financial Scrutiny" of the RSC', *RSC Annual Yearbook 1983/84*, p. 120.

4 The Royal Shakespeare Theatre Trust was originally called the Shakespeare Theatre Trust.

5 Caroline Lees, 'Shakespeare and the Money Men', *Evening Standard*, 20 January 1994.

6 See Sheila Hancock, *Ramblings of an Actress*, London, Hutchinson, 1987, pp. 61–62.

7 See, for example, Michael Pennington in Michael Bogdanov and Michael Pennington, *The English Shakespeare Company: The Story of the Wars of the Roses, 1986–89*, London, Nick Hern Books, 1990, p. xi and Kenneth Branagh, *Beginning*, London, Chatto & Windus, 1989, p. 164. An example of the RSC's problems can be seen in the 1982/83 season, when of the 144 actors hired, only 64 worked a full contract.

8 In 1986 *The Sunday Times* accused Nunn and Hall of exploiting their positions at their respective subsidised companies for personal gain. They sued the newspaper. Hall later pulled out for financial reasons but Nunn continued and after several years settled out of court once the paper had published a reluctant apology. In the wake of the furore, Kenneth Cork, in his report for the Arts Council on the state of English theatre, made recommendations concerning the percentage of earnings from a commercial transfer that should be returned to the originating theatre.

9 For a detailed examination of the Swan effect, see Graham Holderness, 'The Albatross and the Swan: Two Productions at Stratford', *New Theatre Quarterly*, vol. iv, no. 14, May 1988, pp. 152–58, and Peter Womack, 'The Sign of the Light Heart: Jonson's "New Inn" 1629 and 1987', *New Theatre Quarterly*, vol. v, no. 18, May 1989, pp. 162–70.

## FIVE: CRISIS AND MODERNISATION

1 Interview with Benedict Nightingale, *The Times*, 12 January 1991.

2 Quoted in *RSC Annual Report 1990/91*, p. 1.

3 Nightingale, op. cit. 'Why We Do What We Do', May 1991.

4 RSC governance was unique. Governors were self-selecting, unlike at the NT where they were government appointed. Of about eighty governors, some 85 per cent were members of the Court of Governors and around twenty-five were elected members of the Council on a three-yearly basis. A smaller finance and general purposes committee (up to eight strong) had more immediate involvement in RSC affairs. Under the first set of new arrangements, which coincided with the start of Noble's leadership, this body became the executive committee. The 2000 changes created a new board of governors to replace the Council. Shorter terms of

membership and an age cap were introduced as well as different categories of governor, such as emeritus and honorary. The RSC's corporate governance involved a network of committees and boards; for example, the board of the Royal Shakespeare Foundation is the development committee of the RSC Council.

5  *RSC Annual report*, 1996/97, p. 2.
6  Plymouth, unlike Newcastle, is situated in a relatively sparsely populated area. This made attracting audiences for a short season of many performances difficult. Added to the lack of sufficient support from the local council and the Arts Council declining to make up the shortfall for a further year was the problem of gaining sponsors, a problem the RSC had expected.
7  RSC statement, 'The RSC New Deal'. Online: www.rsc.org.uk (September 2001).
8  See Michael Billington, 'The Tempest', *The Guardian*, 19 September 2001.
9  For example, the City raised its grant for 1994/95 by £400,000 when the Arts Council grant was at a standstill. The dreadful appointment from the Milk Marketing Board of Detta O'Cahain as the Centre's director raised tensions but did not alter the basic relationship between the RSC and the Centre.
10  John Birt was director-general of the BBC from 1992–2000. He introduced widespread reforms that caused much controversy and became a byword for the excesses of managerialism.
11  Quoted in *The Independent*, 2 February 1993.

## SIX: BEYOND THE BARD

1  Chapter 1 of *The Empty Space*, London, McGibbon & Key, 1968, is called 'The Deadly Theatre'.
2  Peter Brook *et al.*, 'Artaud for Artaud's Sake', *Encore*, no. 49, May–June 1964, vol. 11, no. 3, pp. 20–31.
3  Peter Brook, 'What About Real Life', *Crucial Years*, London, Max Reinhardt, 1963, p. 21.
4  Peter Brook, Preface to Jan Kott (translated Boleslaw Taborski), *Shakespeare Our Contemporary*, London, Methuen, second edition, revised, 1967, p. x.
5  Peter Hall, 'Shakespeare and the Modern Director', in John Goodwin (ed.), *The Royal Shakespeare Theatre Company, 1960–63*, London, Max Reinhardt, 1964, pp. 41–42.
6  For example, Barry Jackson's pioneering modern dress *Cymbeline* (1923) and *Hamlet* in plus-fours (1925) or Orson Welles's production of *Julius Caesar* (1937) staged like a Nuremberg rally.
7  George Orwell's review of *Applesauce* in *Time and Tide*, 7 September 1940.
8  Hall, op. cit., p. 41.
9  The Mona Lisa reference is quoted in David Addenbrooke, *The Royal Shakespeare Company: The Peter Hall Years*, London, William Kimber, 1974, p. 98. Hall uses it again in *Making an Exhibition of Myself*, London, Sinclair-Stevenson, 1993, p. 176. The RSC was criticised for directorial indulgence by, among others, Val Gielgud, *Years in a Mirror*, London, Bodley Head, 1965, and John Russell Brown, *Free Shakespeare*, London, Heinemann, 1974.
10  Peter Hall, (Goodwin, John, ed.), *Peter Hall's Diaries: The Story of a Dramatic Battle*, London, Hamish Hamilton, 1983, p. 209.
11  The criticism was particularly sensitive when it came from the likes of the eminent Oxford University professor Nevill Coghill and Ivor Brown, a long-standing friend of Fordham Flower and contributor to Stratford publications.
12  Hall, *Making an Exhibition of Myself*, p. 175.

13 John Barton argued with Kenneth Muir, and the scene was set by Gareth Lloyd Evans, another critic who had taken the RSC to task, *The Manchester Guardian*, 26 November 1964.

14 There were many influences behind this style, from scholars such as Muriel Bradbrook (e.g. her 1932 *Elizabethan Stage Conditions*) to, most crucially for Hall, Harley Granville Barker's *Prefaces to Shakespeare*, written in the 1930s. He saw fluid staging in Tyrone Guthrie's productions and, in terms of use of space, recalled Michael Warre's 1947 set for the Old Vic *Richard II* and Tanya Moiseiwitsch's 1951 Stratford histories. Hall also knew about space because he had done his own lighting. He says he learned about the importance of recognising the presence of the audience from seeing Grock and other comedians.

15 For example, Aeschylus's Orestean trilogy (1904) and a new play, *The Piper* by Preston Peabody (1910). Ben Jonson's *Every Man in His Humour* was seen in 1937. It was followed by *She Stoops to Conquer* (1940 and 1945), three Sheridan plays, *The Rivals* (1941), *School for Scandal* (1942) and *The Critic* (1943), Jonson's *Volpone* (1944 and 1952) and *Dr Faustus* (1946 and 1947).

16 Harold Hobson, *The Sunday Times*, 18 December 1960.

17 Peter Brook, '"Endgame" as "King Lear"', *Encore*, Jan.–Feb. 1965, pp. 8–12. The production was supervised by Beckett.

18 The RSC planned to stage a Lope play in 2004.

19 Stratford had a tradition of Christmas shows, so the idea was not new. *Toad of Toad Hall*, for example, appeared regularly at the Shakespeare Memorial Theatre in the late 1940s and early 1950s. The RSC's Christmas shows were very popular and became important box office earners for the company. According to the RSC, *The Lion, the Witch and the Wardrobe* attracted 40,000 first-time attenders in its initial outing.

20 Planning was a perilous business. John Arden wrote an adaptation of Goethe's *Ironhand* for the RSC but then decided to withdraw it because he preferred to have a new play of his produced, *The Workhouse Donkey*, which was presented by the National Theatre in waiting at Chichester. The RSC was set to produce Arnold Wesker's *Chips With Everything* when the Royal Court rejected it but lost the play when the Royal Court changed its mind. The RSC let Peter Shaffer's *The Royal Hunt of the Sun* go with its director John Dexter to the NT and later also lost the race with the NT to stage Tom Stoppard's *Rosencrantz and Guildenstern Are Dead*. The RSC dropped its plan to produce *Peer Gynt* with Paul Scofield when it learned that the Old Vic was planning to mount the same play using the same text.

21 The relationship between Harold Pinter and the RSC was effectively ended when Hall became artistic director of the National Theatre and Pinter accepted an invitation to become an associate director there.

22 The story of the dispute is complicated. Disagreements over interpretation between the playwrights and the RSC artistic team grew to a point where the playwrights asked for a company meeting but were denied one because the production was close to opening. Arden and D'Arcy, members of the Society of Irish Playwrights, believed this refusal breached their contract and decided to strike. A picket was established at the Aldwych Theatre. During a preview, the playwrights came on stage in an attempt to hold the meeting they had been seeking but a rough vocal vote by the audience led them to conclude the majority of the audience did not wish to listen to them. They departed. The RSC made clumsy attempts to invite them to appear on stage after the official first night but were rebuffed by the playwrights. The dispute triggered a public debate on the rights of the playwright.

23 During *The Representative*, Joseph Behrmann, an actor who had spent four years in concentration camps, stood outside the Aldwych Theatre wearing the Star of David

as if to say, 'Never forget'. There had been much media comment on the play and protests from Catholics at the RSC's decision to present it. The censor made a few cuts to soothe certain Catholic sensibilities and requested that under-sixteens be barred. The RSC programme carried a supplement offering views on the play and its content, and debates were held on television as well as after the show. It was following threats to Michael Williams, who played Adolf Eichmann, the leading Nazi recently executed for his war crimes against the Jewish people, that a policeman was stationed at the stage door.

24  The company saw itself as part of a new playwriting network, complementing rather than competing with other theatres. RSC drama was often written on a scale and with an ambition of purpose denied most other theatres through lack of resources. The type of play the company presented meant that for some writers their RSC work would rarely be revived in Britain because of the demands the plays made. Other plays, such as *Piaf* or *Les Liaisons Dangereuses*, have more easily entered the general repertoire.

## SEVEN: SHOTS IN THE DARK

1  George Rylands was the leading force behind the Marlowe Society, which had been founded to revivify late fifteenth- and early sixteenth-century plays, the productions of which Hall had seen as a schoolboy. Hall played Tybalt in a Marlowe Society student production of *Romeo and Juliet*, which Rylands directed and which enjoyed sufficient attention to have a showing in two London theatres. As to how Shakespeare's words might have sounded in his day, Hall admits no one knows, but he advances a view shared by others that contemporary Americans come closer than their British counterparts. Apart from collapsing the vast diversity of accents in the USA into one 'all American' voice, this reflects an unconsciously patronising, almost colonial view. Matthew Warchus's RSC production of *The Winter's Tale* (2002) pursued the point and had the British actors use American accents.

2  *Word of Mouth 1* and *2* were made in 1980. A series was proposed but not agreed. The idea was revived and made into nine London Weekend Television programmes, *Playing Shakespeare*, broadcast on Channel 4 in 1984.

3  In 1998 there was a 'Forum on Verse Speaking and Classical Text' at the National Theatre Studio triggered by an article written by Adrian Noble saying actors coming to Stratford from drama schools were less well equipped to handle Shakespeare's language than before.

4  Peter Hall, 'Shakespeare and the Modern Director', in John Goodwin (ed.), *The Royal Shakespeare Theatre Company, 1960–63*, London, Max Reinhardt, 1964, p. 45.

5  Michel Saint-Denis, *Theatre: The Rediscovery of Style*, London, Heinemann, 1960, p. 18.

6  Article by A.C.H. Smith, RSC Club newspaper *Flourish*, no. 4, summer 1965.

7  Michel Saint-Denis (ed. Suria Saint-Denis), *Training for the Theatre: Premises and Promises*, London, Heinemann, 1982, p. 78.

8  Quotations taken from unsigned and undated internal RSC document 'Stratford Studio' written in 1962 by Michel Saint-Denis, held in private collection of Abd'elkader Farrah.

9  RSC production manager Desmond Hall oversaw the building of the hut. No one I have spoken to can recall who designed it but Sean Kenny's sketch for a small auditorium in Stephen Joseph (ed.), *Actor and Architect*, Manchester, Manchester University Press, 1964, p. 61, is similar to what became the Studio and later The Other Place, as pointed out by Marion J. Pringle in *The Theatres of Stratford-upon-Avon 1875–1992: An Architectural History*, Stratford-upon-Avon, Stratford-upon-Avon Society, 1994.

10 An example of the Studio directly influencing the repertoire would have been Clifford Williams's proposed production of *Timon of Athens* using half masks but actor resistance and the director's ill health led to the abandonment of the production in 1963 – a further blow to the prestige of the Studio. The RSC did stage the play, directed by John Schlesinger, in 1965.

11 Brook used the phrase in a LAMDA Theatre Club member's pamphlet, 1964.

12 Phrase used by the actor Clifford Rose in an interview with the author.

13 Interview with the author.

14 *RSC Annual Report 1991/2*, p. 5.

15 Letter to Adrian Noble, 24 September 1988, in Edward Bond (edited and selected by Ian Stuart), *Letters I*, Luxembourg, Harwood Academic Publishers, 1994, p. 135.

16 Ibid., p. 144.

17 In addition to Bond's own writings on Theatre Eventing and interviews with Cicely Berry, information on the RSC workshop was taken from Ian Stuart, 'A Political Language for the Theatre: Edward Bond's RSC Workshops, 1992', *New Theatre Quarterly*, vol. x, no. 39, August 1994, pp. 207–16.

18 Bond, op. cit., p. 163.

19 The author attended this workshop.

20 As well as having a showing to a selected audience at the end of the fortnight, a few individual company members watched some sessions. Steven Pimlott thought Boal's techniques helped the director to see what the actors were creating rather than helping the actors to be creative. Katie Mitchell used some of the techniques herself in later rehearsals of *The Mysteries*. She thought they were revelatory, a way of structuring how one was operating.

## EIGHT: PUBLIC ACCOUNT

1 As well as film and television exploitation, which are mentioned in this chapter, the RSC had recordings issued, e.g. Argo brought out excerpts of Shakespeare productions and *The Hollow Crown* in 1962. The company later was involved in video but not to any great extent, although in 2003 it announced it was planning a video game based on *The Tempest*.

2 Quoted in Peter Hall, *Making an Exhibition of Myself*, London, Sinclair-Stevenson, 1993, p. 148.

3 *The Times*, 5 December 1972.

4 Peter Hall (Goodwin, John, ed.), *Peter Hall's Diaries: The Story of a Dramatic Battle*, London, Hamish Hamilton, 1983, p. 48. Hall himself was a member of the Arts Council 1969–72.

5 See Antony Sher, *Beside Myself*, London, Arrow, 2002, p. 192.

6 Peter Brook, *The Empty Space*, London, McGibbon & Key, 1968, p. 23.

7 For further commentary on this see Catherine Prentice and Helena Leongamornlert, 'The RSC Goes Walkabout: "The Dillen" in Stratford, 1983', *New Theatre Quarterly*, vol. xviii, part 1 (no. 69), Feb. 2002, pp. 47–58.

8 Peter Hall, 'Shakespeare and the Modern Director', in John Goodwin, John (ed.), *The Royal Shakespeare Company 1960–63*, London, Max Reinhardt, 1964, p. 43.

9 With the RSC move to the Barbican, Tony Church, one of the company's leading actors, became director of drama. RSC personnel – directors, actors and members of the technical, voice and literary departments – took part in the school's teaching. With his departure in 1989, the links remained but gradually became more informal. The RSC Trust funded a Guildhall student bursary before the RSC left the Barbican.

10   *The Sunday Times*, 26 June 1966.

11   Peter Brook asked film-maker Peter Whitehead to shoot *US*. The result was a sixty-minute documentary, *Benefit of the Doubt* (1967). Brook made *Tell Me Lies*, his own film of *US* in 1968.

12   Gareth Lloyd Evans of *The Manchester Guardian*.

13   The sixth edition, March 1962, satirises Hall for his ambition.

## NINE: COMPANY OR CORPORATION?

1   For example, Peter Brook's production of *A Midsummer Night's Dream*, itself an example of collective discovery, benefited from a last-minute suggestion by John Barton. He disliked what he saw but offered helpful advice. He believed the audience would be confused by the conventions Brook was employing and suggested the vocabulary of the production be made clear at the outset, as if displaying the equipment of a gymnasium. This helped Brook and the designer Sally Jacobs set up the production properly when the actors first appeared. (Sally Jacobs interview with the author.)

2   Hall demonstrated this capacity early on at the RSC several times. In 1961 he sacked his Romeo ten days before the production opened. In 1962 an ugly incident had less artistic mitigation. Cyril Keegan Smith, the long-standing head of wardrobe who encouraged young people and had lent Hall and his friends costumes when they were students, was sacked by Hall over an apparently minor dispute concerning the costuming process of *King Lear*.

3   Michael Murray, *Encore*, no. 42, March–April 1963, vol. 10, no. 2, pp. 14–22.

4   Peter Hall, 'Avoiding a Method', in *Crucial Years*, London, Max Reinhardt Ltd, 1963, p. 19.

5   Ian Holm, 'Reflections of an Ex-small Part Actor', *Encore*, no. 42, March–April 1963, vol. 10, no. 2, pp. 23–25.

6   Quoted in David Addenbrooke, *The Royal Shakespeare Company: The Peter Hall Years*, London, William Kimber, 1974, p. 159.

7   Peter Hall records in (Goodwin, John, ed.), *Peter Hall's Diaries: The Story of a Dramatic Battle*, London, Hamish Hamilton, 1983, p. 286, that in 1975 Trevor Nunn tried to form a RSC co-operative of about two dozen actors but only three agreed to participate, others sensing that he was not going to share power equally with the group. In 1976, however, four of the six Stratford productions were co-directed in another experiment in company ethos.

8   Arnold Wesker sued the RSC for breach of contract. After eight years the company settled out of court but for about a sixth of the income Wesker believed he had been denied.

9   These lists were not fixed, e.g. some associates graduated to honorary status, some were dropped.

10   Gerald Jacobs, *Judi Dench: A Great Deal of Laughter*, London, Weidenfeld & Nicolson, 1985; Joy Leslie Gibson, *Ian McKellen*, London, Weidenfeld & Nicolson, 1986.

11   Brian Cox, *Salem to Moscow: An Actors' Odyssey*, London, Methuen, 1991, p. 68.

12   Antony Sher, *Year of the King: An Actor's Diary and Sketchbook*, London, Chatto & Windus – The Hogarth Press, 1985; Nigel Hawthorne, *Straight Face*, London, Hodder & Stoughton, 2002.

13   Robert Stephens, with Michael Coveney, *Knight Errant: Memoirs of a Vagabond Actor*, London, Hodder & Stoughton, 1995, p. 172.

14   Sheila Hancock, *Ramblings of an Actress*, London, Hutchinson, 1987.

15   Kenneth Branagh, *Beginning*, London, Chatto & Windus, 1989.

16  Quoted in A.C.H. Smith, *Orghast at Persepolis: An account of the experiment in theatre directed by Peter Brook and written by Ted Hughes*, London, Eyre Methuen, 1972, p. 20. Institutional racism in British theatre was identified and discussed at a conference held at Nottingham Playhouse (12–13 June 2001), from which a report was issued, 'Eclipse: Developing Strategies to Combat Racism in Theatre', London, Arts Council of England, 2002. Neither the RSC nor the National Theatre was represented.

# BIBLIOGRAPHY

Addenbrooke, David, *The Royal Shakespeare Company: The Peter Hall Years*, London, William Kimber, 1974.

Adler, Steven, *Rough Magic: Making Theatre at the Royal Shakespeare Company*, Carbondale and Edwardsville, Southern Illinois University Press, 2001.

Artaud, Antonin, *The Theatre and its Double*, London, Calder & Boyars, 1970.

Arts Council of Great Britain, 'Royal Shakespeare Company, 1990' appraisal report, London, Arts Council of Great Britain, 1990.

Barker, Francis, Hulme, Peter and Iversen, Margaret (eds), *Uses of History: Marxism, Postmodernism and the Renaissance*, Manchester, Manchester University Press, 1991.

Barton, John, *Playing Shakespeare*, London, Methuen, 1984.

Barton, John, in collaboration with Peter Hall, *The Wars of the Roses*, London, British Broadcasting Corporation, 1970.

Bate, Jonathan, Levenson, Jill and Mehl, Dieter (eds), *Shakespeare and the Twentieth Century: The Selected Proceedings of the International Shakespeare Association World Congress 1996*, London, Associated University Presses Inc., 1998.

Beauman, Sally (ed.), *The RSC's Production of Henry V for the Centenary Season*, Oxford, Pergamon, 1976.

—— *The Royal Shakespeare Company: A History of Ten Decades*, Oxford, Oxford University Press, 1982.

Bennett, Susan, *Performing Nostalgia: Shifting Shakespeare and the Contemporary Past*, London, Routledge, 1996.

Berry, Cicely, *The Text in Action*, London, Virgin Publishing, 2001.

Berry, Ralph, *Changing Styles in Shakespeare*, London, Allen & Unwin, 1981.

—— *On Directing Shakespeare: Interviews with Contemporary Directors*, London, Hamish Hamilton, 1989.

—— *Shakespeare in Performance*, Basingstoke, Macmillan, 1993.

Biggs, Murray *et al.* (eds), *The Arts of Performance in Elizabethan and Early Stuart Drama*, Edinburgh, Edinburgh University Press, 1991.

Billington, Michael, *Peggy Ashcroft*, London, John Murray, 1988.

Blakemore, Michael, *Next Season*, London, Weidenfeld & Nicolson, 1969.

Bloom, Harold, *Shakespeare: The Invention of the Human*, London, Fourth Estate, 1999.

Bogdanov, Michael and Pennington, Michael, *The English Shakespeare Company: The Story of the Wars of the Roses, 1986–89*, London, Nick Hern Books, 1990.

Bond, Edward, (edited and selected by Ian Stuart), *Letters 1, 2, 3 and 4*, Luxembourg/Amsterdam, Harwood Academic Publishers, 1994, 1995, 1996, 1998.

Bott, John, *The Figure of the House: An Illustrated Record of the Building of Stratford's Theatre*, Stratford-upon-Avon, Royal Shakespeare Theatre, 1974.

Branagh, Kenneth, *Beginning*, London, Chatto & Windus, 1989.

Brook, Peter, 'Oh for Empty Seats', *Encore*, Jan. 1959.

—— '"Endgame" as "King Lear"', *Encore*, Jan.–Feb. 1965.

—— *The Empty Space*, London, McGibbon & Key, 1968.

—— *The Shifting Point: Theatre, Film, Opera 1946–87*, New York, Harper & Row, 1987.

—— *The Threads of Time*, London, Methuen, 1998.

Brook, Peter, Cannan, Denis, Hunt, Albert, Jacobs, Sally, Kustow, Michael, Mitchell, Adrian, Peaslee, Richard and Stott, Michael, *US: The Book of the Royal Shakespeare Company Production*, London, Calder & Boyars, 1968.

Brook, Peter, Haigh, Kenneth, Marowitz, Charles and Saint-Denis, Michel, 'Who Alienated Konstantin Stanislavski?' (text of a discussion), *Encore*, no. 43, May–June 1963, vol. 10, no. 3.

Brook, Peter, Hall, Peter, Saint-Denis, Michel and Shaffer, Peter, 'Artaud for Artaud's Sake', *Encore*, no. 49, May–June 1964, vol. 11, no. 3.

Brown, John Russell, *Shakespeare's Plays in Performance*, London, Penguin, 1969.

—— *Free Shakespeare*, London, Heinemann, 1974.

—— 'Another Kind of Shakespeare: Small, Cheap, Exciting', *Theatre Newsletter*, British Theatre Institute, no. 19, May 1979.

Bryant, Chris, *Glenda Jackson: The Biography*, London, HarperCollins, 1999.

Cairns, Adrian, *The Making of the Professional Actor*, London, Peter Owen, 1996.

Callow, Simon, *The National: The Theatre and Its Work 1963–1997*, London, Nick Hern Books, 1997.

Chambers, Colin, *Other Spaces: New Theatre and the RSC*, London, Eyre Methuen and Theatre Quarterly Publications, 1980.

—— *Peggy: The Life of Margaret Ramsay, Play Agent*, London, Nick Hern Books, 1997.

—— '"Home Sweet Home": Stratford-upon-Avon and the Making of the Royal Shakespeare Company as a National Institution', in Cartmell, Deborah and Scott, Mike (eds), *Talking Shakespeare*, Basingstoke, Palgrave, 2001.

Chambers, Colin, and Prior, Mike, *Playwrights' Progress: Patterns of Postwar British Theatre*, Oxford, Amber Lane Press, 1987.

Cohn, Ruby, *Modern Shakespeare Offshoots*, Princeton, Princeton University Press, 1976.

Cook, Judith, *Directors' Theatre*, London, Harrap, 1974.

—— *Shakespeare's Players*, London, Harrap, 1983.

Cork, Kenneth, *Cork on Cork*, Basingstoke, Macmillan, 1988.

Cox, Brian, *Salem to Moscow: An Actors' Odyssey*, London, Methuen, 1991.

Cox, Frank, Interview with Peter Hall, *Plays and Players*, May 1964.

Cox, Murray (ed.), *Shakespeare Comes to Broadmoor: 'The Actor Comes Hither' – The Performance of Tragedy in a Secure Psychiatric Hospital*, London, Jessica Kingsley, 1992.

Craig, Edward Gordon, *On the Art of the Theatre*, London, Heinemann, 1956.

Daniell, David, *Coriolanus in Europe*, London, The Athlone Press, 1980.

Darnley, Lyn, 'A History of Voice Teaching in Britain', unpublished M. Phil. thesis, University of Birmingham, 1994.

Daubeny, Peter, *My World of Theatre*, London, Jonathan Cape, 1971.

David, Richard, *Shakespeare in the Theatre*, Cambridge, Cambridge University Press, 1978.

Dexter, John, *The Honourable Beast: A Posthumous Autobiography*, London, Nick Hern Books, 1993.

Dollimore, Jonathan and Sinfield, Alan (eds), *Political Shakespeare: Essays in Cultural Materialism*, Manchester, Manchester University Press, 1994.

Donohue, Walter (ed.), 'The Warehouse: A Writer's Theatre', no. 8, the Third Series (1979–80) Theatre Papers, Devon, Department of Theatre, Dartington College of Arts, 1979.

Dover Wilson, J., and Worsley, T.C., *Shakespeare's Histories at Stratford, 1951*, London, Max Reinhardt, 1952.

Drabble, Margaret, *The Garrick Year*, London, Weidenfeld & Nicolson, 1964.

—— 'Stratford Revisited: A Legacy of the Sixties' (Gareth Lloyd Evans lecture, 1988), Shipston-on-Stour, The Celandine Press, 1989.

Drakakis, John (ed.), *Alternative Shakespeares*, London, Methuen, 1985.

*Eclipse: Developing Strategies to Combat Racism in Theatre*, London, Arts Council of England, 2002. Report of conference held in Nottingham, June 2001. Available online: www.artscouncil.org.uk/publications/docs/eclipse.doc.

Elsom, John, *Postwar British Theatre*, London, Routledge & Kegan Paul, 1976.

—— (ed.), *Is Shakespeare Still Our Contemporary?*, London, Routledge, 1989.

Elsom, John and Tomalin, Nicholas, *The History of the National Theatre*, London, Jonathan Cape, 1978.

Evans, Malcolm, *Signifying Nothing: Truths True Contents in Shakespeare's Texts*, Hertfordshire, Harvester Wheatsheaf, 1989.

Fay, Stephen, *Power Play: The Life and Times of Peter Hall*, London, Hodder & Stoughton, 1996.

Gambling, Trevor, and Andrews, Gordon, 'An Analysis of the Financial Policies of a Major Theatre Company, 1968–78', unpublished report, University of Birmingham, c.1979.

Gaskill, William, *A Sense of Direction: Life at the Royal Court Theatre*, London, Faber & Faber, 1988.

Gay, Penny, *As She Likes It: Shakespeare's Unruly Women*, London, Routledge, 1994.

Gibson, Joy Leslie, *Ian McKellen*, London, Weidenfeld & Nicolson, 1986.

Gielgud, Val, *Years in a Mirror*, London, Bodley Head, 1965.

Gottlieb, Vera and Chambers, Colin (eds), *Theatre in a Cool Climate*, Oxford, Amber Lane Press Ltd, 1999.

Grady, Hugh, *The Modernist Shakespeare: Critical Texts in a Material World*, Oxford, Clarendon, 1991.

Greenblatt, Stephen J., *Shakespearean Negotiations: The Circulation of Social Energy in Renaissance England*, Oxford, Clarendon, 1988.

Grene, Nicholas, *Shakespeare's Serial History Plays*, Cambridge, Cambridge University Press, 2002.

Greenwald, Michael L., *Directions by Indirections: John Barton of the Royal Shakespeare Company*, Newark, University of Delaware Press, 1985.

Guthrie, Tyrone, *A Life in the Theatre*, New York, McGraw-Hill, 1959.

Habicht, Werner, Palmer, D.J. and Pringle, Roger (eds), *Images of Shakespeare: Proceedings of the Third Congress of the International Shakespeare Association, 1986*, London, Associated University Presses, 1988.

Hall, Peter, (Goodwin, John, ed.), *Peter Hall's Diaries: The Story of a Dramatic Battle*, London, Hamish Hamilton, 1983.

—— *Making an Exhibition of Myself*, London, Sinclair-Stevenson, 1993.

—— *Exposed by the Mask: Form and Language in Drama*, London, Oberon, 2000.

Hallio, Jay L., *Understanding Shakespeare's Plays in Performance*, Manchester, Manchester University Press, 1988.

Hancock, Sheila, *Ramblings of an Actress*, London, Hutchinson, 1987.

Harbage, Alfred, *Conceptions of Shakespeare*, Cambridge, Mass., Harvard University Press, 1966.

—— *Shakespeare without Words and Other Essays*, Cambridge, Mass., Harvard University Press, 1972.

Hardt, Michael and Weeks, Kathi (eds), *The Jameson Reader*, Oxford, Blackwell, 2000.

Hawkes, Terence, *Shakespeare's Talking Animals*, London, Edward Arnold, 1973.

—— *Meaning by Shakespeare*, London, Routledge, 1982.

—— *That Shakespearian Rag: Essays on a Critical Process*, London, Methuen, 1986.

—— (ed.) *Alternative Shakespeares vol. 2*, London, Routledge, 1996.

Hawthorne, Nigel, *Straight Face*, London, Hodder & Stoughton, 2002.

Hayman, Ronald, *The Set-up: An Anatomy of the English Theatre Today*, London, Eyre Methuen, 1973.

Hewison, Robert, *Culture and Consensus: England, Art and Politics since 1940*, London, Methuen, 1995.

Holland, Peter, *English Shakespeares: Shakespeare on the English Stage in the 1990s*, Cambridge, Cambridge University Press, 1997.

Holderness, Graham (ed.), *The Shakespeare Myth*, Manchester, Manchester University Press, 1988.

—— 'The Albatross and the Swan: Two Productions at Stratford', *New Theatre Quarterly*, vol. iv, no. 14, May 1988.

—— *Shakespeare Recycled: The Making of Historical Drama*, Hertfordshire, Harvester Wheatsheaf, 1992.

Holm, Ian, 'Reflections of an Ex-small Part Actor', *Encore*, no. 42, March–April 1963, vol. 10, no. 2.

Howard, Jean E., and O'Connor, Marion F. (eds), *Shakespeare Reproduced: the Text in History and Ideology*, London, Methuen, 1987.

Hunt, Albert, and Reeves, Geoffrey, *Peter Brook*, Cambridge, Cambridge University Press, 1995.

Houseman, John, *Unfinished Business: A Memoir*, London, Routledge, 1990.

Jacobs, Gerald, *Judi Dench: A Great Deal of Laughter*, London, Weidenfeld & Nicolson, 1985.

James, Emrys, 'On Playing Henry IV', *Theatre Quarterly*, vol. 7, no. 22, autumn 1977.

Joseph, Stephen (ed.), *Actor and Architect*, Manchester, Manchester University Press, 1964.

Joughin, John L. (ed.), *Shakespeare in National Culture*, Manchester, Manchester University Press, 1997.

Kamps, Ivor (ed.), *Materialist Shakespeare: A History*, Oxford, Oxford University Press, 1991.

Kennedy, Dennis, *Foreign Shakespeares*, Cambridge, Cambridge University Press, 1993.

Kershaw, Baz, *The Politics of Performance: Radical Theatre as Cultural Intervention*, London, Routledge, 1992.

Kott, Jan (translated Boleslaw Taborski), *Shakespeare Our Contemporary*, London, Methuen, second edition, 1967.

Kruger, Loren, *The National Stage: Theatre and Cultural Legitimation in England, France, and America*, Chicago and London, The University of Chicago Press, 1992.

Kustow, Michael, *Theatre @ Risk*, London, Methuen, 2000.

Lebrecht, Norman, *Covent Garden, the Untold Story: Dispatches from the English Culture War, 1945–2000*, London, Simon & Schuster, 2000.

Littlewood, Joan, *Joan's Book: Joan Littlewood's Peculiar History As She Tells It*, London, Methuen, 1994.

Loney, Glenn, *Peter Brook's Production of 'A Midsummer Night's Dream'*, Chicago, Dramatic Publishing Co., 1974.

—— (ed.), *Staging Shakespeare: Seminars on Production Problems*, New York and London, Garland Publishing, 1990.

Marowitz, Charles, *Confessions of a Counterfeit Critic: A London Theatre Notebook 1958–71*, London, Eyre Methuen, 1973.

—— *The Marowitz Shakespeare*, London, Boyars, 1978.

—— *Burnt Bridges*, London, Hodder & Stoughton, 1990.

Marowitz, Charles, Milne, Tom and Hale, Owen (eds), *The Encore Reader*, London, Methuen, 1965.

Marowitz, Charles and Trussler, Simon (eds), *Theatre at Work: Playwrights and Productions in the Modern British Theatre*, London, Methuen, 1967.

Marsden, Jean I. (ed.), *The Appropriation of Shakespeare: Post-Renaissance Reconstructions of the Works and the Myth*, New York, Harvester Wheatsheaf, 1991.

Marshall, Norman, *The Other Theatre*, London, John Lehmann, 1947.

Marwick, Arthur, *The Sixties*, Oxford, Oxford University Press, 1998.

Membery, York, *Ralph Fiennes: The Unauthorised Biography*, London, Chameleon Books, 1997.

Miles, Patrick, 'Chekhov, Shakespeare, the Ensemble and the Company', *New Theatre Quarterly*, vol. xi, no. 43, August 1995.

Miller, Jonathan, *Subsequent Performances*, London, Faber & Faber, 1986.

Mullin, Michael with Muriello, Karen M. (ed.), *Theatre at Stratford-upon-Avon: A Catalogue-Index to Productions of the Shakespeare Memorial/Royal Shakespeare Theatre, 1879–78*, 2 vols, London, Library Association; Westport, Ct., Greenwood Press, 1980.

Mullin, Michael, *Theatre at Stratford-upon-Avon. First Supplement: A Catalogue-Index to the Productions of the Royal Shakespeare Company, 1979–93*, Westport, Ct., Greenwood Press, 1994.

Mulryne, J.R. and Shewring, M. (eds), *This Golden Round: The Royal Shakespeare Company at the Swan, 1986–88*, Stratford-upon-Avon, Mulryne and Shewring, 1989.

—— *Making Space for Theatre: British Architecture and Theatre since 1958*, Stratford-upon-Avon, Mulryne and Shewring, 1995.

Murray, Michael, 'Diary of a Small-Part Actor', *Encore*, no. 42, March–April 1963, vol. 10, no. 2.

Normington, Katie, 'Little Acts of Faith: Katie Mitchell's *The Mysteries*', *New Theatre Quarterly*, vol. xiv, Part 2, no. 54, May 1998.

Novy, Marianne (ed.), *Cross-Cultural Performances: Differences in Women's Re-Visions of Shakespeare*, Chicago, University of Illinois Press, 1993.

O'Connor, Gary, *The Secret Woman: A Life of Peggy Ashcroft*, London, Weidenfeld & Nicolson, 1997.

—— *Paul Scofield: The Biography*, London, Sidgwick & Jackson, 2002.

Ogden, James and Scouten, Arthur H., *Lear from Study to Stage: Essays in Criticism*, London, Associated University Presses, 1997.

Osborne, John, *The Meiningen Court Theatre 1866–1890*, Cambridge, Cambridge University Press, 1988.

Parker, Patricia and Hartman, Geoffrey (eds), *Shakespeare and the Question of Theory*, London, Methuen, 1985.

Pearson, Richard, *A Band of Arrogant and United Heroes: The Story of the Royal Shakespeare Company Production of 'The Wars of the Roses'*, London, The Adelphi Press, 1990.

Prentice, Catherine and Leongamornlert, Helena, 'The RSC Goes Walkabout: "The Dillen" in Stratford, 1983', *New Theatre Quarterly*, vol. xviii, part 1 (no. 69), Feb. 2002.

Priestley, Clive, 'Financial Scrutiny of the Royal Shakespeare Company, vols I & II', London, Office of Arts and Libraries, 1984.

Pringle, Marian J., *The Theatres of Stratford-upon-Avon, 1875–1992: An Architectural History*, Stratford-upon-Avon, Stratford-upon-Avon Society, 1994.

Quayle, Anthony, *A Time to Speak*, London, Barrie & Jenkins, 1990.

Rissik, Andrew, 'What Has Happened to the Stratford Voice?', *New Theatre Quarterly*, vol. 1, no. 3, August 1985.

Rubin, Leon, *The Nicholas Nickleby Story: The Making of the Historic Royal Shakespeare Company Production*, London, Heinemann, 1981.

Rutter, Carol, *Clamorous Voices: Shakespeare's Women Today*, London, Women's Press, 1988.

Saint-Denis, Michel, *Theatre: The Rediscovery of Style*, London, Heinemann, 1960.

—— (ed. Suria Saint-Denis), *Training for the Theatre: Premises and Promises*, London, Heinemann, 1982.

Selbourne, David, *The Making of A Midsummer Night's Dream*, London, Methuen, 1982.

Shafer, Elizabeth, *Ms-Directing Shakespeare: Women Direct Shakespeare*, London, Women's Press, 1998.

Shaughnessy, Robert, *Representing Shakespeare: England, History and the RSC*, Hertfordshire, Harvester Wheatsheaf, 1994.

Shepherd, Simon and Womack, Peter, *English Drama – A Cultural History*, Oxford, Blackwell, 1996.

Sher, Antony, *Year of the King: An Actor's Diary and Sketchbook*, London, Chatto & Windus – The Hogarth Press, 1985.

—— *Beside Myself*, London, Arrow Books, 2002.

Sinden, Donald, *A Touch of the Memoirs*, London, Hodder & Stoughton, 1982.

—— *Laughter in the Second Act*, London, Hodder & Stoughton, 1985.

Smith, A.C.H., *Orghast at Persepolis: An Account of the Experiment in Theatre Directed by Peter Brook and Written by Ted Hughes*, London, Eyre Methuen, 1972.

Speight, Robert, 'The Old Vic and Stratford-upon-Avon, 1960–61', *Shakespeare Quarterly*, vol. 12, no. 4, autumn 1961.

Steinberg, Michelene (ed.), *Flashback: A Pictorial History 1879–1979 – One Hundred Years of Stratford-upon-Avon and the Royal Shakespeare Company*, Stratford-upon-Avon, RSC Publications, 1985.

Stephens, Robert with Coveney, Michael, *Knight Errant: Memoirs of a Vagabond Actor*, London, Hodder & Stoughton, 1995.

Stuart, Ian, 'A Political Language for the Theatre: Edward Bond's RSC Workshops, 1992', *New Theatre Quarterly*, vol. x, no. 39, August 1994.

Styan, J.L., *The Shakespeare Revolution: Criticism and Performance in the Twentieth Century*, Cambridge, Cambridge University Press, 1977.

Taylor, Gary, *Reinventing Shakespeare: A Cultural History from the Restoration to the Present*, London, Vintage, 1991.

Trewin, J.C., *Shakespeare on the English Stage*, London, Barrie & Rockliff, 1964.

—— *Peter Brook: A Biography*, London, Macdonald & Co., 1971.

Tynan, Kathleen, *The Life of Ken Tynan*, London, Weidenfeld & Nicolson, 1987.

Tynan, Kenneth, *Tynan Right & Left*, London, Longmans, 1976.

—— *A View of the English Stage, 1944–65*, London, Methuen, 1984.

Ustinov, Peter, *Dear Me*, London, Heinemann, 1977.

Walter, Harriet, *Other People's Shoes: Thoughts on Acting*, London, Penguin, 2000.

Wapshott, Nicholas, *Peter O'Toole*, London, New English Library, 1983.

Wardle, Irvine, *The Theatres of George Devine*, London, Jonathan Cape, 1978.

Wells, Stanley, *Royal Shakespeare: Four Major Productions at Stratford-upon-Avon*, Manchester, Manchester University Press, 1977.

Wells, Stanley and Stanton, Sarah (eds), *Cambridge Companion to Shakespeare on Stage*, Cambridge, Cambridge University Press, 2002.

Wiener, Martin J., *English Culture and the Decline of the Industrial Spirit 1850–1980*, Cambridge, Cambridge University Press, 1981.

Williams, David (ed.), *Peter Brook: A Theatrical Casebook*, London, Methuen, 1988.

Woddis, Carole (ed.), *'Sheer Bloody Magic': Conversations with Actresses*, London, Virago Press, 1991.

Womack, Peter, 'The Sign of the Light Heart: Jonson's New Inn, 1629 and 1987', *New Theatre Quarterly*, vol. v, no. 18, May 1989.

## SERIES:

Brown, Ivor, *The Shakespeare Memorial Theatre 1951–53*, London, Max Reinhardt, 1953.
—— Introduction to *The Shakespeare Memorial Theatre 1954–56*, London, Max Reinhardt, 1956.
—— Introduction to *The Shakespeare Memorial Theatre 1957–59*, London, Max Reinhardt, 1959.
Brown, Ivor and Quayle, Anthony, *The Shakespeare Memorial Theatre 1948–50*, London, Reinhardt & Evans, 1951.
Goodwin, John (ed.), *The Royal Shakespeare Company 1960–63*, London, Max Reinhardt, 1964.

*Players of Shakespeare*, Cambridge, Cambridge University Press:
Brockbank, Philip (ed.), *Players of Shakespeare*, 1985.
Jackson, Russell and Robert Smallwood (eds), *Players of Shakespeare vols 2 & 3*, 1988 and 1993.
Smallwood, Robert (ed.), *Players of Shakespeare vol. 4*, 1998.

*Shakespeare in Performance* series, Manchester, Manchester University Press:
Bulman, James C., *The Merchant of Venice*, 1991.
Cousin, Geraldine, *King John*, 1994.
Dawson, Anthony, *Hamlet*, 1997.
Desen, Alan C., *Titus Andronicus*, 1989.
Gilbert, Miriam, *Love's Labour's Lost*, 1992.
Halio, Jay L., *A Midsummer Night's Dream*, 1994.
Hodgdon, Barbara, *Henry IV Part Two*, 1993.
Holderness, Graham, *The Taming of the Shrew*, 1989.
Leggatt, Alexander, *King Lear*, 1991.
Loehlin, James N., *Henry V*, 2000.
McMillin, Scott, *Henry IV Part One*, 1991.
Potter, Lois, *Othello*, 2002.
Richmond, Hugh M., *King Richard III*, 1989.
—— *King Henry VIII*, 1994.
Shewring, Margaret, *King Richard II*, 1998.
Warren, Roger, *Cymbeline*, 1989.

*Actors on Shakespeare*, London, Faber & Faber:
Fielding, Emma, *Twelfth Night (Viola)*, 2002.
Redgrave, Corin, *Julius Caesar*, 2002.
Walter, Harriet, *Macbeth (Lady Macbeth)*, 2002.

## SHAKESPEARE MEMORIAL THEATRE/ROYAL SHAKESPEARE COMPANY MATERIAL

(Few internal documents from the first decade of the RSC are held in the company archive at the Shakespeare Centre, Stratford-upon-Avon. Peter Hall wished to keep the archive in the theatre for the first ten years but by 1970 he had left the company. No one knew of his plan and the material was thrown away.)

'Theatre Records' of the Shakespeare Memorial Theatre and Royal Shakespeare Theatre Company held in the Shakespeare Centre, Stratford-upon-Avon plus miscellaneous programmes, leaflets, photographs, cuttings and memoranda.

RSC annual reports of Council (governors' annual reports)

RSC Yearbooks 1978–88.

*Crucial Years*, RSC pamphlet, London, Max Reinhardt, 1963.

RSC Club newspaper *Flourish* (1964–74) and *RSC Newspaper* (1974–75), *RSC News* (1980–90), *RSC Magazine* (incl. *RSC News*, 1990–).

# INDEX